JOHN HICK

AN AUTOBIOGRAPHY

ALSO BY JOHN HICK

The Fifth Dimension: An Exploration of the Spiritual Realm
God and the Universe of Faiths

EDITED, WITH BRIAN HEBBLETHWAITE

Christianity and other Religions: Selected Readings

JOHN HICK

AN AUTOBIOGRAPHY

ONEWORLD
OXFORD

JOHN HICK: AN AUTOBIOGRAPHY

Oneworld Publications
(Sales and Editorial)
185 Banbury Road
Oxford OX2 7AR
England
www.oneworld-publications.com

ISBN 1–85168–392–5

Cover design by Design Deluxe
Printed and bound in the USA by McNaughton & Gunn

Contents

For
Jonathan, Emily,
Rhiannon and Alexander

Preface

I have been writing this memoir for several years in odd moments between other writing projects. The initial motive was to satisfy the curiosity of my grandchildren, when they are quite a bit older, about Grandad John. I would have been very interested if my own grandparents and parents had left something of the same sort, and I imagine that almost anyone at some stage in their life would like to know more about their forebears. But as I got into it I have found this journey down memory lane to be a thoroughly enjoyable experience in itself – except of course for some very painful memories also encountered on the way. Producing most of it has been made easy by the diaries and letters and other documents lying in a large trunk in the attic, so that much of the book has virtually written itself.

Having spent half my working life in the USA I tend to use both American and British spelling indiscriminately and have not tried to make it consistent throughout. Because of its original orientation to the family and a few friends the result is less formal and probably more frank than it might otherwise have been. However I have avoided any uncharitable revelations while retaining honest, if sometimes critical, judgments of the work of others in the same field. Despite all its faults I hope that the result may be of interest to some of those who have read one or more of my books and would like to know (as I often do with books that I read) a little more about the author.

John Hick
20 January 2003

1

A shipping family

Usually it is only noble or notable families that have a family tree going back before the registration of births, deaths and marriages in England in 1837. The Hicks have never been either noble or notable but because they lived continuously in the same small town, Scarborough, we have a tree going back to a John Hick (1699-1780) who married Ann Thornton (1700-79) and which now (2002) covers nine generations. Beginning in 1685, and increasing considerably during the eighteenth and nineteenth centuries, Scarborough was quite an important port for ocean-going vessels and until the advent of iron ships beginning in the 1820s wooden ships were still being built on the foreshore at Scarborough.[1] Muster Rolls of ships were compulsory from 1786. The first Hick ship on these lists, though not the first to sail, was the *Plough*, built in Scarborough in 1786 and owned and captained by a James Hick. (This was a brigantine, others being barques or snows[2] and, from 1878, steamships). The Scarborough firm that built most of their wooden ships was Tindalls and we get a glimpse of the economics of the industry from the brigantine *Providence Success*, 212 tons, 84 foot long, owned and captained by Walter Pantland senior, which was built by Tindalls in 1796 for £1200 ('hull only') – the equivalent of £60,000 or up to twice that today.[3] In 1787 'there belonged to the port of Scarborough 33,400 tons of shipping, the prime cost of which was £450,000; the number of seamen was 1,500'.[4]

As early as the third generation that we know anything about some of the Hicks seem to have been doing quite well. At any rate if we assume that the magnificent grandfather clock, with the ship which rocks with each swing of the pendulum, made about 1800, was originally bought by Thomas Hick (son of John Hick and Mary Hawson) – which would account for its coming down to Cousin Mercia, who left it to me – Thomas must have been fairly prosperous. There is also a scale model of the *Mary Hick*, a sailing barque of 430 tons, built in Sunderland in 1856, owned by P. Hick, Sr, P. Hick, Jr and Thomas Hick, which went down off Santa Anna in the Gulf of Mexico in September 1879.

The ships normally had two or more joint owners, and between 1775 and 1913 ninety-one were owned or part-owned by Hicks.[5] (This includes four fishing vessels of 30–40 tons, perhaps small trawlers of the kind that were still sailing from Scarborough when I was a boy.) Sailing in those days was obviously a dangerous occupation, for forty-seven of the ninety-one ships were lost at sea – in the Atlantic, the North Sea, the Mediterranean, the Baltic, the Bosphorus, off North and South America, and as far away as Tasmania, three going down with all hands. The best way that I have found of getting a sense of what it must have been like to be in charge of an ocean-going sailing ship is from C.S. Forester's Hornblower novels, for example, *Hornblower and the Hotspur*, where there are detailed descriptions of how the captain used the various different sails in changing weather conditions. However after steam ships came in none of the Hick ships were lost. Their steamers included the Dale line, named after eight Yorkshire dales. These would be 'tramp steamers' carrying cargoes all over the globe.

The only ship for which I have some voyage accounts is the steamer *Lockton*, 757 tons, 123 horse power, registered in 1882 and owned by James Bailey Hick. It seems that the ship cost £21,250 to build. Its first voyage was from 1 December 1882 to 23 January 1883, carrying 1408 tons of coal at 6s 6d a ton from Sunderland to St Nazaire, and then 1508 tons of iron ore at 10s a ton from Bilbao to Middlesborough, at a total cost for the voyage of £1232-7-0, with a profit ('balance due to steamer') of £348-7-0. Most voyages made a profit though a few made a loss. Subsequent voyages made profits of £607, £232, and £259, with a 'balance due to J.B. Hick' in 1883 of £45-2-11, in 1884 of £764-15-0, and in 1885 of £794-9-9. (For today's value one has to multiply by between 50 and 100.) The ship was sold in 1889 to James Knott and renamed the SS *African Prince*. There is a letter of October 1891 from James Knott to Albert Edwin Hick, in his capacity as a solicitor, in which Knott is explaining the poor performance of the ship in the African trade. First, she was detained on the coast so that a voyage that should have taken three months took four and a half with running expenses of £12 a day. And then

> the new Master in whose charge I had placed her made a complete mess of the whole voyage and completely ruined all the arrangements I had made ... It appears ... that he was troubled with a religious mania and I must admit that in all the course of my experience I never heard of such a performance as he has made with the *African Prince* ...

There is also some information, though not financial, about another steamer, *Wydale*. She was an iron schooner-rigged steamship, built in South Shields by John Redhead & Co. in 1881, owned by Pantland Hick Jr, captained by B.W.Hick, and carrying Lloyd's highest rating of 100 A1. However in 1884 she collided off the Isle of Wight with a small sailing vessel whose crew of two were both drowned. A Board of Trade inquiry blamed the captain of the *Wydale* for sailing too fast and his certificate was suspended for three months. In 1887, more happily, he was able to rescue the crew of a large sinking American schooner, the *Baymore*. In 1887, Pantland Hick sold the ship to a Glasgow firm, and in 1900 she was sold again to a Spanish firm. Finally, she ran aground off Burniston, near Scarborough, and became a total wreck.[6]

Interesting information about some of the ships comes from cousin Mercia Bell (who died in 1996) in a letter to grandson Jonathan when in 1995 he was doing a school project on ships:

> After Captain Cook's discoveries [Cook sailed from Whitby, near Scarborough] in the New World in the latter part of the 18th century the need for merchant ships expanded and a great many of the [Scarborough] townsmen became ship-owners. Some were well established before the Hicks, but the distinction of the Hick family was that it managed to go on the longest. Before the end of the 19th century it was the only family to own a deep-sea fleet based on Scarborough. For that reason it became, for the period, of great importance to the town, providing opportunities for seafaring jobs and a living for traders in marine requirements ...

Pantland Hick Junior was running the firm for the last 30 or more years of the century, until he died in 1900. Times had changed and the harbour was no longer suitable for the ever larger vessels. The Hick steamers [the Dale line] were sold [the last in 1905] and Scarborough was no longer a ship owning port.

The sea-faring Hicks were however remembered with pride and gratitude for many years. When my [Mercia Bell's] grandfather, Burlinson Walker Hick, died in 1917 no fewer than ten former captains of Hick ships presented themselves at the cemetery to escort him to his rest.

In another letter cousin Mercia says that when her mother was married at St Mary's [Scarborough] in 1905

every ship in the harbour below was decorated, as her ancestors, the Herberts and the Hicks, had been ship-owners, Master Mariners and Harbour Commissioners for so long.

It had always been the case that most Scarborough ship-owners had been to sea first and owned ships later. Scarborough was a small town until the railway came in the 1840s and it often happened that there were marriages between ship-owning families [Walker, Tindall, Hick, Herbert, Hawson, etc.]. It was no wonder when sons of such marriages wanted to go to sea. If they did, they went to sea at the age of 14, so that they could become master mariners by the time they were 21. Your [Jonathan's] great-great-grandfather, Edwin Hick, had five brothers who went to sea very young and became Master Mariners. These were Thomas, Pantland Junior, James, Burlinson Walker Hick, and William.

Another cousin, Sylvia Spooner, provides some information about Thomas, the eldest, who was her grandfather. He was a master mariner and seems to have owned some ships, and in 1859 he was sent by a London company of which he was a shareholder to transport mining machinery to a mine in the Northampton district of Western Australia, in which silver and lead had been discovered. But after waiting almost two years in vain for further orders about the machinery it was off-loaded and left on the beach, where apparently some large pieces can still be seen. Later he lived in London and became a Ship and Insurance Broker, and in 1877 was given the Freedom of the City of London.

Continuing with Mercia's information,

It was Pantland Hick Junior who came ashore to take over after his father, Pantland Hick Senior, who had earlier taken over from his father Thomas, who had built up the ship-owning business in the first part of the 19th century. In spite of the dangers of sailing ships, some intrepid young wives accompanied their husbands on long voyages. Mary Herbert was one of them and James Hick's wife another. Sometimes, in the sailing vessels, it took a matter of years rather than months to sail right round the world (as they sometimes did) delivering and picking up cargoes from place to place as they went. Mary had her first child, my uncle Herbert Hick, born at sea half way between Chittagong and Colombo in 1873. They were then in 'Syringa', which was still only a wooden ship [and was wrecked off Maryland, USA, in 1887].

The 'Mercia' turned out to be a rather special ship. She was a fast one and could, in good conditions, rival the speed of the famous tea-clippers. On one run, south of Cape Leewin, she achieved 1,198 miles in four days, an average of nearly 300 miles a day. She was the last foreign-going Scarborough sailing ship. My grandfather and grandmother, little Herbert Hick, the Mate, the crew, the hens, the sheep, the cargo and a clever dog, all sailed the high seas in 'Mercia'. . which was known in her high hey-day as the Pride of Scarborough. . (There is a framed photo of a painting of the 'Mercia')

The Hick ships do not seem to have had many adventures, but in his young days as Master of 'Syringa' B.W. Hick was once cast ashore on an almost deserted island in the Dutch East Indies and had a long row to Batavia to get help to pull the ship off. On another occasion he rescued the crew of a German ship, including the Master's wife and baby, in the south Pacific. He was presented with a bulldog but got no other reward. In 1882 Admiral Beresford intended to bombard Alexandria, where there were anti-foreign riots. He requested that British ships in the vicinity should go to convey the British citizens to safety. Both James Hick and B.W. Hick were on their way to the Black Sea at the time and both diverted their ships to the rescue.

On the back of the oil painting of *Concord*, built in 1830, a snow of 224 tons, 54 foot long, with a crew of 10, it is recorded that when in 1845 she was captained by Thomas Hick, aged twenty-one, on his first voyage a Finnish whaler circled the ship and an old whale hand shouted 'That whale means mischief.' It did, for it charged and stove in the ship's side and the crew had to abandon it in strong seas and were rescued by another ship.

Sylvia Spooner relays two more stories which she had heard from Mercia.

In the early 19th century a Hick ship was sailing into the Tyne at the time of a flood and saw a wooden cradle floating out to sea. Inside there was a baby, a girl. They fed her through the spout of a teapot until they tied up and she was united with her parents. Subsequently her parents brought her as a young girl to thank the Captain Hick who had saved her life.

The other story sounds legendary though it may not be: 'During the Napoleonic wars a French ship appeared in Scarborough Bay. No naval vessels being in sight a Hick ship left harbour to chase her. She turned and fled. Subsequently came a message to say she would not fire on a Hick ship.' (There was a Hick flag, which can be seen on the picture of the *Mercia*.) Yet another story from Mercia is that at some point during the Napoleonic wars a Hick ship was in a French port and the captain was interned but escaped disguised as a servant of a family who were travelling by coach out of France, and so eventually got home.

Although the first recorded Hick vessel was the *Mary*, a small boat of 40 tons and a crew of three, owned in 1775 by John Hick, and there were others continuously since then, the family business only really began to flourish at the end of the Napoleonic wars[7] and was at its height through the second half of the nineteenth century. Pantland (1803–1887) was a master mariner and owner of four ships in 1851 and was part-owner of the *Mary Hick*, whose model still sails on in a glass case. He retired ashore at the age of forty-one and became a town councillor, a President of Trinity House (a home for retired seamen), a President of the Merchant Seamen's Hospital, a member of the Harbour Commission, a Director and Trustee of the Savings Bank and a Director of the Scarborough Gas Company; while his brother Thomas owned seven ships; and his brother Michael, a master mariner, owned two ships and was part-owner and master of another; and a JP. Pantland married Mary Burlinson Walker, who owned twenty-one ships, so that two ship-owning families were united. They had eleven children, of whom two died in infancy. Of the seven sons, Thomas was a master mariner; Pantland junior (of whom there is a fine photo in his mayor's robe, skilfully touched up by an artist) was a master mariner, and a JP and alderman and mayor of Scarborough in 1883–4; James was a master mariner; Burlinson Walker, also a master mariner (referred to in Mercia's letter above), was owner and master of the *Mercia*. Between them they owned the Dale line of steamships. Until 1900 Pantland Hick was still running the business from an office in Scarborough, with a branch office in Cardiff run by his brother William, and two other brothers had shipping agencies in Liverpool and London.

In a note added to his list of the ships Captain Sydney Smith (a retired Hick captain) says

> Hicks kept in the outer harbour at Scarborough a pontoon upon which vessels could be placed at high water. It was then allowed to ground at low water and the sluices opened so that it emptied itself of water. The sluices were then closed and the pontoon floated with the vessel upright upon it, the last vessels to use it being the barques 'Coral Isle' [built 1861] and 'Olive Branch' [built 1868]. This enabled the bottom to be painted and underwater repair work done. I cannot find the date it was disposed of.

The old wooden chest currently in the conservatory is part of the shipping story. Apparently it is a late George III period walnut brass-bound cellarette converted to a travelling box and made about 1830. There was a note inside the lid by my mother, Aileen:

> Leeds, August 1987. 'Old Richardson', as he was always known to us, was one of the first people Mark took me to see when we were first married [in 1917]. He lived in one of the Sailors' Cottages on the way to the harbour, and had always sailed in one of the Hick ships and had sailed all his life. It seemed to me then that he was an old man, and he often came to see us. I think that Mark saw that he was well looked after. One day he arrived carrying this box, and told me that it had been all round the world with him, and that everything he had was kept in this box and that he would like it to stay with the Hicks and that he would like to give it to me. (I hope I was suitably impressed.) [My wife] Hazel always liked it, and I want her to have it. It must be very dirty. I think I kept coal in it - but have always used it and valued it. So here it is for Hazel with my love, and certainly with old Richardson's regards. Aileen.

And then there is another piece of paper on which she has added, 'In the night that I had written this, a man came to me in a dream and said, "You are wrong about old Richardson – he lived in a Seamans' Dwelling, nothing to do with a cottage at all." So awake, I was wrong, and asleep I was right.' I (John) also remember being taken to visit old Richardson when I was a child but I can remember nothing about him except that he was a friendly old man.

The only one of the brothers in my grandfather's generation who did not go into shipping was my grandfather himself, Albert Edwin (1846–1900), who became a solicitor, setting up on his own in Scarborough at the age of twenty-three or four. Later he took a younger partner and the firm when I knew it was Hick & Hands, a small provincial firm in a Dickensian gas-lit office doing mostly rather unexciting work such as conveyancing and probate. Albert Edwin was Deputy-Coroner for Scarborough, president of the Scarborough Hospital, a trustee of the South Cliff Congregational Church, president of the Mechanics and Literary Institute, treasurer of the Band of Hope Union – he was a keen teetotaller – was a Liberal-Unionist ('though he took no very active part, and was highly esteemed by both parties'), was connected with the Scarborough Amateur Rowing Club, and owned a farm at Staintonedale and was also part-owner of two of the fishing vessels that came at the tail end of the shipping business after all, the rest were larger ships no longer based in Scarborough.

Edwin and Maria had two sons, my father Mark and his brother Norman. I have a very dim memory of Granny Maria, who died when I was four, as a Queen Victoria-like figure sitting in state in the loggia at Athol House (Fulford Road, South Cliff, Scarborough). When she died in 1926 she left the house to her two sons. Mark evidently bought Norman's share and we lived there all the time whilst I was growing up. Norman was trained as an architect but, I think, hardly ever practiced. I believe that he designed the Hutton Buscel post office, and apart from that only a cottage which he had built to give to a couple when they retired after serving Norman and his wife Marjorie for many years – a decent thing to do which was entirely in keeping with his character as I remember it. He and Marjorie lived in a lovely old house in Hutton Buscel, near Scarborough – the house had once been an inn, and the story is that some of Cromwell's troops were billeted there on their way to besiege Scarborough castle.

Edwin died at the age of only fifty-four of a heart attack after
visiting his farm, finding that some stakes had not been driven into
the ground that should have been, and doing it himself. He died in
the train on the way back to Scarborough. He was described by the
Coroner, who had known him for over thirty years, as 'one of the
most honourable of men, and one who had ever had the best
interests of the town at heart.' I know that his son Mark, who was
only twenty when Edwin died, always remembered him with great
admiration and affection.

On my dining room wall I have a group photo of the Hicks of my
grandfather's generation, taken probably in the 1880s or '90s; also a
photo portrait of one of them, Pantland, in his mayor's robe, and
one of another, William, also in some official robe. The group photo
is an excellent piece of photography, well arranged and very clear.
This is from the time when they were the leading shipping family in
Scarborough. The first word that comes to my mind in looking at
them is solidity. They are men most of whom have been at sea for
many years, have faced dangers and hardships, and who have been
successful in life. They look to me like a group of ancestors of whom
one can be proud. William has a big moustache and a scowl, but all
the others look relaxed and kindly, and well contented with life.

On my mother's side her mother, Lucy Hirst, was a Cocker before
her marriage. The story of the Cocker family, spreading over
Yorkshire, Van Dieman's Land, Melbourne, British Columbia,
Mexico, Tonga and Michigan, has been well traced by cousin (the
Venerable) Mark Dalby.[8] It is an interesting story, but I cannot
recount it here. The only individual among them whom I want to
mention is the first academic in the family, the Rev. Benjamin
Cocker who became professor of philosophy at the University of
Michigan and published several books, including *Christianity and
Greek Philosophy* (1870), *Lectures on the Truth of the Christian Tradition*
(1872) and *The Students Handbook of Philosophy* (1881). I have sampled
some bits and would say – if I can without impertinence about an
ancestor – that they were good in their time but of no intrinsic
interest today. (Perhaps in another hundred years, if any of my own
books are referred to, it will be in much the same terms.) The other
academic on the Cocker-Hirst side was uncle Eddy, Edward Wales
Hirst, of whom more later.

NOTES

1. See James Buckley, *The Outport of Scarborough 1602–1853*, apparently printed privately, presumably in Scarborough, no date.
2. A brigantine was a two-masted vessel with square rigged foremast and fore-and-aft rigged mainmast. A barque had its aftermost mast fore-and-aft rigged and its other (usually two) masts square-rigged. And a snow was 'a small sailing-vessel resembling a brig, carrying a main and foremast and a supplementary trysail mast close behind the mainmast; formerly employed as a warship'.
3. For the figure of £60,000 I have multiplied by 50, the figure used by Roy Jenkins in his *Gladstone* (1995), p. 149. However the historian Hugh McLeod believes that the figure should be more like 100. See extended note in chap. 2.
4. Joseph Brogden Baker, *The History of Scarborough*, London: Longmans, Green, 1882, p. 370.
5. The list was made by Captain Sydney Smith, who was Deputy Harbour Master at Scarborough and Senior Warden of the Scarborough Trinity House.
6. *Scarborough Evening News*, 25 October 1974.
7. James Buckley, *The Outport of Scarborough*, p. 104.
8. Mark Dalby, *The Cocker Connection*, London & New York: Regency Press, 1989.

2

Childhood, schools and family

My earliest datable memory is of being told at the age of two that I now had a sister, Shirley. I don't recall that this was then of any interest to me. This was at 7 Westbourne Grove in Scarborough. When I was four we moved into Athol House, which was then large and with a decent sized garden. But at the end of the 1939–45 war Mark and Aileen divided it into two and sold one half. Later they also sold most of the remaining garden for a bungalow to be built. All this presumably to support their finances – which prompts me to speculate a little about those finances.

Mark's father, Albert Edwin the solicitor, married Maria Day, daughter of a successful woollen mill owner in Dewsbury, said to have been a hard business man though he also contributed generously to the building of a new Congregational church in Dewsbury. There is a letter dated 22 November 1881 from Edwin in Scarborough to his wife Maria who was in Dewsbury visiting her mother, telling Maria the contents of her father's will, he having recently died and the solicitor administering it apparently being in Scarborough. He left between £50,000 and £60,000 (the former being the equivalent today of either two and a half or five million, the latter either three or six million, depending on whether one multiplies by 50 or 100[1]) to Maria and her two brothers in equal shares. So Maria may have inherited the equivalent, on the lower total of £50,000, of either £750,000 or £1.5 million, and on the higher figure of £60,000, either £1 or £2 million – or in each case somewhere between, but nearer the higher figure. I speculate that her wealth made it possible for Edwin to do so much in the way of public service in the town rather than spend all his time cultivating the law practice. Maria lived in Athol House after her husband's early death, dying herself at the age of seventy-six when, I presume, she left her two sons half her estate each, amounting on the 1881 multiple, to between £350,000 and £800,000 on the lower figure, or between £500,000 and £1 million on the higher one. However, I don't know by what to multiply from 1926, when Maria died. Nor do I know whether whatever sum she inherited was either increased or eroded during her lifetime. But whatever the amount of his own inheritance, I speculate that it will have made it easier for my father Mark also, who would probably have increased his inheritance on the stock market, to pursue his real interest, which was tennis, at the expense of his work as a solicitor. But more about that later.

We seemed to be a well enough off middle class family, employing a cook and a maid, an occasional handyman, at one time a nanny and later a tutor. However in 1939 some big investment in the east, I think in rubber, failed and there was an economising regime as a result. I don't know whether this was a major financial disaster for Mark or only a set back, but probably the former. He had – like many of his generation – no pension scheme and was, I think, living on capital during his last years. When he died in 1962 Aileen was left owning Athol House (half the original house) but not much more. There was however an assortment of smallish family Trusts from which Aileen received the income during her life. (My sister) Shirley put a lot of effort into forcing the almost criminally inefficient family solicitor to dig these out and account for them, and quite enjoyed harassing and threatening him on behalf of us all, to good effect. At Aileen's death in 1988 Pem, Shirley and I each received, if I remember rightly, some three or four thousands pounds. (I was by then fairly well off and passed my share on to my children, Ele, Mark and Pete).

Returning to childhood in Athol House, my main memory is of the three of us playing endless enthralling games in the nursery, which was a large room on the second floor. We had a lot of bricks – ordinary builder's bricks – and lots of toy soldiers and other lead figures, and built towns and castles illuminated with flashlight bulbs strung together on long wires attached at one end to a battery. We would play happily for hours on end, though of course with occasional quarrels and fights as well. There were also many happy hours spent playing on the sands and amongst the rocks and pools at Children's Corner in the south bay, with occasional ice creams and also donkey rides and Punch-and-Judy shows on the foreshore and paddle boats on the mere. The family hired each summer one among the rows of wooden 'bungalows' on the sloping south bay cliff facing the sea, consisting of a small room and a minute kitchen, with space in front for deck chairs, where we spent a lot of time each summer. My memory is of long, sunny warm days, but I'm not sure that the weather can really have been as good as I remember it.

One early memory is of the Christmas atmosphere which seemed magical. I remember looking down through a window after dark at the Salvation Army band grouped round a lamp post (the street lamps then being gas and lit by hand); and feeling the present-filled stocking in the early morning and then going to sleep again until it was light; and the Christmas tree with its small red candles clipped onto the branches and lit with magical effect – much more romantic although much less safe than today's coloured electric bulbs. I would say that my pre-prep-school childhood and school holidays were very happy, the same being true of Pem and Shirley.

Pem (Pentland), two years older than me, has had an unusual career involving early experiments in butterfly farming (before the 1939–45 war selling to the then numerous collectors of exotic foreign butterflies was still a viable small-scale business), later cinema and theatre ownership, and then a spectacular entrepreneurial success in creating Flamingo Park, a zoo near Malton in Yorkshire. In 1960 car ownership was rapidly increasing and his idea, which proved correct, was that people would be looking for places in the countryside to visit. In addition to hundreds of private cars, dozens of charabancs brought visitors from all over Yorkshire. His wife, Nora, ran the restaurants and bars which also proved highly profitable. She later wrote an account of the whole Flamingo Park episode.[2] Pem's basic plan was to build up a successful business and then sell it at a large profit. But in selling the Zoo he was badly cheated, and has been doing a variety of other things since and now lives in Italy, so that we communicate mainly by email.

Shirley, two years younger than me, has also had an interesting and sometimes remarkable career. She trained as a social worker in child-care, specialising in fostering and adoption and later serving as a Guardian ad Litem in the juvenile courts. She has also developed an expertise in play therapy for problem children in schools. She married Norman Leak when he was Tutor at Westminster College, Cambridge, and then a Presbyterian minister, serving the church in various ways as youth secretary, editor of the denominational journal and minister of various congregations, eventually retiring early through ill health. But Shirley's physical fitness puts us all to shame. When she was seventy one she won the silver medal in her age group at the World Triathlon Championship in Mexico; and has long been and still is a keen golfer. She has an enviable gift for enjoying life in all its details to the full. I have been much closer to her than to Pem, with shared holidays, visits and long phone conversations.

Returning to my own story, prep school, today's primary school but up to at least thirteen, was awful. The private school that I went to, Lisvane, just round the corner from Athol House, had some good but some very bad aspects. On the good side, I made several true friends, BP (Brian Parker), Hutch, Wood, Monty Motum – the characters along with J in the gang stories which I told to the children when they were very young. I have remained in touch with BP ever since and we last met for a delightful day together in Scarborough when I was there with some of the family for a hotel weekend. Hutch also was a close friend, though I lost touch with him sometime after the war and he was, I believe, killed in a plane crash sometime in the 1950s. At Lisvane he and I once made a pact which required us to be celibate and not to drink alcohol, on pain of the lapsed party paying the other a fine of one guinea!

At Lisvane I enjoyed being a Cub and then a Scout. But the school was owned and run by a man who turned out to be mentally unbalanced and ended up in prison for impersonating an army colonel. He looked the part, as an imposing military-type figure who successfully fooled the parents. But there was a lot of bullying of the boys by the staff themselves, including the head. This was not the sexual abuse that we hear so much about these days, nor being physically assaulted, but more a matter of being shouted at and intimidated, although there were also canings – quite common and accepted in schools in those days – and I came in for that once. I don't now remember a lot of detail, but I do remember once being made by one of the masters to wear a wicker waste-paper basket over my head and stand in a large cupboard; and since I still remember it this must have had an effect on me. But as this was our only experience of school life we all took the bullying for granted as normal and did not even think of complaining to our parents. It is not mentioned in the very brief entries in my Charles Lette's School-Boy's Diaries. Today such treatment would quickly become known and treated as criminal child abuse. One unfortunate Lisvane boy was reduced to a nervous wreck and spent years under psychiatric treatment.

From the bits of diary when I was twelve I find that I had some good but more bad days at Lisvane, but with no details; that I read H.G.Wells' *An Outline History of the World*; that I kept an exact account of my income and expenditure (the amounts seldom exceeding 6d), and had measles, an operation to remove tonsils, a camping holiday, an air-gun, and a small printing set on which, amongst other things, I printed a paper against fox-hunting.

As a child I was painfully shy. As a teenager not much less so. Basically I probably still am to some extent although it is covered over by the adult persona. However I had a natural bent for what I later learned was philosophy. I remember the relief at turning sixteen because it seemed less precocious to be reading the kinds of book that I was reading. This would probably not be precocious today when the young seem to grow up much quicker than two generations ago. I have no diary for age sixteen, but at seventeen I was reading Nietzsche, particularly *Zarathustra*, which I thought (rightly I think) to be a truly great work, being stirred particularly by Nietzsche's splendid independence of mind; and Leibniz, particularly the *Monadology* which I found fascinating, Mill's *Utilitarianism*, and was also interested in Schopenhauer, A.N.Whitehead's *Science and the Modern World*, Freud's *Totem and Tabu*, Russell's *The Problems of Philosophy*, and was thrilled by C.E.M. Joad's *Guide to Philosophy*. It was a revelation to read about Plato, Descartes, Locke, Berkeley and Hume, and above all Kant. From my diary,

> I wonder whether thinking is necessary. I think it is for some people and not for others. It is for me! (July 1939)

> Bought for 1/- a fairly good copy of Thomas Hardy's *Under the*

> *Greenwood Tree* ... I now have a vast gold mine of literature. I am
> surrounded in my bedroom by some of the best books in the
> world. Good books should cost nothing. They are beyond price
> (July 1939).

Another book that I loved was Lin Yutang's *The Necessity of Living*,
about Chinese wisdom for life. My then Me was obviously a bit of a
bookish nerd.

Around this time I was put in touch with Uncle Eddy, Edward
Wales Hirst, Aileen's uncle. He was then retired, but had been a
Lecturer in Christian Ethics at Manchester University and in the
United Methodist and Hartley Colleges. As the only academic
member of the family he took a kindly interest and was very helpful
to me. He was the author of several books - I still have three of them,
published in 1919, 1928 and 1949 – and had received a DLitt from
London University. I had a small hand in the last of his books,
making a number of suggestions for improving the style, usually by
deleting redundant phrases, and typing it for him and reading the
proofs. Although few today can have heard of E.W. Hirst, he made
his own distinctive contribution to Christian ethics at the time. He
was in fact ahead of his time in taking account of ancient Chinese
thinkers. After writing his last book he very generously gave me his
library, a fine collection of early twentieth-century philosophical
books, including the great Hastings Rashdall multi-volume
Encyclopedia of Religion and Ethics, a valuable and very useful reference
work though now long superseded.

At one time Uncle Eddy wrote to Aileen after reading an essay that
I had sent him called 'The Dreamer's Vision', recommending that I
should go to a University; and when I was about to become an
articled clerk at Hick & Hands, the legal document requiring a stamp
duty of £80 – then a lot more than £80 today – he intervened again,
suggesting that I should test my aptitude for philosophy by going for
a couple of terms to Manchester University and then if this seemed
feasible become a regular student there for a BA and then a PhD,
hoping for a University teaching career. But in the end it was decided
(I acquiescing) that the Law was the safer prospect, and that I could
read philosophy in my spare time. The lesson there seems to be:
beware of giving prudent career advice to teenagers.

Although this was not at that time on the cards, I did in fact later go to a University – Edinburgh. Uncle Eddy then introduced me to a friend of his, D.S. Cairns, retired professor and principal of one of the Scottish theological faculties. Uncle Eddy's handwriting was so bad that I spent some weeks trying to trace a principal D.S. Cavins, but when I managed to make contact he was very kind, inviting me to tea from time to time. He was rather absent-minded and sometimes happily enjoyed his own tea and cakes without remembering to offer me anything after the first cup and the first slice of cake. In a much later diary, for 1953,

> Reading the unfinished autobiography of D.S. Cairns, recently published. It is well written. I remember him as a somewhat Johnsonian figure, vast and untidy. He was very kind to me. I visited him a number of times at Mayfield Terrace, arguing about pacifism and talking about many other things. I went to him once when [after the war] I was very concerned about the European blockade, asking his support for the famine relief movement. After thinking about it for a day or two he said that he was willing to sign the draft letter to the papers which I had written, but suggested trying to get the four religious leaders of Scotland to do so. He rewrote it, in a more specifically non-pacifist spirit, and it was published over the signatures of the Moderator of the Church of Scotland, the Episcopal primus, Roman Archbishop and the President of the Free Church Council. The last time I had to do with Dr Cairns was when he sent a letter supporting my application to the Appellate Tribunal.

Returning to Uncle Eddy, his handwriting, together with my own, produced an amusing misunderstanding as we corresponded about philosophical questions. At one point I wrote that various contemporary philosophers thought in a way that was homocentric (human-centred), but Uncle Eddy read this as homosexual and wrote several delicate and embarrassed letters before the misreading was corrected.

Returning to Lisvane, at a certain stage Pem, for some health reason that I have forgotten, was being educated at home by a tutor (a very nice chap, known as the Great H, with whom we kept in touch on-and-off for years afterwards) and I left Lisvane to join him. After this I went as a boarder to Bootham school in York, apparently because Mark had known and been impressed by the head, Donald Gray, during the 1914–18 war. I was only there for the two years 1937 and '38, when I was fifteen and sixteen. My memories of Bootham are wholly good. Its Quaker atmosphere meant that each pupil was treated as an individual and was encouraged to fulfil his own potential. The day began with an assembly with five minutes of silence and then announcements. On Sundays we processed through York to one of the Friends' Meetings, sitting opposite the girls from the Mount school. As Lisvane had been exceptionally bad, Bootham was exceptionally good and I flourished there. I read a lot – I remember, for example, being gripped by Thoreau's *Walden*. The Penguin sixpenny paperbacks began in 1935, and soon after that the Penguin Classics, Thoreau's book being one of the first batch, and then the Pelicans in 1937. Another discovery was the nature mystic Richard Jefferies' *The Story of My Heart*. The Penguins (fiction) and Pelicans (non-fiction) and Penguin Classics were a tremendous benefit to many thousands of people, encouraging us to buy books and extend our range of reading. I also began to enjoy writing and had something published in the school magazine. I even find, to my surprise, that I wrote some rather stodgy verse:

> Moving through Earth's star spangled skies,
> Creeping o'er Earth's dark shadowed slopes,
> Thrusting through veils of misty cloud,
> Ray of the Sun brings Morn of Hopes!
>
> Now in the dawn stands forth a light.
> Earth in her path revolving turns,
> Bringing from East to West the sun.
> Day to the Planet Earth returns!

My prose writing was originally rhetorical and emotive until, one day, thinking about a phrase I had just used, 'the mystic winds of war', I realised that it was meaningless and resolved in future to write as accurately and lucidly as I could – which I have tried to do ever since.

Whilst we all, I think, enjoyed Bootham, that does not mean that we were model schoolboys all the time. Some of us managed to get an imprint in wax of the key to the door out to the grounds and make keys for ourselves by filing down blanks, using them to go out from time to time and climb over the wall into the town to visit a cinema. And on one occasion I put fireworks with a long fuse under the small wooden platform on which the master sat, so that they went off during the class – childish but true. An annual Bootham treat was Chocolate Jumbo's Strawberry Vit, a feast put on for us at Rowntree's chocolate factory by the head of the firm. I also first became aware of politics and the wider world at Bootham. We had interesting visiting speakers, including some MPs. The Spanish Civil War was being fought and we collected money for milk for children on the Government (anti-Franco) side.

I left Bootham after only two years without having taken any significant exams to became an articled clerk at Hick & Hands, at a time when the thought of war was beginning to cast its shadow over everyone's minds.

I have been referring here to Mark and Aileen because this may make it easier for you to see them as real people, but in fact we never called them that – they were Dad and Mam. I was very pleased when my own children on their own initiative in their teens began to call Hazel and me by our first names. Mike was the first to do this, put up to it I suspect by the others.

My relations with Aileen were always good. She was a wonderful mother, always loving and understanding, devoting herself utterly to the interests of her children and later also her grandchildren. After Mark's death she was financially vulnerable but showed great courage in setting up her own business, a souvenir shop at Pem's Flamingo Park; in dealing with sometimes very difficult lodgers in Athol House; and in her old age living on a small income in a flat in Leeds (with Pem in the flat above), living with a cancer which however remained stationary for many years, and increasingly painful arthritis, but always, with much use of the telephone, close to her children and grandchildren. She was a wonderful person, and I regret that during her life I took this for granted and seldom made a point of telling her

But my relations with Mark, in my teenage years and later, were often bad. On his side, he was politically conservative whilst I was a socialist, he was disappointed that I switched from the Law to the Presbyterian ministry, and during the war he was a conventional patriot whilst I was a conscientious objector. During the First World War he had been a lieutenant in charge of a howitzer battery. As the second war approached there was continuous tension. For example,

Had a bad quarrel with Dad at dinner today. I do not know how it began, and I myself was more of a spectator than a combatant, but Dad was very annoyed over my lack of patriotic bias in viewing history! M. appeared in tears afterwards asking me not to let it happen again (July 1939).

But although he seemed to me at the time to be irrationally resistant to new ideas, Mark was far from unintelligent. On the contrary, for he played both chess and bridge for Yorkshire. According to a pen portrait of him in the Scarborough *Evening News* in 1946, on one occasion

> he was one of 25 players who played [the world chess champion] Dr Alekhine simultaneously, and he survived from eight in the evening until two in the morning, when he resigned. In a similar game played by Tarkover [another grand master] against a smaller number of opponents Mr Hick secured a draw.

Looking back, the breach was all as much my fault as his – except that I was a teenager when it started and he a mature adult – and then later I was away from home a good deal, at Edinburgh, in the Friends Ambulance Unit, at Belford, and then in the US – about all of which later. He must have had money worries after the investment failure in the east, and a genuine patriotism stirred up by the war, and a worry about his reputation in the town with a conchie son. The rift was perhaps understandable on both sides, but I am very sorry that it was not healed later when it might easily have been with a sufficient effort on either side. He was, I am sure, basically a very decent, kindly and loving parent. I am profoundly thankful that nothing like that father-son rift has recurred in the next generation.

Mark's central interest, as I have mentioned, was tennis. He was a very good player, only a notch or two down from the top players. He was one of the British seeded players at Wimbledon from 1912 to 1925, apart from the war years, and would have played on the centre court in 1921 if rain had not rearranged the matches. He won the North of England championship three times, the Yorkshire championship five times, winning the cup outright; and was Scarborough champion thirty times in a row, apart from the war years. In those days – before and after what came to be called the Great War – Wimbledon as he and Aileen described it was a relatively small affair in which everyone knew everyone and it was a delightful social as well as a great tennis occasion. The players were all amateurs – professionals in those days were coaches who were not allowed to play in the competitions. Mark was famous for throwing the ball exceptionally high when serving. He played for the pleasure of playing, and went on long after he had ceased winning, taking to doubles with a younger partner when he could no longer play high-level singles. He played a good deal on the continent, and every Easter Aileen and he went to Cannes for a tournament and holiday there. (It was there that Aileen reported seeing a wealthy fat man waddling about, 'almost too rich to walk'.) Mark also played for Scarborough at hockey. Later, in his fifties, he took up bowls, and quickly became good enough to win various Scarborough and Yorkshire championships.

Alas, I was never really reconciled with him before his death, and was in the United States when he died. This was in 1962, when he had suffered from heart attacks for a year or more. From my diary for August 1961:

'Scarboro' Pa feeling a little better, and I am glad that these last days are more tolerable, for he is not expected to last much longer. Noticing a faded rose in the garden of the new house [in Princeton] I thought of the vanished world of his hey-day – Wimbledon in the 1920s, the Riviera before World War II, camping with John Byass in Harwood Dale ...

Hick & Hands was a small firm consisting of the two partners, one legal executive and one typist. Its offices were above a chemist's shop in the middle of town, reached by grimy stairs, the rooms still lit by gas, dusty and with shelves of old documents, and with a letter book in which every letter sent out was placed, the book then being pressed in a vice, leaving a copy of each before they were posted. So letters to do with every case were in the same book instead of in separate files. When I remember it I am astonished by the contrast with my son Mark's Wragge & Co in Birmingham, with its currently more than a hundred partners, some six hundred fee earners, and with over a thousand people in the firm altogether, being the biggest on one site outside London. Mark had a tough time getting where he is now as a partner in this highly reputed firm. He started out as a barrister and then requalified as a solicitor, involving a lot of hard work and a lot of determination. His special field is now insurance law, overseeing a portfolio of cases dealing with warranty and indemnity insurance in the case of large corporate transactions, often involving millions or tens of millions or even more of pounds, as well as professional negligence insurance, etc. The cases seldom get to court but are usually settled by negotiation and Mark has proved to be an extremely successful negotiator. He is essentially a 'people person', establishing good personal relations with colleagues, employees, opposing solicitors, etc. I am proud of him, for this and his other qualities and achievements, as I am also of Ele and Pete.

Returning to Hick & Hands, whilst I was an articled clerk I walked down with my father Mark across the Valley Bridge at 9.15 and back at 12.45, and down again at 2.15, returning at 4.15. He then went to the South Cliff Club to play bridge and talk with his pals about the news and the stock market. He also often went out mid-morning for coffee with them. As I have suggested earlier, I think that initially this rather relaxed life, in which the business did not expand much, was possible because he had inherited quite a lot from his mother, though it seems that this was lost in the failure of what I remember as the rubber investment. But, until his last years, when heart trouble and financial worries progressively beset him he had, I would think, a pretty enjoyable life, though alas overshadowed during the war by my being a conscientious objector.

NOTES

1. Roy Jenkins, in his *Gladstone* (1995), p.149, and again in his *Churchill* (2001), uses a factor of about 50 to translate the Victorian value of the pound into its present day value. But my colleague the historian Professor Hugh McLeod says that for the later Victorian period one should multiply by about 100. He says (in an email to me):

> In the later Victorian period, £50 a year was generally reckoned to be the poverty line. £100–150 a year was the income of the better paid working class, and £150 represented the bottom end of the middle class. £300 was more middle-middle class, and £500 or more indicated someone who was very comfortably off. Someone with over £1,000 a year could be counted as wealthy, and with £5,000 you would be considered very wealthy. To get some kind of equivalent of these figures in present-day terms, I think you would have to multiply by about a hundred.

He adds that such calculations are difficult because, e.g., in Victorian times a middle class family would have a full-time live in maid, but not today, but today such a family might well go on annual overseas holidays, but not in Victorian times.

2. Frances Hick, *Zoo Lady* (Ventnor, Isle of Wight: Olympia Press International, 1992).

3

Religious exploration and conversion

From Bootham, which I left before any major exams, I became an articled clerk at Hick & Hands. In those days few provincial solicitors took Law degrees – so far as I remember, only one at that time in Scarborough – the rest having qualified through the Law Society's exams. I had some special tutoring at home and passed the Law Prelim, which was I suppose somewhere between GCSE and A-levels today, and went twice a week by train to Hull to attend law lectures at what was then the University College, now the University of Hull. The first lecturer was good, according to my diary, and the second abysmally bad, doing little more than read to us out of the text book which we all had. But I had attended extra-mural lectures on philosophy in Scarborough by professor T.E. Jessop and was now allowed to attend his lectures at Hull to a class of three, the other two preparing for the Presbyterian ministry. One of these, Dan Beeby, having served as a missionary in China and Taiwan, is now almost a neighbour in Selly Oak, and we enjoy meals together from time to time in spite of the fact that he retains his doctrinal fundamentalism of Hull days. The other, Bryan Dawson, has also had a long ministerial career abroad and in this country but has moved on a long way from his early fundamentalist theology, and we quite recently reconnected to our mutual pleasure.

'Prof. Jess' was very learned (in Greek, Latin, German, Italian and French), and more a historian of philosophy than an original philosophical thinker. As well as having edited Berkeley's *Principles* he also wrote about the Italian Lakes, Christian Ethics, and the Treaty of

Versailles. He was a major influence to whom I owe much in encouraging my philosophical bent and we kept in touch. He later stayed with us in Princeton and in Cambridge, and we corresponded from time to time. He was always supportive and helpful.

At seventeen I was busy writing, including an essay on 'Equality of Income' and another on 'The New Renaissance'. (This was after I had decided to try to write lucidly!) I read a lot by leftish authors, including G.D.H. Cole, Stafford Cripps, Bernard Shaw, H.G. Wells, Bertrand Russell, and the great eighteenth-century critic of religion Tom Paine. This was the time of Victor Gollanz's Left Bookclub, reasonably priced in its yellow jackets. Hutch, who had gone to a grammar school in Ripon but had an uncle and aunt in Scarborough whom he visited, introduced BP and me to the latest poetry – W.H. Auden and Christopher Isherwood. A friend of Granny's, of her own generation, Miss Dickson – I don't think I ever knew her first name; she was just Dicksie, – who had been one of the first woman journalists, helped me to develop the art of writing. Incidentally, when in December 1914 Scarborough was shelled during a rapid raid on the east coast by a German warship she had happened to be in York for the day. But the news agencies, assuming that she had been in Scarborough, telegrammed for her account of it and she wrote the first-hand account that was read all over the country! An amusing item from my diary: 'Miss Dickson has a strong superstition that a member of the family always dies in December, the 18th being the most dangerous day. Being ill she naturally thought and came to believe that she would die next Monday. But a few days ago an old distant relative aged over 90, whom she hardly knew, died, thus stepping into the breach, and Dixie is now much more cheerful' (16 December 1939).

It seems that I was helpful to her one winter, and she wrote these nice lines:

I send a word of greeting from my lonely prison cell
To which I've been confined for days, yet I am fairly well.
My life in gaol's been bettered by a very faithful friend
Who daily scaled the snowy heights to reach me and to lend
To life that hope that, minus him, quite surely would have fled,
For no one else dare mount the steps that to my dwelling led.
He posted piles of letters – Christmas, as you can guess.
He saw I didn't starve or die of utter loneliness.
He got me ink and stamps and 'notes', bearding the Banker's den

> To find them, so that I could have the wherewithal – you ken?
> It was no 'damsel in distress' who sadly called for aid,
> But for a dull old lady, who was snow-bound, that he made
> His daily journeys through the slush and snow and bitter cold,
> Which makes his kindness greater – her gratitude untold.

Whilst on the positive side I was a great reader, on the negative side I was very smug and a cultural and intellectual snob (as indeed I still am, or at least the latter), and a very naive if also quite intelligent youngster. There are diary comments such as 'Murder on the Second Floor' was 'the least undesirable play I have seen for a very long time'. (Scarborough then had a good repertory theatre, the plays alternating with the York theatre.) 'Within a few feet of me there were fifteen dead animals draped around the ladies.' Aunt Grace (not actually an aunt but a family friend), referring to working-class children evacuated from the coastal towns to the country said 'something about not too much soap having been used by some people so one heard; to which I replied that sometimes some people hadn't got too much money so one imagined' (September 1939); and, 'We get up in complete darkness, have breakfast in unnatural electric light, spend half the morning in Medieval gloom and pouring rain, and day dawns at about mid-day' (November 1939). Having heard Archbishop William Temple defending the war, 'He is an entertaining old heathen! . . . The Archbishop of York ought to be one of the most Christ-like men in the world, but he is a politician, spiritually not greatly above the average' (October 1939). And some theosophical pamphlet 'was not a good example of a well-written booklet – too full of assertions without proofs'.

For my second term at Hull instead of commuting I lived in a students' hostel in Cottingham. The war had now begun, and the bombing of Britain. Hull with its port and huge storage facilities was a target and we all took our turns in overnight fire-watching teams at the college to put out any fires from incendiary bombs. Shortly after dark, as we stood on the roof there would be a distant rumble growing gradually louder, and then searchlight beams stabbing the sky and anti-aircraft fire, and then the bombs exploding. I was on duty during the two successive nights when the centre of Hull was destroyed:

> Two nights ago we had the worst air-raid Hull has had so far. From about 8 at night to after 1 in the morning there was almost

continual sound of gunfire and H.E. bombs. Occasionally there was the very alarming sound of bombs coming nearer and nearer in tremendous rippling waves. Several times we heard the shriek of bombs quite close, but none of them exploded. Fire bombs were showered down. There were several dozen in the College grounds. The preliminary casualty list gave over 100 casualties, about 30 killed and many seriously wounded. (11 March 1941)

It was at Hull that I experienced a powerful evangelical conversion to fundamentalist Christianity. But before coming to that, what was my previous religious state? As children we had been taken to the nearby parish church, presided over by the Reverend 'Fishcake', and found the services infinitely boring and totally off-putting. Granny (Aileen's mother) was into all sorts of religious explorations and I was interested in all of them with her. Quite apart from this she was a marvellous Granny, two of her familiar sayings when we were very young being 'Boys will be boys', which I approved of, and 'Cleanliness is next to godliness', of which I did not approve so much. In these religious explorations she took me to lectures by British Israelite speakers, whom I found highly unconvincing. I must have been a visiting lecturer's nightmare because I not only asked questions, and then further questions about the answers, but also sent in written questions: 'Got a series of answers to my questions on British Israelism which I addressed to the Rev. Claude Coffin. Only 3 out of 8 are satisfactory. I have prepared a series of replies to them'! (February 1939).

Earlier Granny provided hospitality in her house just up the road to the then well-known Welsh evangelist, George Jeffreys, founder in 1926 of the Four Square Gospel Alliance (later the Elim Pentecostal Churches) and some of his fellow evangelists when they held a revival mission in Scarborough, I then being twelve. Jeffreys was a powerful charismatic preacher and also a healer – though whether his healings went beyond a strong placebo effect I do not know. When the party left there was a farewell prayer meeting in Granny's dining room and we children were included. I was kneeling at a chair when Jeffreys, coming round the circle, laid his hands on my head. I immediately felt a strong physical effect, like an electric shock except that it was not a sharp jolt but a pervasive sensation spreading down through my body. I was in floods of tears – not of sadness or fright but, I suppose, a tremendous emotional impact. Although people who have never experienced such things pooh-pooh them I am in no doubt that there are individuals through whom a real psychic force of some kind flows.

I also sometimes went with Granny to the Methodist Central Hall where 'Tubby' Newman (later a president of the Methodist Conference) preached. He bounded back and forth across a very wide pulpit and once leaned out so far that we could all see, with fascination, that he was finding it difficult to get back.

Mother's equally keen religious experimenting took a different form. In the wake of the First World War Spiritualism flourished and she and some of her friends took it up. She believed (at least ninety per cent) in a spirit Doctor Lascelles who spoke through a London medium, Mr Simpson. She and her friends also used the ouija board (a board with a circle of cards with the letters of the alphabet, and an upturned tumbler in the middle on which two sitters each placed a couple of fingers and it then moved and spelled out a message). They recorded masses of 'messages', none of them so far as I know of any real significance. Aileen also attended seances when in London; and once the famous (or infamous) materialisation medium, Helen Duncan, performed in Athol House. She would produce 'ectoplasm' which built up into life-size white figures who spoke and were supposed to be recognised by members of the audience. In this case there was an audience of about twenty, each paying a fee which went to Mrs Duncan. She arrived (smelling of gin, according to Aileen) with a male assistant, and two lady members of the audience took her to another room where she undressed, was searched and clothed in a loose black dress. She then sat on a chair in a corner which had been curtained off, with a low wattage red light outside the curtains and the rest of the room in darkness. The curtains were open for a while after she sat down and her assistant then closed them. We all sang some hymns, and then presently there was a voice from behind the screen and figures, consisting of a head and a long white robe, emerged one at a time into the dim red light and spoke, some of them apparently being recognised as deceased relatives by members of the audience. I don't remember what the figures said – probably something to the effect, 'I'm happy here on the Other Side.' And then in due course the curtains were opened again and Mrs Duncan, in trance in the chair, began to wake up. This was presumably a typical performance. I found it totally unconvincing, and my own theory was that the assistant who closed the curtains contrived in doing so to throw her some tightly packed white material and then took it back again as he helped her out of the corner into another chair at the end. However in 1933 and again in 1943 she was convicted of fraud and the second time sentenced to nine months in prison. Her spiritualist supporters said that sometimes she was genuine but sometimes nothing happened and she cheated to fill the gap. At any rate I was sure that she was cheating the time I saw her, although my theory about how she did it is only a theory – another was that she swallowed some very thin muslin-like material and regurgitated it behind the curtain.

On the few occasions when I have had a seance with a professional medium in London, the medium going into a trance and then a deceased person supposedly speaking through him or her, I have been quite unconvinced. But I have a strong rationalist streak and spiritualists say that this inhibits genuine communication!

This rationalist streak comes out quite often in the diaries. For example,

> Mrs Ball sent me recently the horoscope which I challenged her to make out for me. It is an Analysis by the Science of Numbers and Solar Biology! Apparently I ought to vibrate to the number 2. She traces (by 'impressions') five previous incarnations. But I will keep the document itself – it runs to ten typed pages – as a prize evidence of superstition in this twentieth century.

I'm afraid it is long since lost.

I am not however in any doubt as to the reality of ESP (extra-sensory perception, or telepathy). And I am impressed by some of the communications recorded in the early days of the Society for Psychical Research. I was a member of the Society for many years, reading its regular publications, having joined at the suggestion of my Oxford doctoral supervisor, H.H.Price, who was one of the most highly intelligent people I have known, and author not only of important books on epistemology but also of fascinating philosophical discussions of psychical research, or parapsychology as it is known today.

Aileen was herself very 'psychic'. For example, shortly after Pem was born she went into the bedroom where he was sleeping and saw her father, who had died a year earlier, apparently entirely solid and standing at the foot of the cot, looking at the baby. Panicking, she rushed downstairs to tell Mark that there was a man in baby's room. At another time, when we were holidaying in a country cottage, she woke one night to see a pretty, smiling young girl, dressed in the style of a hundred or so years ago, standing at the foot of her bed. There were several other apparitions and strange events.

But the most remarkable were her two healings. One was of a man whom she knew, called Wardle, who had been badly wounded in the Canadian navy during the 1914-18 war. One day she heard that he had collapsed onto the floor and been taken to the hospital. From her account:

> Sir Barclay Monagham from Leeds (the most famous surgeon in the north at that time) had been to see him (because of a Canadian pension, or something of that sort) and could do nothing for him because of his internal condition, & had given him the choice of staying in hospital or going home; and he was now at home in very severe pain & having morphia. I went straight to his house (by the Mere) & found him practically dead – only his eyes could open & he muttered 'sleep'. His wife said he had no normal sleep for several days & nights and that he was dying. His coffin had been ordered – apparently normal in their circle. His wife & children were weeping round his bed. I have no idea what made me do what I immediately did. But I heard myself saying in a very authoritative voice, 'Mrs Wardle, please take the children into the kitchen & and I will soon have Wardle asleep.'
>
> They left the room & I drew the curtains & knelt down beside him & put my hands on his head and prayed that I could be used to help him. I don't think he saw me or knew me – he was hardly alive – but I began to talk to him in this authoritative voice saying 'You are very tired & and you will have a long quiet sleep, and when you wake up you will be well.' This is exactly what happened – he slept for hours (if I remember rightly Mrs Wardle said he slept for 8 hours – but I can't be sure), and he was able to sit up and eat when he woke up – he got better every day & in three weeks he walked through the thick snow to see me, about a mile and a half away. He became quite well and eventually moved somewhere on the south coast where he started a Zoo. I knew his Scarborough doctor (now dead) & asked him about Wardle – he said 'what would I not give to see his inside!' – and that his recovery could only be called a miracle.

Her other healing was of a doctor friend whom we knew for many years. After leaving Scarborough he lived near London, and it was there that Aileen did much the same for him, when he was desperately ill but unexpectedly recovered rapidly.

One of Aileen's friends was a Theosophist who lent me some theosophical literature – theosophy being a nineteenth-century western philosophy created out of elements of Hinduism and Buddhism by Madam Blavatsky, founder of the Theosophical Society in 1875. Her successor, Annie Besant, proclaimed a young Indian, Krishnamurti as the coming world teacher – a role which he later disavowed, spending his life outside the theosophical movement and giving useful spiritual teaching, mostly in the United States. I was attracted by theosophy as the first coherent religious philosophy that I had met – much more so than the Christianity I knew. But after a while I consciously dismissed it, with its precise levels of existence and invisible spheres and ranks of angelic beings, as too neat and tidy and professing to know too much. What I gained from it however was an interest, which continued until my evangelical Christian conversion and then hibernated for many years, in the eastern religions.

At this time, whilst working during the day as an articled clerk, I often walked half way up Oliver's Mount to a particular comfortable spot under a tree to read for an hour or so before the sun went down I have always liked to record special moments, and there were several under my Thinking Tree. For example,

> It is so perfectly peaceful and beautiful now that I cannot bear not to give myself a note to remember it by. I came out this evening to sit in the sun and read again Thoreau's *Walden*. The woods are sloping up to my left and I am lying at the foot of the first tree. I cannot possibly convey in words the beauty of them, just trees on a green slope, in the warm sun, alone, with the sheep and two brown horses in the field on my right below me, mostly quite still. Below that the mere is shining blue and cool. Birds are twittering in the trees. It is literally too beautiful for words (5 May 1940).

I see that in 1940 (aged eighteen) I already had a view of life's problems and difficulties rather like that in my parable of the two travellers in *Faith and Knowledge*, first published in 1957. In 1940 I wrote:

Imagine yourself trudging through a seemingly endless stretch of dangerous bog, with snakes and other horrors by the way; if your idea of it depends on what you see on the way, then you may well be miserable – your chances of getting through appear small, and in any case you don't know what it is leading you to; but if you have previously studied a map of the journey, and you knew that the bog wasn't really so deep as it seemed, that there were no snakes except in your imagination, and that on the other side of the bog was just the place you had always dreamed of, the journey would be a joyous one, and you would inspire all your fellow travellers with hope and courage (16 January 1940).

As well as the diary I kept a 1940 notebook of philosophical reflections, aphorisms, a literary form learned from Nietzsche, and with many references to Nietzsche, about whom I planned a book the first chapter of which got written and long since lost. One or two of my eighteen-year-old aphorisms:

Every question of right and wrong, and thus of what we ought to do in any circumstances, ultimately depends on what we, at our stage of spiritual evolution, conceive, consciously or subconsciously, to be the purpose of life, for morality must be based on the true nature of the Universe ... I myself believe that the purpose of life as we can know it is the perfecting of every individual soul by the transmuting of all evil into good, and that thus every action is right which assists in this process, and every action wrong which hinders it.

Reality is ethical and consists of God, who cannot be regarded as finite or infinite, or as having any or no form, or by any other analogy from the physical universe, but can only be comprehended 'mystically', by reason of the divine spark in each of us.

To be personal is to be finite. God is not finite and therefore not personal. But the personal being with whom we can get into contact in prayer etc., whilst being finite, may yet be larger than the extent of our consciousness and therefore infinite in relation to us and our needs.

Every question is an open question, because when it is closed it is no longer a question.

Always remember that to be discontented with life really means that you are discontented with yourself.

A book (not including novels) should be as short as possible –

not some usual and conventional length. It should be completely lucid and precise, with no vagueness, no implying rather than stating, no mere rhetoric.

Nazism and the war against Nazism are not two separate things, a disease and a cure, but one big disease, generated by almost the whole of Europe.

And in November 1939,

At the moment, and for years to come, we shall be living in a world gone mad. There will be no news, no facts, only propaganda. We shall be mentally debased by the foul atmosphere, and despised by most people once the war feeling has been fully worked up.

One of my earliest published pieces, in the Hull students' journal, before my conversion, was called 'On the Importance of Heresy'. This was about an attitude to life: heresy, I said, 'is that salutary state of mind in which everything is seen as alive and mysterious and worth looking at'. Reading all this now I see how my intellectual development has been surprisingly consistent apart from the interruption of the evangelical years.

This then was the background to my conversion experience. I believed absolutely in some sort of divine reality, though not the God of Christian orthodoxy. Clearly I was in a religiously questioning and open state. Having written about my conversion experience before I will quote from those accounts.

As a law student at University College, Hull, at the age of eighteen, I underwent a powerful evangelical conversion under the impact of the New Testament figure of Jesus. For several days I was in a state of intense mental and emotional turmoil, during which I became increasingly aware of a higher truth and greater reality pressing in upon me and claiming my recognition and response. At first this was highly unwelcome, a disturbing and challenging demand for nothing less than a revolution in personal identity. But then the disturbing claim became a liberating invitation. The reality that was pressing in upon me was not only awesomely demanding and but also irresistibly attractive, and I entered with great joy and excitement into the world of Christian faith.[1]

and discussing momentary religious experiences,

An experience of this kind which I cannot forget, even though it happened forty-two years ago [from 1982], occurred – of all places – on the top deck of a bus in the middle of the city of Hull, when I was a law student at University College, Hull. As everyone will be very conscious who can themselves remember such a moment, all descriptions are inadequate. But it was as though the skies opened up and light poured down and filled me with a sense of overflowing joy, in response to an immense transcendent goodness and love. I remember that I couldn't help smiling broadly – smiling back, as it were, at God – though if any of the other passengers were looking they must have thought that I was a lunatic, grinning at nothing.[2]

I would say now that there was a genuine impact upon me of the ultimate divine Reality and that I was conscious of this in the way then available to me. For my closest friends at Hull were members of the Inter-Varsity Fellowship, the evangelical campus organisation; and throwing in my lot with them I accepted as a whole and without question the entire fundamentalist theological package – the verbal inspiration of the Bible; creation and fall; Jesus as God the Son incarnate, born of a virgin, conscious of his divine nature, and performing miracles of divine power; redemption by his blood from sin and guilt; Jesus' bodily resurrection, ascension and future return in glory; heaven and hell. Among the hymns that we sang a couple of lines have stuck in my mind (perhaps because they are so visually off-putting), 'There is a fountain filled with blood, drawn from Immanuel's veins.' It was later, but still in my fundamentalist period, that I almost became engaged to the fundamentalist daughter of a fundamentalist family. Happily – in retrospect – this was only 'almost' because marriage with her would, long term, have been a disaster.

I now decided, almost automatically, to switch from the Law to train for the Christian ministry. I was not positively enjoying the Law, but would have stayed with it, presumably for the rest of my working life, but for this conversion. The ministry meant for me in practice the Presbyterian ministry simply because my IVF friends happened to be members of the then Presbyterian Church of England. I was a whole-hearted evangelical fundamentalist for the rest of my time at Hull and during my first year at Edinburgh, which I went to for an Arts degree before going on to theology, and also through my time in the Friends

Ambulance Unit. At Westminster College after the war, and during my three years as a minister at Belford, and still during the three years at Cornell, and then at Princeton Theological Seminary, I was still a highly orthodox but no longer fundamentalist Christian. I remember, at Westminster, being profoundly shocked by an Australian graduate student who did not believe in the divinity of Christ – though of course much later I came, retrospectively, to agree with him.

Although I have since been a critic of evangelical theology, seeing it as a form of doctrinal (and sometimes also biblical) fundamentalism, with all the dangers of the fundamentalist mind-set, I can nevertheless genuinely understand the evangelicals' point of view, having once fully shared it for several years. But this fact has made the criticisms particularly resented. One survey declares that I

> had the regrettable effect of snapping evangelicalism in general back to a hunkered-down sense of defensiveness – especially with regard to Christology. Hick was especially problematic in this case because he was himself an apostate evangelical. Hick's shadow over evangelical Christology has been long.[3]

I was not myself aware of this, but it may be true. But I hope that as well as making some evangelicals more defensive I have helped others to move beyond their doctrinal fundamentalism. A number of people who had assumed that they had to choose between the traditionally orthodox Christian beliefs which the churches still profess but which those outside find incredible, and on the other hand an entirely non-religious stance, have said that they have felt liberated by reading one or other of my books. For there is a vast range of possibilities beyond these two alternatives.

NOTES

1. Dennis Okholm and Timothy Phillips, eds., *More Than One Way?*, reissued as *Four Views on Salvation in a Pluralistic Age*, Grand Rapids, Michigan: Zondervan, 1995 and 1996, pp. 29–30.
2. Michael Goulder and John Hick, *Why Believe in God?* London: SCM Press, 1983, reissued 1994, pp. 40–41.
3. Douglas Jacobsen and Frederick Schmidt, 'Behind Orthodoxy and Beyond It: Recent Developments in Evangelical Christology', *Scottish Journal of Theology*, Vol. 45 (1992), p. 519.

4

A conchie

It is, surely, to the credit of both Britain and the United States that they recognise that some people have a conscientious objection to taking part in the mass homicide that we call war. In the 1914–18 war conscientious objectors were sometimes very harshly treated in Britain. Many were imprisoned and some were forcibly dressed in army uniforms, taken to the front, given an order which their conscience required them to disobey, sentenced to be shot but later reprieved. There were some 60,000 conchies in the 1939–45 war but nothing so drastic happened to us, although a few who refused any alternative service – and all honour to them, although I did not share their viewpoint – had a hard time in prison.

I was one of the majority who thought that it was impossible totally to opt out of the war but that we should do something constructive rather than destructive. I went before a Tribunal and was allowed to join the Friends Ambulance Unit as a form of alternative service. I received some criticism and condemnation on the home front but none whatever from the soldiers whom I encountered abroad. There we wore army uniform, but with our own shoulder flash with a red cross and the letters FAU. That we were conchies was sometimes puzzling to the conscripted soldiers but we were accepted as individuals who were in the same boat as themselves. Some members of the FAU were killed in action but I myself never came under fire or in danger of death. It was life in what someone has called the margins of chaos. I was, on the whole, doing interesting and satisfying work, interspersed with quite a lot of waiting around and doing very little.

Why was I a conscientious objector in the 1939–45 war? Was this not as well justified a war, on the Allied side, as any? Yes, I think it was. It would have been a terrible disaster for western civilisation if Nazism had finally triumphed. The Jewish Holocaust – we did not know about it until the end of the war, although the government did – might well have become total. The Nazi ideology would have dominated Europe, perhaps for generations, and it would have been a long time before 'Christian' civilisation re-emerged.

But something else is also true. Imagine a visitor from outer space observing the human race. She would see the wars that have occurred throughout our history as attacks of mass insanity. She would see in every generation sections of the human species turning upon and seeking to destroy one another, driven by mutual fears, suspicions, greeds and hatreds, and using the escalating means of destruction that their technologies provide to kill or maim thousands or millions of their fellow human beings, making others vulnerable to dangerous diseases, laying waste towns and cities, and leaving many of the survivors permanently damaged in body or mind. And focusing on Europe in the twentieth century she would see the 1914–18 war, blundered into by short-sighted politicians and generals and developing under its own impetus into the mindless slaughter of millions. And then she would see the settlement after it, again reached by short-sighted and sometimes vindictive politicians, creating the conditions within which Hitler later came to power, leading to another world war which might otherwise never have happened, again involving the slaughter of millions. (This was also the analysis of John Maynard Keynes, the great economist and one of the most intelligent people of his generation, who in *The Economic Consequences of the Peace* argued that the punitive Versailles Treaty and continuing punitive treatment of Germany were sowing the seeds of the next war.[1]) She would be witnessing a vicious cycle of violence leading to more violence and creating the possibility, as the means of mass destruction escalate into nuclear and germ warfare, that the human race, with hundreds of millions killed and the infrastructures of civilisation destroyed, may batter itself back into the stone age.

Further, war degrades our human nature, suppressing its best potentialities and encouraging its worst. As the historian Eric Hobsbawm says,

> the First World War was a machine for brutalizing the world, and these men [the early Italian Fascists, of whom 57% were ex-servicemen from the First World War] gloried in the release of their latent brutality ... [More widely, there was] the emergence of a relatively small, but absolutely numerous, minority for whom the experience of fighting, even under the conditions of 1914–18, was central and inspirational; for whom uniform and discipline, sacrifice – of self and others – and blood, arms, and power were what made masculine life worth living.[2]

There was indeed the reality of comradeship and the satisfaction of a temporary meaning in life which many otherwise lacked so that in wartime they were, paradoxically, more alive than in peace time! But she would also observe, here and there, individuals and small groups standing up and saying that all this is madness. Would she not see the spread of their point of view as the best hope for humankind? But on earth this could only be more than an abstract ideal if those individuals and groups acted on it by refusing to join in the mutual hatred and destruction, and accepting for themselves any penalty that this involved. And this is what the conscientious objectors did. Some took the very simple and straightforward position that one cannot imagine Jesus dropping bombs on inhabited cities, shooting or bayoneting or riding in a tank with guns blazing, and that anyone who was trying to be a disciple of Jesus could not possibly do that. Others, including myself, shared that conviction but went beyond it to a wider consideration.

There is a short-term and a long-term view. The short-term view was that in the given situation of 1939, regardless of how it had come about, it was necessary to fight back against Nazi Germany and later against Japan. The long-term view was that in the larger situation it was necessary to stand up for the truth that the apparently endless cycle of wars, escalating in destructive force, constitute the insane self-destruction of humanity. Once war has begun it is too late for the radically different outlook and policies that might have prevented it from ever happening. But it is not too late to point stubbornly for the sake of the future to the way out of the vicious cycle of mutual destruction. In theory one could hold that both points of view are correct, with some, the large majority, having a vocation to act on the one and some, the small minority of conscientious objectors, a vocation to act on the other. In practice we all simply acted out the moral insight that gripped us. I, for one, respected the right of soldiers to be soldiers, with the terrible work that they sometimes had to do, whilst being quite clear that I could not be one myself.

It has not been given to many successfully to combine non-violence with effective political action. The greatest historical example is Mahatma Gandhi. A number of contemporary examples are described in Hagen Berndt's book *Non-Violence in the World Religions*,[3] which I read recently – and found that I know three of them, Desmond Tutu, Mohammed Arkoun and Farid Esack.

In the 1930s I joined the Peace Pledge Union ('I renounce war and I will never support or sanction another') founded by Canon Dick Shepherd, whose nearly 150,000 members then included a number of people who were very well known: George Lansbury (Leader of the Labour Party,1931–35), Charles Raven (Regius Professor of Divinity at Cambridge), Donald Soper (well-known Methodist leader), Bertrand Russell, C.E.M. Joad, Aldous Huxley, Laurence Housman, Middleton Murray, Vera Brittain, Rose Macaulay, Dame Sybil Thorndike – though most of them did not continue as members throughout the war.

Editorials in the Friends Ambulance Unit Chronicle were in dialogue form, such as the following:

I see John Hick is running to four pages once again.
Yes; and using words like 'normative'. Do you know the meaning of 'normative'?
No.
Nor do I. First he put 'operative', but he crossed it out. It might give us a clue. But I like what I can understand.
What do you like?
I like this: 'To refuse to do wrong is sometimes, in its immediate context, itself a wrong. Thus in different ways both the pacifist and the non-pacifist do evil that good may come.'
So what does he do about it?
Well, he says, 'There is a practical solution, in terms of vocation.'
Do you agree?
Yes.
I'm not so sure. It may be all right for him, but for a lot of people

> in the FAU pacifism is a simpler thing than that. Reading John
> Hick would unsettle them.
> Don't you think it's time they were unsettled?
> I'm not so sure.
> Well, what else are we to put in the Chronicle?
> What, indeed.

As a c.o. I met a deeply distressing opposition from my father. I was
in Hull when at the age of eighteen I had to register. It makes me sad
now to re-read the letter in which he said,

> Your attitude, as I expect you know, has been the greatest sorrow
> in my life, apart from the deaths of my father and mother ... I
> also suspect – but I may be wrong – that your mind was
> deliberately poisoned by some vile creature at York [i.e.
> Bootham] ... I think you should appreciate, if it has not already
> occurred to you, that at any rate for a time there is the possibility
> it would be very unpleasant for an out and out c.o. to live in a
> town where his record was known – and, perhaps, difficult to
> carry on business there (5 February 1940).

This may have been before I had decided not to be an 'absolutist' but
to seek alternative service. I still remember, after agonising about this
for weeks, waking up one morning with the utterly clear conviction,
all doubts and worries banished, that I should take the latter course.
(I seem to have an active unconscious mind which has guided me at
critical moments.) I think also that Mark's feeling of revulsion and
shame may have been slightly assuaged when I arrived home in
uniform on embarkation leave.

During the war there were about a thousand members of the FAU,[4]
mostly men but also some women doctors and nurses. In general we
were 'middle class', and quite a number were either recent university
graduates or, like me, in the middle of a university course. I recently
saw some photos taken by another FAU member and was struck by
what a lively and interesting lot, for the most part, we looked. Several
whom I knew became so fascinated by medicine that after the war they
trained as doctors. Sam Macilwain, for example, with whom I stayed in
contact for many years, was older than me and had been a seaman,
first officer on a merchant ship. After the war he trained as a doctor –
not an easy thing to do in his thirties – and spent the rest of his career
as a happy and professionally fulfilled country GP. A number, such as

Theo Cadoux and Peter Ure, had careers as academics. Some, such as Hallam Tennyson, worked for the BBC. A few were later to become nationally well-known – Gerald Gardiner, already a barrister when in the FAU, became Lord Chancellor in Harold Wilson's Labour government;[5] Richard Wainwright became a Liberal MP and chairman of the Liberal Party. Another whom I did not know personally, Roy Ridgway, served a term in prison as a c.o., and then joined the FAU, 'saving the lives of injured men in the midst of heavy fighting' according to his obituary, and after the war editing the BMA's News Review, being one of the founders of the Medical Campaign Against Nuclear Weapons and one of the team who received the Nobel Peace Prize on behalf of International Physicians for Prevention of Nuclear War; and Freddy Temple (nephew of archbishop William Temple), who became an Anglican bishop. Those I worked with included Donald Swan of Flanders and Swan; Lewis Waddilove, an extremely able man who was in charge of the FAU's work in the Middle East when I was there and who went on to do all sorts of interesting things including being chairman of the Rowntree Trust and then of Shelter, doing much to promote the development of housing associations (receiving a CBE); Gordon Tilsley, with whom I was in the same group in Greece, has been a successful solicitor and Town Clerk of Norwich; and many more who have also contributed positively to society in a wide variety of different ways. And there were certainly a great many others whom I do not happen to know about.

Having been accepted by the FAU I reported at its training camp at Manor Farm, Northfield, in Birmingham, only a couple of miles or so from where I now live. This was the fifteenth camp. I don't remember just how many there were of us new recruits, but probably about fifty. The camp commandant was Michael Cadbury, whom I met again from time to time in Birmingham until his death. The training was a mixture of physical exercise and basic medical training – something between first aid and the training of a paramedic today, including, for example, how to deliver a baby. One day the Quaker theologian H.G. Wood, who had recently become the first professor of theology at Birmingham University, came to talk to us and I was asked to express our thanks – I little thought that twenty-five years later, when a new chair had been created in his name, I would become the H.G. Wood professor in the theology department.

From Northfield I was sent as one of a section of about six to work in St Alfeges Hospital in Greenwich as a ward orderly doing the dirty work of administering bottles and bedpans, portering, taking pulses and temperatures, etc. My second, brief, love was a nurse there called Googie (Guggenheim). In August 1940 there were two hundred and thirty FAU members in British hospitals, some doing whatever unskilled jobs needed to be done and some receiving training and in a few cases (but not me) quite advanced training. In the great majority of cases hospital work in Britain was a prelude to service overseas, early on in the war in Finland and Norway where the first fighting took place; running medical clinics in Syria and Ethiopia; the China Convoy; later throughout the North Africa campaign; later again in refugee camps in the Middle East and relief work in the Balkans; and after the Allied invasion of Europe driving ambulances and looking after the wounded there.

After what was probably two or three months at St Alfeges I was sent to the Royal Infirmary in Edinburgh to train in the path. lab. To start with I was given the lowliest of jobs, which was to look after the guinea pigs used for tests. I can claim that I was good at this, reducing the rate of guinea pig deaths from disease from several a day to none a day. Others in our section were working as orderlies and porters. Because those who were portering had to get up at some unearthly hour, those of us who were working more civilised hours took over the porters' work once a week to give them a lie in. My memory of this is of taking corpses of patients who had died during the night on trolleys to the mortuary. There were two possible routes. One was through a network of underground passages, manoeuvring round sharp bends, crouching under roof pipes, and up and down an occasional step. The other route, which I preferred, involved going out of doors, sometimes in wind and rain, and crossing a sloping yard, trying to prevent the corpse from falling off on the way.

We lived in an empty ward but had our meals with the rest of the staff. But one day mother and Shirley came to visit us and cooked a meal in our ward kitchen. When they opened the unused oven a family of mice jumped out! We made friends with some of the nurses and some of the junior doctors. And having completed a first year at Edinburgh university I was also able to keep in touch with some university friends.

After these months of 'training' in home hospitals I was considered ready to go overseas – something that we all, aged about twenty, ardently desired. I did the mechanics course at Failand, near Bristol, learning to drive cars and lorries, and basic mechanics including how to dismantle and reassemble an engine – a skill which I have been careful never to use! And then a return to the Northfield camp for an embarkation course, followed by embarkation leave, and then to Liverpool for departure to the Middle East.

Whilst I was away from home amusing things happened at Athol House, as later recounted by Aileen. A group of soldiers were billeted there and were befriended by her. They were a motley lot of conscripts, including professional thieves and other interesting characters. They loathed their officer whom they said they would shoot when they got to the front, and so when Mark, who played bridge with this officer at the South Cliff Club, suggested bringing him home for a meal she absolutely vetoed the idea. The soldiers used all the coal stored in the window seats of the various upstairs rooms which they occupied, to keep themselves warm, but when they left for the invasion of the continent Aileen found that they had scrounged enough coal to leave them full again. She thoroughly enjoyed their presence, which lightened the load of anxiety from the fact that Pem and I were both overseas. I met him once, in Cairo, but apart from that our wartime paths did not cross.

NOTES

1. See Robert Skidelski, John Maynard Keynes:Vol. 2, *The Economist as Saviour, 1920–1947*, and e.g., Eric Hobsbawm, *Age of Extremes*, pp.30–1.
2. Ibid., p.125.
3. Hagen Berndt, *Non-Violence in the World Religions*, London: SCM Press, 2000.
4. The official history of the FAU in the Second World War is *Friends Ambulance Unit* by A. Tegla Davies, London: Allen & Unwin, 1947. See also *Pacifists in Action: The Experience of the Friends Ambulance Unit in the Second World War*, ed. Lyn Smith, York: William Sessions Ltd., 1998.
5. Gardiner took on the job of Lord Chancellor on condition that the death penalty would be abolished, and he was also responsible for a number of other important legal reforms. Geoffrey Robertson says,

   I once asked Gerald Gardiner why it was that as Lord Chancellor in the first Wilson government he refused to hold sensitive conversations in his office or his house. 'I believed they would be bugged by the security services.' But how could you believe that? 'Because, you see, I'd been a pacifist during the war' ... For this reason, Gardiner and Elwyn Jones, the Attorney General, were in the habit of discussing sensitive subjects in a car going round and round Trafalgar Square. ('We trusted the driver.')

Geoffrey Robertson QC, *The Justice Game*, London: Chatto & Windus, 1998, p. 133.

5

With the Friends Ambulance Unit in Egypt

From Liverpool we sailed in January 1944 for Egypt in a luxury liner, the *Stirling Castle*, converted into a troop ship. Shortly after the war I wrote an account of most of my time in the FAU abroad and what follows is largely from that.

Although expecting to be treated as the lowest form of military life, as civilians we were in fact ranked on the ship – I don't know why – with the warrant officers, which meant eating off plates instead of mess tins and sleeping in bunks instead of hammocks. Our immediate fellow-passengers, sergeant-majors of the regiment on board, were hard-bitten, hard swearing, army types, many of them professional soldiers. The leader of our FAU section had the (presumably notional or honorary) rank of major – he was nearly twice as old as most of us and looked every inch a major – the second-in-command was a captain, and the two doctors and the women were all lieutenants. We joined a convoy of some twenty ships escorted by four corvettes and sailed well out into the Atlantic to avoid the U boats, before swinging back towards Gibraltar. The main battle against the U boats was then over but there were still some marauders at large and outside the Straits there was a submarine scare – rapid changes of formation, the corvettes scurrying about dropping depth-charges and a plane flying low over the water searching for the raider. We were of course all at emergency stations and in life-jackets.

One soon discovered the proper use for the life-jackets which had to be carried at all times – they were very comfortable deck seats, and we spent much of the day sitting on them, reading, talking, using pocket chess sets, or just looking at the waves. But the sea soon ceased to be a novelty, except when schools of porpoises could be seen rolling in the water nearby. As we sailed further south the foam at the ship's wake became phosphorescent in the darkness and streamed out behind like a cascade of gleaming pearls and flashing diamonds showering into the water. The night sky was another splendid sight, the whole starry dome shifting and swaying as the ship's mast moved rhythmically across it. We passed Gibraltar during the night with the lights of Algiers and Spanish Morocco on one side and the black shape of the Rock on the other and moored beneath it a brilliantly lighted hospital ship. For several more days we were in sight of the mountains of North Africa, range upon range of snow-capped peaks gleaming in the sun.

On the morning of the fifteenth day we woke to see in the distance, instead of the familiar sea, a city lying on the horizon and the ship moved slowly in amongst swarms of small fishing boats and dhows weighed down almost to the waterline with cargo. This was Port Said. Then we saw all the eagerly anticipated suggestions of the East – minarets, luxurious palm trees, squat oriental houses, and natives in their rags and turbans. Clashing with all this were huge advertisement boards for British whiskies and cigarettes. We moored at the mouth of the Suez Canal and could see up it like a long road stretching into the desert, flanked by palm trees.

Having disembarked we went straight by train to GHQ Southern, a large military camp at Maadi a few miles outside Cairo. There we slept on the concrete floors of cool brick huts and a large mess building was allotted to us as lounge, office and dining room. Everyone immediately developed a phenomenal appetite and did true justice to the abundant fruit and to such novelties as sweet potatoes. Here we met for the first time an institution which is universal in the army in eastern countries – native servants in the messes. The only time when I felt a reaction to this was later, at El Shatt, where we had Egyptian servants who were suddenly replaced by volunteers from the Yugoslav refugees. The 'wogs' were to be dismissed without notice or compensation and with precautions which suggested that they were all unconvicted thieves. There had not in fact been any special boom in theft; though after they left, when some were probably hanging about in the neighbourhood without work, organised thefts became so serious that the camp guards were issued with arms. At the meeting when it was decided to sack the 'wogs' I disgusted the army officers, who then composed the greater part of the mess – mostly South Africans with strong racist prejudices – by proposing that instead of having them searched and marched off under guard, we should treat them as servants rather than as slaves and give them each a few piastres from the mess fund in lieu of notice. It was pointed out heatedly that it had never been the custom to treat the wogs as anything but wogs – i.e., as lesser beings having no rights in relation to ourselves.

To return to GHQ Southern, our first official contact with the army was unfortunate. We were wrathfully informed that a lavatory which we had been in the habit of using was for the exclusive use of the general. The army was also very perturbed by our failure to salute officers. This was a problem which cropped up everywhere. As civilians we were not obliged to salute anyone outside our own organisation, and certainly would never have dreamed of saluting anyone in it. We did however of course return salutes received by mistake, as happened all too frequently owing to the curious braid on our battle-dress and the red crosses on the drill shirt worn on the shoulder where an army officer wears his 'pips'. These often caused the mystified 'other ranks' to salute as a precautionary measure. Once in Cairo I met a string of soldiers, the first of whom saluted me, with all the rest then following suit, with me of course returning the salutes to my acute embarrassment.

Maadi village was a luxurious residential suburb of Cairo. In the early spring the main road had flowering trees arched across it and the gardens were a glorious mass of colour. Nearby, in drab sandy contrast, was the Arab village of Maadi which I visited during a typhus control exercise when we sprayed the inhabitants with DDT, the then new anti-louse powder with which the recent terrible Naples typhus outbreak had been controlled. This other Maadi was a filthy breeding place for all kinds of diseases. There were donkeys, oxen, and hens in most of the back-yards and ground-floor rooms. In one house there was a bundle of grass on a small landing, where a goat lived. However the people, especially the children, thoroughly enjoyed being disinfested.

We all visited Cairo itself during our first few days and were shown round by some of the Unit men living there. The FAU's HQ was a large flat in a block next to Bab-el-Louk station where one arrived by train from Maadi. It was a splendid flat and to stay there on leave or on business was always a pleasant interlude. Most of the people working in the HQ office had gone through the North African campaign, roughing it in the desert and coming under fire, and we late-comers benefited from the good impression they had made with the army. But in the Middle East the Unit's work was now to lie less and less with the army and more with refugees. Our own party of about thirty was the first to come out specifically as a relief force ready to go into the Balkans, and all later parties in this part of the world were likewise destined to work with civilians. At some point, when MERRA (Middle East Relief and Refugee Administration), later to be UNRRA (United Nations Relief and Rehabilitation Administration) was created, we came under its auspices.

My written account includes a good deal about Cairo with its palaces and mosques, and the Sphinx and Pyramids, essentially tourist stuff which I omit here. In spite of thoroughly enjoying all this I sympathised with Thoreau when he wrote,

> As for the Pyramids, there is nothing to wonder at in them so much as the fact that so many men could be found degraded enough to spend their lives constructing a tomb for some ambitious booby, whom it would have been wiser and manlier to have drowned in the Nile, and then given his body to the dogs.

I disliked Cairo, as it was then, with its racial tensions created by the occupying British lording it over the Egyptians. The only time I found Cairo tolerable was when I saw it from the balconies of the 15th Scottish General Hospital where I spent a month with jaundice. The hospital was a large building by the river and once the first phase of the disease was over life was very pleasant. In the evenings the dhows on the Nile, with their triangular sails spread, were a sight worth seeing. Hugh Russell was in the same ward, which was of course for 'other ranks', i.e. ordinary soldiers, and one day this fact caused consternation among the authorities. Lady Russell, wife of Russell Pasha, the British Commandant of the Egyptian police and a relative of Hugh's, came and asked for Lord Russell, which was Hugh's title as a son of the Duke of Bedford. There was brief panic, for a lord could hardly fail to be an officer who had been put in with 'the men' by some dreadful blunder.

At the beginning of 1944 refugees from the Dalmatian coastline of Yugoslavia were reaching the Middle East in large numbers. They had fled with the aid of the British navy from the regions devastated by the fierce three-cornered fighting between Tito's Partisans, the German army of occupation, and Mihailovitch's royalist Chetniks. A number of camps were rapidly being set up in Egypt and Palestine for these people, most of whom were arriving with all that remained of their possessions on their backs. After a few weeks at Maadi I was sent to a camp to house some 25,000 refugees which had just been set up at El Shatt in the Sinai desert some fifteen miles north of Suez. The camp had only been in existence for a few days and order was just beginning to emerge from the initial chaos. It was being run by a mixture of South African army officers (most of whom had been sent there because their units did not want them) and a number of civilians, including members of the American Near East Foundation, the British Red Cross, International Voluntary Service for Peace, American Mennonites and ourselves. The FAU soon became the largest single NGO (non-govermental organisation) group there.

I wrote an impression for *Bootham*, the school magazine:

It is early morning, and as the long train slowly comes to a halt on the sidings, hundreds of refugees gaze at the sandy scene before them. In the foreground is the desert, with a white mass of tents visible in the distance, and in the background the dark mountains of the Sinai peninsula. It is still early when there is the sound of a multitude of voices in the distance. Presently moving specks are visible and soon a vast crowd begins to arrive in eager groups. These are earlier arrivals who are now trooping down to the siding to look for relatives and friends. They mingle with the little parties huddled round their scanty luggage and inevitably delay the loading operations. The new refugees throng up wooden steps to the waiting lorries, grimly clutching their precious belongings. The back clangs up, someone chalks a number on the side and the lorry moves off on a rough improvised track of wire netting laid on the sand towards the metropolis of tents that is to be their new home.

In a few days they have sorted themselves out into family groups and begun to feel at home. The tents, of a large double-roofed army pattern, are pitched in pairs, each pair housing an average of eighteen people. Men, women, and children all live together, with no partitions and almost the whole floor space occupied by low beds two or three feet apart. The complete absence of privacy must be one of the most irksome conditions of this new life. Another trial is the dim illumination after dark, with only one hurricane oil lamp in each double tent.

Almost every tent has its portrait of Tito and a few family photos and postcard views of home. Many have small crosses or crucifixes and rosaries and pictures of the saints and biblical scenes. Each tent also has its own improvised furniture made of wooden boxes and pieces of timber. Little bits of coloured ribbon sometimes hang on the walls. Often a design is traced with pebbles outside the door. In such ways as these the refugees make their tents as home-like as they can. For the most part they are kept spotlessly clean, although the same care does not extend to anything outside the living quarters. There is constant effort to impress on them the need to keep the dining areas and lavatories clean. All meals are cooked and eaten in large dining tents. The food, as to both quantity and quality, is generally approved, though no one wants to eat a great deal because of the heat.

Each section of the camp elects its own executive committee, responsible for the details of administration. The camp as a whole is proudly of the partisan movement, and some of the leaders are men of genuine power and ability.

Probably the happiest are the artists and craftsmen – carpenters, painters, tin smiths, tailors, etc. – who are working at their old occupations and so feel less deeply uprooted than their fellows. But many of the old men and women, of hardy peasant stock, have withstood the rapid change of climate, surroundings and mode of life remarkably well. As for the younger people, change has been the staple diet of recent years and their sense of social revolution seems to overshadow all lesser changes.

The camp hospital was housed in a large brick building with a corrugated iron roof, built as a mess when this had been the site of a military camp. The building was divided into three wards with about thirty beds each. The patients were of all kinds, and had not yet been sorted out even into different sexes let alone diseases. There were no case sheets or charts. The hospital kitchen had barely been opened. Everyone was working all hours trying to reduce the place to some kind of basic order.

Only the infectious cases had been segregated and put into some twenty tents, which constituted the isolation block. There were cases of typhoid and typhus, erysipelas and mumps; children with diphtheria, measles, and whooping cough; a young Italian prisoner with gonorrhoea; and several cases of 'psychosis maniacalis', doped with bromide. A staff of about twenty girls had been recruited from among the refugees. These were all completely untrained – in anything except guerilla warfare – and only one spoke English and one a little French. An army Sister, one of four lent to help start the hospital, and myself had to try to establish an elementary medical routine and generally to try to create a medically passable isolation hospital.

The medical staff of the camp varied from time to time, but during most of the period there was Dr Dodd, a good physician and a good man, from the Near East Foundation, as principal medical officer; a British army doctor and a Yugoslav and an Indian army doctor working in the out-patient tents of the three subsidiary camps. In addition to the four fully trained Sisters there were five FAU men, one acting as hospital quartermaster, one as dispenser, one in charge of the kitchen, one looking after the whole hospital at night, and one in the isolation block. I started in the isolation tents and later was in charge of the hospital at night.

In addition to the partisan nurses in the tents there were about a dozen Yugoslav Red Cross nurses in the main building. The Yugoslav Red Cross was a royalist organisation recruited from those living in Egypt. As royalists they were at first hated by most of the partisans, although they were freely serving them. They were all well educated, speaking good French (but no English), mostly from well-off families, and with a certain innate gentleness and tact, in contrast to the rough and sturdy peasant girls in the group of refugee nurses. Most of these latter had served with the partisan forces and one in particular was a celebrated sharp shooter. They had a passionate loyalty to the partisan movement and lived in a Russian Revolution-like atmosphere. The normal way of saying hello was a dramatic 'Zdravo' or 'Smrt Fascisma' (Death to Fascism), with the communist clenched-fist salute. But they were tireless workers, totally dedicated to the cause.

The first phase of medical work at El Shatt included mass inoculations and vaccinations. The day after they arrived each new batch of refugees had to go through the double ordeal of being disinfested with soap and water, and inoculated against typhus. For this daunting reception several tents were pitched end to end with a rope gangway through them. Those wielding the syringes stood at tables beside the gangway and inoculated the people as they filed past, arms having been cleaned with spirit by helpers at the entrance. Dr Dodd showed me how to inoculate and vaccinate and I took part in most of these unpopular ceremonies. The proceedings were pandemonium from beginning to end – children screaming and kicking, timid old folk trying to run away, and helpers struggling valiantly to keep order. We worked on a crude system, which was however the only way of dealing quickly with such a large number of people, given our very limited supply of instruments. Most of the syringes held 10cc and were emptied into ten arms one after the other with the same needle. Using half a dozen needles to a syringe each needle lay in spirit for five to ten minutes at a time. This was appalling by normal medical standards but was the best we could do and better than no sterilisation at all. There was generally one syringe filler to two inoculaters. In this way one could inoculate several hundred people a day. When vaccinating we worked in pairs, one laying on the vaccine with a scalpel and the other scratching it in with a hypodermic needle.

We ourselves lived in a horseshoe-shaped row of tents near the mess. These were about twenty feet by twelve and housed four of us. We had precarious canvas-covered beds which were not above collapsing in the middle of the night; one hurricane lamp; cut-down petrol tins for washing; and one or two packing cases for furniture. Life was made tolerable by the coolness of the nights in welcome contrast to the 110 or more degrees in the shade during the heat of the day. Chocolate and boot polish melted during the day and became solid again at night. Going out of the tent around midday was like stepping into a solid stifling oven. But however intolerable the day, after a shower and change of clothes the heat was forgotten in the luxurious coolness of the evening.

At the beginning of the summer there was a wretched period of sandstorms. The sand found its way into everything – one's hair, eyes, ears, nose; one's shoes, shirt, bed; and even between the pages of a closed book. Whilst writing a letter one had to blow off a film of dust which settled every few seconds. The floor of the mess was covered with sand during a storm, in spite of the door and shutters, and a cup of tea always had a deposit of sand at the bottom. The worst nuisance was that a storm generally blew down several tents. Ours disappeared once into the night, and nearly all our possessions with it. The hospital tents had to be constantly watched.

After a period in charge of the isolation hospital I moved on to a job which, whilst intensely interesting, also involved at the time a good deal of anxiety. There was no properly trained person available to take charge of the hospital at night, and three of us had to take turns in doing this as best we could. Dr Dodd, or one of the other doctors, could be woken in case of dire emergency, but they all worked at full pressure during the day and could not afford to be disturbed at night unless it was absolutely necessary. There were generally three Yugoslav Red Cross nurses on duty in the main building, and four of the partisan girls in the tents. There was also an ambulance driver standing – or rather sleeping – by.

There were always some worrying patients in the hospital. In the case of heart diseases, for instance, Dr Dodd told me what to do in case of various signs, and I had to be ready to give an injection of heart stimulant – something which, in an English hospital, must be specifically ordered in writing by a doctor and the dose checked by someone other than the person administering it. One nightmare case was a child with diphtheria, in so serious a condition that I might have to perform an emergency tracheotomy – cutting through the throat into the windpipe and inserting a breathing tube (which I knew how to do, but had never actually done) – to save the child from choking to death. As her breathing became more and more difficult I prepared the instruments; for if breathing ceased the patient could not wait fifteen or twenty minutes for a doctor. Fortunately the crisis passed without reaching the point at which natural breathing became impossible, and the child gradually recovered.

There were other anxious moments of many kinds. Frequently a man would come in to say that his wife was having a baby. The ambulance went out to collect her and she was put in the small surgical theatre and at what I judged to be the right time I fetched Dr Dodd to do the delivery. Once, as the baby was appearing, the theatre was plunged into darkness, the dynamo having failed. Another time the baby's foot, instead of head, emerged prematurely, and I rapidly fetched Dr Dodd who was able to turn it round and make a safe delivery. One night the British military police rang up from the other side of the Canal to say that they were bringing in a maniac who had evidently swum across from our camp. With one of the nurses interpreting he described what was evidently a persecution mania: he heard someone speaking to him out of the air and ground and threatening him with an instrument which sounded like a burning glass. Fortunately he accepted quietly an offer of a bed for the night in the ambulance drivers' tent and was taken next day to a mental hospital in Suez. Another mental case was less co-operative. He had become dangerously violent and had tried to kill a neighbour. He had to spend most of the night tied up with four volunteers from the camp to watch him. There were in fact quite a number of mental breakdowns from time to time among the refugees, uprooted as they were from their homes, transported to a bleak, alien, intolerably hot place in the desert, and facing an unknown future.

In the interval of these excitements we generally had a midnight tea-party in the hospital kitchen – in fact several each night. At first the partisans refused to sit with the royalists, but eventually politics were forgotten. The partisan refugees eventually returned to Dalmatia and I presume that the royalists remained in Egypt.

As in all hospitals, there was the tragedy of children and old people dying, and the living mourning them. But the unstinting hard work of both groups of nurses, and the fortitude of the patients, who found themselves in an ill-equipped and often amateurishly run hospital in the middle of nowhere, was remarkable. And although the night sometimes brought death, the morning often saw the birth of a new life. I shall never forget the early mornings when I stepped out of the hospital as the eastern sky was first tinged with a glow of light merging into the deep blue of the night, the morning star shining through the cold air and the camp lying silent below on the sand. Then day rapidly advanced and the stars gave way. As the light grew stronger a range of mountains in the west stood out for a short time with a majesty which was soon lost when the full glare of the sun had covered everything with its uniform and unbearable brightness.

As the camp hospital gradually became more organised the period of emergency medical work for which the FAU was best fitted was superseded. My next job was to take charge of the education system in Camp 1, where there were about a thousand children of school age, about forty teachers, half of them professionals, some fifty tents and a few broken benches and improvised blackboards. The schools were only able to function for an hour or two a day. I was the 'chief education officer', working with a Yugoslav commissar. The tents were wastefully pitched, and the first thing we did was to get a work gang to re-pitch them so as to provide enough tents for an extra school for a section of the camp which did not have one. I obtained everything that the Quartermaster's store contained in the way of benches, which were then nailed in pairs so as to be less easily stolen. These were used as desks, with seats consisting of petrol cans filled with sand and sealed with concrete – neither comfortable nor healthy to sit on. Carpenters were mobilised to make blackboards, easels, cupboards, rulers and small slates in lieu of exercise books. Having put all this material into the schools I inserted a bloodthirsty notice in the camp newspaper and on notice boards saying that anyone who stole school property would be regarded as a traitor to Yugoslavia and an enemy of the rising generation and would be 'treated accordingly'. What this threat meant was not clear, and was not meant to be clear, but it had its effect. Later the British Council sent some stationery, which was carefully rationed out to the schools; and the teachers began to compile text books, using a page a day of the camp newspaper.

The refugees had their own committees and commissars and part of my job was to get their agreement when proposing any change. There were occasional disputes, as when the senior teachers threatened to strike unless they were given a tent as their common room, even though there were simply no tents available. Again, a leading teacher and his wife set up home in a temporarily empty tent. They could not be allowed to do this but it took hours of argument before they saw this. Doing business through an interpreter is quite an art. One has to have something definite to say, and it has to be said in clear and logical stages. In dealing with committees, social oil in the form of cigarettes was a great help, the cigarettes – from my ration, since I did not smoke – being produced in stages subtly related to the progress of the discussion.

But it was the hygiene officer, who was one of those with whom I shared a tent, who had the most irritating job in the camp. The refugees kept their own tents clean and tidy, but outside they were incorrigibly unhygienic; and in a large camp in a hot climate health depends mainly on hygiene. He had a go-ahead renegade priest as his chief assistant and they kept a large squad of workers busy making new latrines in the right places.

The camp was divided into five sections, and each day there was an inspection of one of these by a duty officer accompanied by a member of the camp committee, some of the Partisan Guard (young men who had not been able, at the time when they were evacuated from Dalmatia, to join Tito's guerilla army), and an interpreter. We took it in turns to be in charge of these inspections, in the interest mainly of hygiene; preventing the inhabitants from living in airless ovens; watching for illness and for stolen property – one generally had to send a truck round to collect it all. But it was natural for the refugees to try to make their new homes as livable as possible and one could only sympathise with them. The most widespread expression of their partisan consciousness, and the most effective in fostering it, was in the universal folk-language of song. The traditional music of Dalmatia – where every town has its own anthem – and the stirring partisan songs, resounded constantly through the camp. A group walking together, a family in their tent, a squad of workers, or one of my education committees, would strike up these songs twenty times a day and be swept along in a common experience of loyalty to the movement. And although we must have seemed to be doing nothing but interfere with their lives, they did in fact generally appreciate our work, and I am sure that if any of us had visited their village of Podgora after the war we should have received a warm welcome.

My last assignment in Egypt was a period of training in the lab. of the army's 63rd General Hospital at Heliopolis in the Cairo area. What I learned (according to my notebook) I shall put in a footnote, only to be read by the medically interested![1] I had been identified within the Unit as someone capable of running a lab., and from Egypt I was sent, with another FAU man, Roger, to an army malaria diagnosis course at Damascus. The course was run by an RAMC major, a bacteriologist, with a friendly and entirely unmilitary

outlook. We used the lab. in the Italian hospital, and Roger and I and
seven soldiers were billeted nearby in an empty house where we slept
on the floor. The group included a sergeant-dispenser, an educated
man who loathed army life; Corporal John and his friend Dave; Bill,
who squinted and was a great talker on all subjects; and others whose
names I have forgotten. Most of them had come straight from the
fierce fighting in Italy and I was surprised, until I heard of their
experiences there, that most of them were taking sedative drugs.
Several were regular visitors to the semi-official local brothel. They all
hated the army and the degraded life it forced on them.

We learned how to diagnose the different types and stages of
malaria by examining blood slides under a microscope, and by the
end of the course we could do this with almost one-hundred per cent
accuracy, Roger and I coming top in the final exam. We worked in
the mornings, siestaed in the afternoons, did two more hours work,
and then read or wandered about in the cool of the evening or sat in
cafes and talked - a small cup of Turkish coffee costing about a
shilling.

It is entirely typical of the army, and therefore of the FAU when
working with it, that in spite of six months in Britain, three in Cairo
and one at Damascus, spent in training as a laboratory technician, I
never had an opportunity to use this and have of course now long
since completely forgotten it.

From Damascus Roger and I travelled back to Cairo via Beirut,
spending a few days with the FAU unit there and visiting the awe-
inspiring Roman ruins at Baalbek. On the way to Beirut we spent a
few days with an FAU group working for the Spears Mobile Clinics
based in the village of Sednaya, where according to a written account
of the work 31,498 patients were dealt with between 1942 and 1944[2].
We lived with the resident unit in a small house on the main street
and slept on the flat roof. There was a famous nunnery in the village,
said to have been founded in the sixth century, and shaped like a
ship, where we were invited for a meal. After a wait of several hours
the meal was magnificent - a vast table piled high with fruits and
meats and cheeses of every kind. Hospitality is everywhere in the
Middle East and crosses all divisions of race and religion.

Arriving back in Cairo, all of us in Egypt were now being
assembled to go into the Balkans.

NOTES

1. It included blood grouping, blood counts, red and white cell counts, haemoglobyn estimation, examination under microscope of sputum, urethral pus, throat swabs, stools, urine – for dysentery, helminths (intestinal worms), malaria, typhus, typhoid, vincents angina, elephantiasis, leprosy, Malta fever, etc.
2. 'The Work of the Spears Mobile Clinics in Syria and Lebanon, 1941–1945', anonymous and unpublished, but lent to me by a local Friend, a relative of whom had been in the Spears unit.

6

FAU in Italy and Greece

Our group of 'Vol. Soc.' teams – there were now other organisations such as the Red Cross also working for UNRRA – traveled together from Maadi to Italy, variously destined for Greece, Yugoslavia and Albania. At Port Said we boarded the troopship *Ormonde*. The women went first class – there being three FAU women in this particular group: Joan, a doctor; Nora, a fully trained nurse, older than the rest of us, a Quaker who had spent her life in the service of others, and who was to lose it in the same service a few months later; and Susie, the life and soul and universal sister of the party, who later married our 'sergeant'. The rest of us were on the troop deck where I just had time to master the art of sleeping in a hammock when the voyage ended. During these four days at sea I spent several hours a day with a battered little red book, *Colloquial Italian*. Italian is a very easy language to learn if one has some French and some faint memories of Latin, and after a few weeks in Italy I could speak it well enough for ordinary daily purposes, though I have long since lost it again through disuse.

One morning I went on deck early and saw an unforgettable sunrise. There was no one about; but the sun seemed a living thing as it rose slowly, silently, majestically, transforming sea and sky. A bank of clouds formed a series of battlemented terraces, and wisps of cloud, reflecting the red glow, stood out like flags on the castle towers. Then, as the sun rose above its cloudy fortress a long drawbridge of shimmering light was let down from the horizon to the ship, and the busy human day began.

We disembarked at Taranto in the heel of Italy, went by train to Bari on the Adriatic coast, and then by truck to the village of Ruvo a few miles inland, where the UNRRA Albanian mission was being assembled. There were ten of us in the FAU unit, I being the laboratory technician. However there was no mobile laboratory scheduled for Albania; my equipment had not arrived, and never did; and whilst in theory we were all trained for different jobs, when we finally got to work (which was not in Albania!) our jobs depended on the needs to be met rather than by what we had come prepared to do, all this being typical of wartime plans.

The three months at our villa, Santa Lucia, waiting for UNRRA to send us into Albania, were an idle interlude. We attended conferences and meetings on the situation in Albania and the relief plans for the country, serviced machinery and stores, and went on 'jangles' round Appulia in one of our three-ton trucks on decayed roads full of potholes, seeing all the places of interest. At Christmas we played Santa Claus to an orphanage in Ruvo, bringing the children out by truck to Santa Lucia for a feast and party, as a brief sparkle of colour in their very meagre existence in the convent, in which they were only kept from starvation by the constant self-sacrificing efforts of the nuns. We were invited in return to a concert at the orphanage, a most pitiful occasion when we had to sit cold and shivering whilst the children, who were even colder, went through their performance. This was just one of thousands of little cells of humanity for whom life is normally hard but who had been squeezed almost beyond endurance by the terrible blight of war.

The move into Albania was held up by political complications. The recent history of this small country had been similar to that of its bigger neighbour Yugoslavia. The old corrupt monarchy had collapsed at the beginning of the war and a communist guerrilla movement had emerged and had now taken over the administration as the Germans retreated. (A British landing a few months earlier had misjudged the strength of the enemy and had been forced to withdraw.) The guerrilla leader was Colonel-General Enver Hoxha, a smaller scale model of Tito. As in Yugoslavia the movement was energetic, disciplined and ruthless. By the end of 1944 the Hoxha regime was established in practically undisputed control of the country. It was not however recognised by either the British or

American governments, which had small military missions there but no diplomatic representation and still officially recognised the hostile regime of the exiled King Zog. This did not concern UNRRA but it did concern the military liaison group, who had to pretend ignorance as to who was in control of the country and sent in a reconnaissance party to treat with whoever they happened to meet without raising any questions of *de jure* status. Hoxha, on the other hand, was anxious to secure international recognition but suspicious of British and American intentions. When he learned that the British intended to send in a military force with the relief personnel he refused to accept them. The proposed force was only a small one (as far as I remember, about 600 men), but even a small well-armed and trained British unit could have out-gunned the ill-armed and ill-trained partisan army and could easily have been a sufficient bridgehead for a larger force.

With that intractable impasse in the background smaller quarrels developed. The Hoxha regime professed to be mortally insulted when the allied mission failed to attend the ceremony for the opening of the National Bank in the capital, Tirana. At about the same time Field-Marshall Alexander was insulted when he offered a Brigadier as his personal representative – this being intended as an honour – and Hozha refused on the common-sense ground that the colonel who was currently head of the military mission knew and understood the country and its problems whereas a newcomer would not. The incident apparently caused telegrams to fly to and fro between the Allied Field HQ at Caserta and Whitehall.

This ridiculous situation, in which much-needed relief supplies were withheld from the Albanian people by the hang-ups of the politicians and military, went on so long and reached such an apparently final deadlock that we began to look for work elsewhere. The civil war had been ravaging Greece and so we terminated our agreement with the Albanian mission and joined the UNRRA mission to Greece. We were told of urgent work on the island of Corfu where thousands of refugees had just been landed from the mainland, and we were to join the FAU unit there which was fresh from the civil war in the Athens area. We received a signal one evening to move the next morning and loaded our trucks at night, floodlighting the yard with the headlights. Once again we carried the hundredweight barrels of soft soap and the hundredweight boxes of hard soap down from the store to the trucks. (I wonder if these boxes were the original cause of my later back troubles.) Loading was completed early in the morning, and after a short break we packed our personal kit and took the road back to Taranto to board a tank-landing craft, able to take trucks, and profoundly glad at the prospect of work.

In fact there was not much to be done on Corfu and before long we moved to the mainland of Epirus (north-west Greece) and to the provincial capital Ioannina. As the Germans retreated the two communist resistance guerrilla forces, ELAS (National Popular Liberation Army, with EAM, the National Liberation Front, as its political arm) and EDES (Greek Democratic National Army), actively harassed them. However whilst EAM/ELAS remained staunchly communist, EDES under Napoleon Zervas moved to the right, opposing ELAS, thereby attracting British support, but was defeated in a pitched battle by ELAS, and its political arm EAM was able to set up a provisional government in the mountains which in fact took control of most of the country apart from Athens and Salonika. But in December 1944 a British force landed at Athens and fought a bitter battle against the ELAS guerrillas in the city, one of our FAU units being in the middle of this. The historian Eric Hobsbawm says that but for the British intervention the Communists would probably have prevailed.[1] But eventually the foreign supported royalists won. When our FAU group arrived at the beginning of 1945 the civil war had just about ended but with pockets of guerrilla forces still in the hills of Epirus.

Apart from this there was a period of peace until civil war between the communists and the royalists broke out again in 1946 – after our own time there – and on this occasion it was American forces that came to the rescue of the royalists. Both the US and the UK have a disastrous history of supporting corrupt regimes.

We made our HQ in Ioannina, a picturesque old town with storks nesting on many of the chimney tops. The guerrillas had been continuously harrying the retreating Germans who had responded by destroying all the villages in their path. Very often the only building left standing was the stone church. The crops had been destroyed but the sheep and goats and other animals had usually been successfully hidden in the hills until the Germans had passed through. To add to the devastation, the two Greek factions, the royalists supported by the British and Americans, and the communists who had done most of the fighting against the Germans, seemed to hate each other as much as they had both hated the Germans: every now and then, for example, someone – a local leader – was found on a road outside his village with his throat cut.

Our FAU unit took on the task of distributing clothes sent from the United States to the people in the destroyed villages. We used the ancient Lion of Ioannina's castle as our store, where the masses of clothes were sorted and useless items, of which there were a surprising number, weeded out. At the same time others of us went out in pairs to tour the villages and report back on their state and their needs. I went with Peter Ure, who was a much better linguist than me and quickly became fluent in modern Greek. (Peter was a brilliant and talented friend who later became professor of English Literature at, I think, Durham or Newcastle but, sadly, died whilst still relatively young.) There were no roads to many of the villages and we walked most of the time, but sometimes rode on mules, going out for a week or so on each trip, usually sleeping on the floor of a church or in the graveyard. We were the first people from outside, apart from the German invaders, whom they had seen for several years and were greeted with great enthusiasm. We were impressed by the positive spirit of these hardy villagers, who were not wasting any time cursing the departed Germans but were getting on with the business of rebuilding their houses and their lives.

When we arrived at a village the first thing was to sit on the ground with the village elders to exchange greetings and drink ouzo, with what seemed to be all the rest of the village standing around in a circle to watch. (Living this outdoor life one could absorb a lot of ouzo without feeling much effect.) We gathered all the information we could from them, supplemented with the evidence of our own eyes. Sometimes a village put on a special feast for us. This took a long time, because a sheep had first to be slaughtered and cooked, and then all the supposedly most delicious bits, such as the sheep's eyes and heart, were offered to us as honoured guests. It would have been a deep insult to refuse them, but I usually managed to palm my piece unnoticed and look as though I was enjoying it.

The archbishop of Ioannina was in Athens serving as regent, but we got on well with the younger bishop Athanasius who was in charge. Because of his contacts with the priests in every village he was often better informed about the state of the area than the Governor of Epirus. On one occasion he put on a splendid dinner for us, and presented me with a copy of the New Testament in Greek, and I gave him mine in English. We attended the great Easter-eve service in his cathedral. The church was packed, everyone with a candle, and with hundreds more standing outside. As midnight approached all the lights went out leaving the cathedral in complete darkness. Then the bishop, dressed in full regalia, appeared dramatically from behind the screen, holding up a light and calling out *Christos aneste*, Christ is risen, then lighting the candles of those nearest him, who passed the flame on so that a wave of light spread back through the church. Outside, people fired their guns into the air and there was jubilation throughout the town. Bishop Athanasius was an efficient leader, but of course a royalist; and before we left he was assassinated on a trip out to some of the villages.

After our reconnoitering trips to the villages, right up to the Albanian border, we drove out with our trucks loaded with bales of clothes, rationed out to each village according to its size, and supervised their distribution. There were always a number of passengers perched on top of the bales, wanting a ride to their village in return for doing the lifting and heaving of the bales.

One day as we hiked across the hills from one village to the next a shepherd shouted out *Hitler apethane*, Hitler is dead. Later we voted by post in the general election at home. There was now a British Council office in Ioannina. In its shop window it started with a large photo of Churchill and a small one of Attlee. As the day wore on they had a bigger picture of Attlee and a smaller one of Churchill. Probably all of us and a large proportion of the troops voted Labour. Some of our Greek friends assumed that Churchill would now be hiding in the hills with his armed followers and were surprised to hear that he merely went to Buckingham Palace to resign and then went home.

By the summer of 1945 the clothes distribution was completed – although never definitively so since there were always deputations from different villages complaining that theirs had not been given its fair share. By a piece of organised good luck which I never under-stood, we were able to drive to Athens and hitch an empty air force cargo plane back to England. After a visit to the FAU's HQ in Gordon Square I demobilised myself and promptly went up to Edinburgh just in time for the beginning of the new university year in October. I had to apply to a Tribunal to be allowed to resume my studies and the Edinburgh Tribunal, of which incidentally Kemp Smith (see next chapter) was a member, refused, for the perfectly good reason that the soldiers had to wait their turn in the long and complex demobilisation process, so why should I be allowed to do it immediately? Whilst seeing this I nevertheless thought that it would be pointless for me to miss a year of my preparation for the ministry, and I appealed. This was supported in person by Dr Hagan, my minister, now a former Moderator of the Church of Scotland, at the meeting of the Appeal Tribunal in Edinburgh, which allowed the appeal. I remember that I was so delighted by this that I could only work off my excitement by walking around Edinburgh for several hours. I did not feel any qualms of conscience about resuming my studies without further delay. Although I had not explored this when I was first called up in 1942 I could probably have claimed exemp-tion then as a candidate for the ministry, though I am glad that I did not. I was better prepared for this and for life generally by my three years in the FAU than I would have been by spending the time at university and theological college.

And so a new chapter of life began.

NOTES

1. Eric Hobsbawm, *The Age of Extremes: The Short Twentieth Century*, London: Michael Joseph, 1994, p. 80.

7

Student at Edinburgh and Oxford

In my first year at Edinburgh, 1941–2, the two philosophy professors, who had stayed on beyond the normal retirement age because of the war, were Norman Kemp Smith in Logic and Metaphysics and A.E. Taylor in Ethics. I did not take a course with Taylor although I heard him on other occasions, but I was deeply influenced by Kemp Smith. He took a continuing interest in some of his students and I kept in touch with him until going to America, and he had died before we returned. These two were succeeded at the end of the war by A.D. Ritchie and John Macmurray. Ritchie was a brilliant expositor and was kind and helpful to his students, but was not an original or powerful thinker and his work has left little trace. Macmurray on the other hand had his own original philosophy and was influential enough for there to be a John Macmurray Society still functioning today. His thought, emphasising community and interdependence rather than individualism, has also influenced Prime Minister Tony Blair. The political journalist James Naughtie says that Blair 'has often cited his discovery of the Scottish philosopher John Macmurray as a turning point in his life'.[1] Macmurray was a popular lecturer and a stimulating teacher in the small honours seminar that he conducted. However in our youthful either arrogance or perspicuity some of us thought that his philosophical system was not fully coherent, and I for one continued to think the same when it was published some years later as his Gifford lectures.

In his recent biography of Macmurray, John Costello says that, 'The more mature students – among them John Hick, the eminent theologian-to-be, and others of great ability – were much more sceptical, and found him vague, elusive and difficult to pin down in argument.'[2] Later, referring to my review of the first volume of Macmurray's Gifford Lectures, *The Self as Agent*,[3] he says,

> John Hick, under the guise of claiming not to know what Macmurray was 'on about', gave a clipped, almost caricaturing exposition of Macmurray's thesis while deliberately offering no judgment on the work at all. From a former student – granted one who did not seem, by reports, to have appreciated Macmurray's style or viewpoint – it was dismissive to the point of insult.[4]

On reading my review again I have to grant that it is more critical than appreciative though not, I hope, 'dismissive to the point of insult'. It expressed my considered judgment, which continued to be as Costello had earlier reported it.

In a fairly long review in the *Scottish Journal of Theology* I began,

> This is a difficult work to review. It is manifestly important; and yet it has a curiously remote and elusive quality ... No one who is acquainted with Professor Macmurray's earlier publications can doubt that he writes from a significantly original standpoint ... The hope that many must have entertained was that he would now make his distinctive insights available, by relating them to the technical problems with which, for the most part, professional philosophers work. Perhaps such a hope is misplaced, and Professor Macmurray's standpoint is too revolutionary to be expressed as a contribution to contemporary philosophical discussions ...[5]

Most of the rest of the review is an extended (not 'clipped') summary of the book, but it must be true that when stated baldly the book's argument does not sound as impressive as in Macmurray's own full-length but more diffuse exposition. However Costello also cites other philosophical reviewers, ending, 'Loose thinking in loose language was their most trenchant judgment',[6] which was a more frankly stated version of my own view.

I nevertheless still feel grateful to John Macmurray for his emphasis that human life is essentially personal and that we are all mutually interdependent. It is presumably this that has struck Tony Blair in stark contrast to Margaret Thatcher's famous, 'There is no such thing as society.' I also empathise with Macmurray as one who had a highly conservative religious upbringing which he later transcended; as a Christian socialist; and as distancing himself from organised Christianity until in his last years he joined the Quakers. But I am still inclined to think that his earlier, and less overtly philosophical, books are more profitable to us today than his Giffords.

The war had held up a number of students who had completed the first or first two or three years of their four-year course, who all arrived back together in 1945, and these included an unusual concentration of people who later went on to successful academic careers – Jim Whyte became principal of St Andrews University's faculty of divinity; Jim Barr became a leading Old Testament scholar, teaching at Oxford and Vanderbilt; Jim Torrance (of the Torrance clan which – unfortunately, in my opinion – dominated Scottish theology for several decades) became professor of dogmatics at Aberdeen; Ian Pitt-Watson after a successful ministerial career in Scotland became professor of homiletics at Fuller Seminary at Pasadena; Ken Rankin became professor of philosophy and head of department at Victoria University in Canada; and Ron Murray became a barrister, a QC, Labour MP for Leith, Lord Advocate in the Labour governments of the 1970s, a privy councillor, and finally as Lord Murray an appeal judge in the Edinburgh high court. I have kept in touch, on and off and to varying extents, with all of them.

Returning to Kemp Smith, I was impressed by his massive coherent mind. He was one of the last of the Idealist philosophers and also a major interpreter of Kant, Hume and Descartes. His translation of the *Critique of Pure Reason* is still widely used, although his *Commentary* on it, once influential, has long since been superseded; his work on Descartes was also influential; and his book on Hume revolutionised Hume studies. I kept in touch with him and have a number of letters from him in his spidery and sometimes almost unreadable handwriting. He was always encouraging. It was through him that I realised the immense importance of Kant, and particularly of his utterly crucial distinction between the not directly experiencable reality-in-itself and our distinctively human consciousness of it formed in terms of the structure of our own minds. I agree with Bryan Magee when he says that, 'I hold the greatest single achievement in the history of philosophy to be Kant's distinction between the noumenal and the phenomenal.'[7] I also agree with Magee that, 'No one who understands the central doctrines of the world's leading religions ought to have any difficulty in understanding this idea', namely that 'reality exists independently of all possible experience',[8] and the 'existence of the transcendental world, a part of reality that is not the empirical world'.[9] (Magee himself however remains an atheist, but the concept of God that he rejects is one which I, for one, also reject!)

Kant's 'Copernican revolution', making the mind central to the process of cognition, seemed to me so significant that I devoted almost all of my final year at Edinburgh to a detailed study of the first *Critique*. I have retained from Kant what today I identify as 'critical realism' – the view that there is a world, indeed a universe, out there existing independently of us, but that we can only know it in the forms provided by our human perceptual apparatus and conceptual systems. Although it was Kant who definitively effected the philosophical 'Copernican revolution', the basic idea was not in fact new with him. It was at least implicit in Locke, and I specially treasure the brilliant earlier statement of Thomas Aquinas that, 'Things known are in the knower according to the mode of the knower.'[10] In Kantian terms, we cannot directly experience the world as it is in itself independently of human observers, but only its phenomenal appearance to us, and it is this distinction that I have later applied to religious experience, distinguishing between the transcendent divine reality, which I call the Real, which is from our human point of view transcategorial (or ineffable) but which we experience as the humanly constructed God figures and non-personal Absolutes of the different religions.

Although Kant himself did not apply his noumenal/phenomenal distinction to religion, it can in fact solve the problem which he did not solve, namely how the noumenal reality can be said to cause the phenomenal reality when causation is itself an aspect of the latter. For if we hold, with the mystical strand of all the great world religions, that there is a spiritual aspect to our own nature that is akin to or continuous with the noumenal divine reality, then causality only enters in on the human level in our overcoming of the ego-centred point of view and thus becoming open to our own deepest nature, which naturally responds to the universal presence of the transcendent divine reality.

In my first year at Edinburgh, in 1941-2, I was a keen member of the Evangelical Union, attending all its lectures and prayer meetings, conducting ward services in the Royal Infirmary, fully immersed in its ethos. When I came back three years later I rejoined but soon found that I was no longer in tune with its biblical fundamentalism. My wider experience during the war had made me more independent in outlook, and my philosophical training was leading me to ask awkward questions. It was then a basic tenet of the Evangelical Union that the Bible is verbally inspired. But how, for example, could one understand the sun standing still for about a day as recounted in Joshua 10:13? In the light of our modern knowledge of astronomy we would have to say that the earth, which rotates at a speed of about a thousand miles an hour, suddenly ceased to rotate. Taken seriously, this is utterly mind-boggling and impossible to believe. Again, can biological evolution responsibly be rejected just because it is contrary to the book of Genesis, written some two and a half thousand years ago? And could it really be an expression of infinite love to sentence the large majority of the human race to eternal torment in hell? And are there not innumerable contradictions between this biblical text and that? And so on. Outside the fundamentalist-evangelical thought world such ideas are bizarre and incredible. But within it these questions are serious and vexing ones and I was aware of a distinct reluctance on the part of the student and faculty leadership to face them, a feeling that they were dangerous, providing openings for the devil to tempt us into back-sliding. And so I drifted away from the Evangelical Union though continuing for many years to be what I would now regard as a very conservative Christian.

My philosophy studies went well. Real philosophers in my opinion are born, not made, and I think that I was born one. Born philosophers usually deal with the big and important issues, whilst the ones who are made often deal in highly sophisticated trivialities. They can be incredibly clever, and yet contribute nothing to our understanding of the universe and our place in it. At least, so say I! The Scottish university system involves a four year undergraduate course, in contrast to the three years in England. But at the end of my third year I sat the final exams just to see how I was faring. Members of the department read my scripts and told me that I would have been awarded a First. So I was confident of one the following year. I spent some of the intervening year at St Deiniol's Library at Hawarden, near Chester, endowed by Gladstone's estate and continuing as a residential library for scholars (the characterful Alec Vidler being then Warden), mainly studying Kant. And when my Finals came round I did receive a First, plus the senior philosophy medal, plus the Vans Dunlop scholarship, which however I declined because I also received something else much more valuable, namely the first Campbell–Fraser scholarship to Oriel College, Oxford. This was open to new philosophy and classics graduates, and was for two years, paying enough to live on comfortably. There were in fact only two philosophy honours finalists that year, Ron Murray and myself, who both got Firsts, but he intended to pursue a career in Law – which he has done with notable success whilst still retaining his interest in philosophy. It was at Edinburgh that I nearly became engaged for the second time, to an American graduate student who however married someone else when she returned to the States. Many years later, when Hazel and I were visiting the University of Virginia, we met Barbara and her husband at the nearby college where they both taught philosophy. We all enjoyed the meeting, none of us having any regrets.

So I graduated from Edinburgh in 1948 and was at Oriel for the next two years. Oxford philosophy was then dominated by Gilbert Ryle, whose *The Concept of Mind* published in 1949 was at the centre of discussion for several years. He had also introduced the notion of the category mistake and had made other important contributions to philosophy, including his editing of *Mind*, and instituting the new two year BPhil degree based on the American PhD – i.e., with taught seminars as well as the writing of a thesis. This was taken by most of the philosophy graduate students at Oxford in my generation. However I came to Oxford with a thesis topic in mind, the relation between faith and belief, and Ryle and his circle were not interested in such issues. I had in fact had the topic of faith in mind whilst at Edinburgh and even earlier.

The philosophy don at Oriel, Richard Robinson, told me that the best epistemologist in Oxford was H.H. Price, the Wykeham professor of logic, at New College. He is described in *The Oxford Companion to Philosophy* as 'a shy, reclusive figure, belonging to no school or group and seeking no disciples'. He was indeed an independent figure, fully aware of Ryle's work and that of the linguistic analysts generally, but pursuing his own agenda. I went to see him in New College and at first found him rather frightening. He looked like Sherlock Holmes – with a hawk-like visage and a curved pipe, but with a rather remote and abstracted air. But I soon realised that the apparent remoteness was shyness and presently got on well with him. He was an ideal doctoral supervisor. I would write a draft chapter and send it to him, and a week or so later we would go out in his ancient car, leaving it for a walk through the countryside. He had the eccentric belief, which I did not presume to question, that one should never leave a car with its hand brake on, and so he always parked on as level a piece of ground as he could find and we wedged stones under each wheel! He knew a great deal about birds and always had his binoculars with him. Our walks ended at a pub where we had some tea, and at this point he pulled my typescript out of his pocket and proceeded to criticise it mercilessly. But at the same time he was encouraging in that he took it seriously and made it possible for me to go back and rewrite it better.

At the end of my two years I had been able to complete and present the thesis. It was examined later that year by Austin Farrer and Ian Crombie. According to my diary,

> I had a very sticky time at the viva. Farrer clearly strongly disagreed with my theory of faith, whilst Crombie also disagreed but was more friendly disposed. Their questioning was wholly on my theory – no reference to the rest of the thesis. This was perhaps so far a good sign. But I did very badly in answering. I got confused and made a poor showing. They gave no indication of the result, but I felt at the end that I had certainly failed. I was extremely disappointed and depressed. My feeling now is that I am more likely than not to have failed. I should hear within a week.

I do however also remember that Crombie gave me a smile as I left the room. And a week later I received a letter from Price to tell me that the examiners had reported favourably to the Lit. Hum. Board which had accepted their report, and offering his congratulations. I had begun to fear that my theory of faith might be nonsense, but perhaps it was not after all. In fact however, when I re-read my thesis after the viva, I wrote, 'I am shocked to see how feeble it is. It is much less well written than I had thought. I shan't encourage anyone to read it, and consider myself lucky to have got a degree on it.' A few months later, 'Today I officially became Dr Hick. The prefix makes me feel very old and grey-haired, and completely bogus!' I have now been reading some of the thesis again after nearly fifty years and much experience of doctoral examining. I would have had no hesitation in passing it. I don't know why I felt so negatively about it at the time, although I would still not advise anyone to bother to read it. The ideas are much better presented in the book into which I later turned it, *Faith and Knowledge*.

Price continued to keep in touch and we met from time to time in both England and the USA as well as corresponding by letter – until his last years, which were tragically clouded and then obliterated by Alzheimer's disease.

As well as rooms in New College Price – or Henry as he became – owned a large old rambling house in Headington Hill on the outskirts of Oxford where he lived with his sister after he retired. The house was full of models of gliders – he was a qualified and once practising glider pilot – and of owls. When I once sent him another owl he wrote,

> Thank you very much for the very nice brass owl. He is now sitting on my mantelpiece looking very dignified. His face is somewhat melancholy and seems to conceal many secrets, which is what an owl's face should be like. Your estimate of about 50 owls in all agrees with those offered by other authorities. But, like other questions of population, it is partly a matter of definition. If there is a picture containing three owls, does this count as three or as one?

I have a lot of letters from him in his neat and almost microscopic handwriting. They are delightful, containing not only interesting philosophical discussions but also whimsical comments drawing on his interest in Roman times. For instance, when he was a visiting professor at the university of California at Los Angeles,

> I have decided that living in California is rather like living in North Africa in the reign of Septimus Severus, when that province was populous, flourishing and well-irrigated; or perhaps it is like living there in the reign of the virtuous and amiable Gordian III.

After Henry's death his literary executor tried without success to get a volume of his papers on parapsychology published, and I was delighted when many years later such a volume, excellently edited by Frank Dilley, appeared in Macmillan's Library of Philosophy and Religion, of which I was the General Editor.[11] This is actually much better than Henry's last small book, *Essays in the Philosophy of Religion* (1972), which is largely about parapsychology. This was a serious interest of Henry's and intensified my own interest in it, prompting me to join the Society for Psychical Research. This is a highly respectable body, publishing research, exposing fraud, and providing a forum for the philosophical work of such people as Price, C.D. Broad and others.

Once when Henry visited Cambridge I took him to see Ely Cathedral, and in the car on the way back he told me of his recent – this was 1965 – vivid religious experience, which he described as an experience of the sense of presence. I asked him to record it in writing, which he did, giving copies to several friends, but with a strict instruction not to publish it during his lifetime. I present it here in an abbreviated third-person account. One Sunday morning, after a late breakfast, Henry found himself in an unusually tranquil and peaceful frame of mind. He felt moved to go into the drawing-room, where there was a writing-chair in the middle of the room, facing the empty fireplace. Then in a gentle and gradual way it began to dawn on him that there was someone else in the room, located fairly precisely about two yards away to his right front. There was no kind of sensory hallucination, either visual or auditory, nothing seen or heard. He was not in the least alarmed, and the experience itself was so absorbing that he did not even feel any surprise at the time. It was just as if he had received a visit from someone he had never met before. They proceeded to have a conversation, though one conducted entirely by exchange of thoughts, about God's love for human beings, including himself. When God is said to love us this is not just some conventionally pious phrase but is to be taken literally. When we love someone we are fond of that person, or he is dear to us. In the same way, Henry was told, God was fond of him and he was dear to God.

Henry had a strong impression of the visitor's personality. He seemed to be very good and very wise, full of sympathetic understanding, and most kindly disposed towards him. He did not know how long the 'conversation' lasted, guessing in retrospect about a quarter of an hour. But gradually he passed from exchanging thoughts with the visitor into a private meditation on what he had said, and after a while he became aware that the visitor was no longer there. The effects lasted for the whole of that day which, Henry said, was certainly the happiest day of his life. But it was something different from ordinary everyday happiness, more tranquil and also more profound, going down to the roots of his personality. He thought that 'joy' was a better word for it.

Who was the visitor? He was quite sure that it was a finite individual like himself. If Henry had been a medieval person, he thought, he would have supposed that this was his guardian angel. At any rate he was by far the most welcome visitor Henry had ever had. As he told me all this in the car, driving back from Ely to Cambridge, I could only respond that he was very lucky. For an ounce of first-hand religious experience is worth more than a whole library of books about it. In terms of my own epistemology of religion, he had undergone a moment of unusual openness to the universal presence of the Real, the Ultimate, which he had vividly experienced in the particular form furnished by his own mind.

I made a number of friends at Oxford. Stan Booth-Clibborn had a room on the same stair in Oriel, later vicar of Great St Mary's, and later still bishop of Manchester. I foretold then, correctly, that he would become a bishop and was not surprised that he was entirely unspoiled by the office. Tony Flew, later a renowned atheist philosopher, was doing research at Christ Church. We have continued to meet and argue from time to time on two continents. Geoff Payman, of Oriel, came one summer on a camping trip through Europe with Shirley and I, stopping at Oberamagau for the passion play. Eric Tomm was one of those doing the new BPhil instituted by Ryle. I had first known him at Hull where he was working in the College library. He made a marriage which his friends saw would be disastrous although we were not able to warn him successfully. He did however have a daughter who was a big plus to balance the minus. Whilst I was at Oriel Eric and his wife lived in a caravan behind a house near the river outside Oxford, so that their address was 'Mrs Lansbury's Rear'. Eric was a keen logician and later became a lecturer at Glasgow University, but never published much or rose in the academic ranks. He parted from his wife and later married, or partnered, someone else very successfully.

I regularly attended the Socratic Club, chaired by C.S. Lewis – he was an excellent chairman, never intruding but keeping the discussion flowing. I also joined all the political societies, and the Union, which was then regularly visited by the top politicians of the day. At one time or another I heard Clement Attlee, George Brown, Herbert Morrison, Ernest Bevin, Stafford Cripps, Harold Wilson. But the most impressive political orator whom I have heard in the flesh was Aneurin Bevan, radical socialist and creator of the National Health Service, at a general election meeting in Edinburgh. He came from another meeting at the end of a long day of campaigning, but the sheer energy of his personality immediately radiated throughout the huge Usher Hall. He spoke with a soft Welsh voice, but perfectly audibly, and was full of fun as well as passion. He was reputed by his enemies to be bitter and vicious, but in fact his uncomplimentary remarks about the Tories came across with good humour.

Winston Churchill was of course also a great platform orator, but in a quite different style. I only heard him on the wireless (as radio was then called), but his addresses to the nation, particularly in 1940 and 1941, were immensely powerful and were indeed historic events in their own right, directly influencing the state of mind of the country and thus indirectly the whole course of the war. I am glad to have heard all these figures. But the only major politician whom I know personally is Clare Short, currently the Secretary of State for International Development in the Labour government, about whom more later.

NOTES

1. James Naughtie, *The Rivals*, London: Fourth Estate, 2001, p. 18–19.
2. John E. Costello, *John Macmurray: A Biography*, Edinburgh: Floris Books, 2002, p. 309.
3. John Macmurray, *The Self as Agent*, London: Faber & Faber, 1957.
4. Costello, *John Macmurray*, p. 331.
5. *Scottish Journal of Theology*, vol. 12 (1959), p. 193.
6. Costello, *John Macmurray*, p. 331.
7. Bryan Magee, *Confessions of a Philosopher*, London: Phoenix, 1997, p. 243.
8. Ibid., p. 189.

STUDENT AT EDINBURGH AND OXFORD 77

9. Ibid., p. 195.
10. Thomas Aquinas, *Summa Theologica*, II/II, Q. 1, art. 2.
11. *Philosophical Interactions with Parapsychology: The Major Writings of H.H. Price on Parapsychology and Survival*, edited by Frank B. Dilley, London: Macmillan, and New York: St Martin's Press, 1995.

8

Theological training

As a newly converted Christian it just seemed obvious to me that I should devote my life to the work of the church, and I became a candidate for the ministry of the Presbyterian Church of England – later to unite with the Congregational Union of England and Wales to form the United Reformed Church. I chose the Presbyterian Church simply because my evangelical friends were in it. It was a relatively small denomination (much smaller, for example, than the Methodists) and had only one training college, Westminster College, Cambridge – not one of the constituent colleges of the university but located in Cambridge and making use of its faculty of divinity. Indeed whilst I was there, 1950–53, H.H. Farmer was both a professor in Westminster College and Norris-Hulse professor in the University. The most important theologian associated with the college had been John Oman (author of two very original and influential books, *Grace and Personality* and *The Natural and the Supernatural,* as well as a number of others) who had died a few years earlier. His successor was H.H. Farmer, whose colleagues were W.A.L. Elmslie for Old Testament, J.Y. Campbell for New Testament, and Roy Whitehorn for Church History. Farmer was first class, Elmslie a stirring Old Testament teacher, J.Y. a supremely lucid New Testament teacher, and Whitehorn a dud as church historian, with no great interest in the subject, but a genuinely important and influential ecclesiastical statesman, representing our church (in which he served a term as moderator) in ecumenical discussions.[1] He was also a very kindly human being. I am afraid I once played a cruel joke on him. I invented a medieval philosophical movement called Pandiculism whose main tenet was that all metaphysical propositions are value judgments (which, so far as I can tell, is meaningless), and asked him in class if Pandiculism had had any influence on the Reformers. He said that he would take notice of the question and answer later. Of course the whole College took note, and in the annual Bardic Ceremony the new Bard, Syd Bell (who later ministered in Calgary, Canada, where we have met once or twice) intoned in his Ode on the freshers:

> First on the list I think is Hick.
> We have no doubt he's good at heart.
> I'm afraid he made a very poor start,
> For despite his bland disarming face
> He came here from the Other Place.
> He'd read a lot of bits and pieces
> And crammed them into some kind of thesis.
> Although he wrote down all he knew
> It didn't help his Greek & Hebrew.
> His philosophy course was a dreadful legacy,
> For ever since he's been spreading heresy.
> The most famous one, and quite ridiculous,
> Was apparently framed by one Pandiculus.
> Despite these little episodes I know you'll join with me
> In congratulating Johnny on receipt of Ph.D.
> Show respect, you freshers, do the trick,
> And doff your caps to Doctor Hick.

The Principal, Waley (Elmslie), was a loveable character and a genius at making the Old Testament prophets live. He was so good at this and at explaining the nuances of key Hebrew words that I was able successfully to get out of learning Hebrew! For the amount that I (and most others) would learn could never replace translations and commentaries, and if we tried to use the text without them we would probably get badly misled. It would be a case of 'a little learning is a dangerous thing'. According to my diary, about halfway through my first term at Westminster,

> I have still not got into a proper routine of work. The main trouble I now locate as Hebrew. It is a difficult language for a non-linguist aged nearly 29, especially when the said non-linguist knows that he will never make use of Hebrew after learning it and

is prevented by it from doing what he is interested in and can do. I find Hebrew utterly burdensome and frustrating. It takes up a lot of time – or would if I did it properly! – and gives me a bad conscience when I follow up the N.T. or church history studies, which I find fascinating [despite the way the latter was taught]; let alone theology, and the job of keeping up with current work in philosophy.

Happily, it seems that Elmslie had himself come to the view that not everyone need do Hebrew. Apparently,

> Principal Elmslie in one of his mischievous, provocative moods, once told the General Assembly in 1942 that he questioned the need for Hebrew and Greek and, during the later years of his reign, reasons were readily found for excusing individual students – whether for constitutional inability to cope or for the physical reason of eye-strain.'[2]

I was very happy to benefit from his, to my mind, very rational attitude.

Westminster was then full and included several American students spending a year in England. They contributed greatly to the life of the College, making it a livelier place than it would otherwise have been. We all had to get used to the differences between British and American English. For example, the College cook was a pretty and charming young woman called Lorna who sometimes joined us at tennis. One day I was to play a doubles game with her against Chuck, one of the Americans, and someone else. As Chuck was not quite ready I said, 'Lorna and I'll go ahead and knock up until you come.' If you know American English you will understand why he looked so shocked. Recalling this reminds me of how careful one sometimes has to be when writing letters of recommendation from the UK to the US or vice versa. For example, 'quite' in American (as in 'She is quite good in epistemology') usually means 'very', whereas in UK English it usually means 'not very'.

The College would have been far from full if it had been confined to candidates for the English Presbyterian ministry. There were only three of us in my own year. One, Geoff, was then a maverick but later became entirely orthodox, and the other, Gordon, was then highly orthodox but later became a well-known radical, which could also be said of me. There were also graduate students living in

Westminster but working mainly in the University, from New Zealand, Australia, Canada and Sweden. The Swede was Krister Stendahl with whom I have kept in touch. He has been a major New Testament scholar, much involved also in Jewish–Christian dialogue, and was dean of the Harvard divinity school when I gave the Ingersoll lecture there.

Whilst at Westminster I also attended John Wisdom's and C.D. Broad's lectures in the University. Wisdom was one of Wittgenstein's closest disciples. He gave two sets of lectures in the same term, one on metaphysics and the other on philosophical psychology. There was however no discernible difference between them – they were Wisdom on Mondays and Wisdom on Thursdays. He imitated some of Wittgenstein's mannerisms, pausing visibly to think, groaning with head in hands or looking up at the ceiling for inspiration. His lectures were completely unstructured and unprepared, and one listened bored stiff to his meanderings until every few weeks he said something, often just a sentence, so arresting and thought-provoking that one came back for more. One such sentence which I have treasured ever since was that doing metaphysics is like finding a pattern in a puzzle picture. This was a brilliant use of Wittgenstein's discussion of seeing-as, and was for me a clue to the nature of religious experience and religious faith.

In one of the several letters that I later received from Wisdom he says,

> Thank you for sending me your paper on The Nature of Religious Faith. [This was written for the XIth International Congress of Philosophy in 1953.] I think you do very well in short space. No, I don't disagree with III. But of course every phrase such as 'lies behind', 'interpretation', 'significance' is liable to revive the old model of someone behind the scenes, as opposed to the model of omnipresent energy. The energy is indeed only partially manifest at any time – eye hath not seen nor ear heard – but the inference to it from its manifestations is, I need not say, profoundly different from the inference to water from its manifestations when these are taken to be the movement of the stream it carries, the wheels it drives. The old comparison of the spirit to the wind is excellent, we may realise afresh. The child doesn't know there is a wind until the mother connects the hurrying clouds with the flying leaves and the feeling on his face. To say there is a wind but

nothing is moving and no one can feel anything is absurd, but this doesn't imply that there would be no wind if we did not exist or couldn't feel it.

I also visited R.B. Braithwaite in his rooms at King's, having been introduced by Henry Price:

> Spent a most pleasant and profitable hour & a quarter with him discussing the nature of faith, etc. – he lying on a sofa and gesticulating with his arms, and never completing a sentence. A very jolly & loquacious man. He calls himself a Christian; but on the strangest grounds. Does not, as a Logical Positivist, believe (or disbelieve) in the existence of God; had the creed omitted when he was baptised in King's College chapel ten years ago; not interested in immortality. But got on well, and had a good talk.

I later, when a lecturer at Cambridge, had some correspondence with him also, but in order to know what the more interesting bits refer to I would have to remember more about the context than I now can. Thus in one letter Braithwaite says,

> Towards the end of August [1963] I had an idea of an original nature which excited me very much, and which I have been working on since. The idea is: Is there a criterion in the principles according to which I act, when the results of my action is partly determined by some factor external to myself, for distinguishing as to whether I take this factor to be general or impersonal? This led me, almost immediately, to the question: Are my principles of action when you (or any other person) are the other participating factor different from what they would be if I believed that you were merely a machine? I believe that I have found such a criterion: it's very subtle, and I'm not yet sure I've got it quite right. (I tried it out at the Moral Sciences Club at its first meeting, and it was received critically but not too badly.) If you're interested I'll tell you more about it when you come to dinner (I haven't yet developed its consequences with respect to theism).

But, alas, I can't now remember what the idea was! Again, in another letter he says, 'I am sorry I exploded about the Divinity Faculty to you at Dorothy Emmet's party. Mackinnon is an eccentric and I was wrong to attribute his views to the Divinity Faculty in general.' But once again I don't now remember what the point at issue was. However Mackinnon was indeed a famous eccentric. More about him in chapter 12.

Whilst referring to people whom I came to know at Oxford and Cambridge I should include Ian Ramsey, who was Nolloth Professor of the Philosophy of the Christian Religion at Oxford, not while I was at Oriel – that was his predecessor L.W. Grensted – but later. I liked him, as I expect everyone who knew him did, and appreciated his encouragement. Referring to the same paper to the International Congress of Philosophy, he says, 'I am sure that what you say about levels and a "total interpretation" is very much on the right lines and I hope there may be a chance in August, if not before, for us to talk about all this together.' And when later he became bishop of Durham, and I was a professor at Birmingham, 'I hope I shall be able to say something helpful about the concept of the Eternal. You would see how much I was indebted to you in that article on Hell, and though I ought to wait until I have heard your paper before saying this, I think we are in complete agreement about Universalism.'

It was while I was at Westminster that I first met Hazel. She was one of a group who had been Student Christian Movement leaders at Oxford, now holding a reunion, and although I had not been an SCM office-bearer myself I knew some of them and was invited to join the group. I was immediately attracted to her. In my diary a little later, 'I am, for the first time in my life, utterly and gloriously in love.' A couple of years later we were married in the Belford church in which I had then recently been inducted as minister, our mutual love developing and increasing for forty-four years until her death.

In my last year at Westminster, the University advertised for a lecturer in the philosophy of religion and Farmer encouraged me to apply. Another of his students, George Galloway, older than me and already teaching in Scotland, also applied. Many years later, as president for that year of the Society for the Study of Theology, I introduced George as speaker at the annual meeting, that year in Bristol, and told the story of how our first meeting had been traumatic but could now be recollected in tranquillity. We had both applied for the same job and after the interviews we were waiting anxiously for the result. The door opened and a member of the committee appeared and beckoned to – the third person who had been interviewed! This was Howard Root. The committee had wanted someone who was willing to develop an interest in other religions and learn their languages, as well as dealing with the traditional topics in the philosophy of religion. At that stage I had no interest in other religions and said so – although I later developed a keen interest in them. Howard said that he was prepared to study them but in fact never did. He became primarily an Anglican theological committee man, active in discussions with Rome, and attending the Second Vatican Council as an Anglican representative. Howard was a confident and polished Oxbridge young man, whilst George and I were in comparison unsophisticated provincials. However in retrospect I am glad that I did not get the job. For I would probably have spent the rest of my career there, missing the much wider and more varied experience that I have in fact had. Not every failure is bad. Indeed each time that I have failed to get a job for which I had applied I have later been glad to have missed it. With one exception, the H.G. Wood chair at Birmingham, all the teaching jobs I have had have been ones for which I did not apply!

When Farmer retired he had hoped that I would succeed him. I was then at Princeton Theological Seminary. People did not apply for the Westminster chair but were nominated by Presbyteries. I took no steps in the matter and don't know whether I was even nominated. The general secretary of the church, a good man who was not however primarily an academic, was appointed. I was not particularly disappointed at the time and retrospectively regard it as another example of a serendipitous miss. Westminster College was a very small affair compared with the Princeton Seminary, where I then was; and when I later went to Birmingham my interests went far beyond training people for the traditional ministry.

Farmer was a fine human being, and one of the two best preachers I have ever heard, the other being Reinhold Niebuhr. In his prime Farmer did important work continuing the Oman tradition and his book *The World and God* (1936) is still, in my opinion, well worth reading. In his Gifford lectures, delivered at Glasgow over two years, he provided a Christian interpretation of religion and the religions, publishing the first set as *Revelation and Religion* (1954). I was at Belford at the time and was one of those who read the proofs for him. Farmer's predecessor, John Oman, had been one of the first British theologians to create a comprehensive religious interpretation of religion. But whereas Oman had a more global understanding of religion Farmer restricted it by definition to the various forms of theism. 'The essence of religion in all its forms,' he said, 'is a response to the ultimate as personal.'[3] This was his explicit starting point. And within theism he held that 'there is given to us through the Christian revelation and faith the normative concept of religion'.[4] Thus other religions can be graded according to their likeness and unlikeness to Christianity; and Buddhism, being non-theistic, was excluded altogether. For 'where the idea of divine personal activity is explicitly repudiated and denied, we must presume that we are no longer in contact with religion in its original, living, creative essence'.[5] And so whereas Oman discussed Buddhism at some length, Farmer said very little about it. But, sadly, this was later to make his treatment of the whole subject seriously out of date. For the definition of religion in exclusively theistic terms has been generally abandoned by historians and philosophers of religion. There is now a considerable Christian interest in Buddhism in several of its forms, particularly Zen, Tibetan and Theravada. And it is incumbent upon the Christian theologian to explain how a religion that is, from a theistic point of view, so totally wrong, can have fruits in human life that are certainly not inferior to Christianity's.

Farmer's departure from Oman's more global outlook had been reinforced by attending the International Missionary Council at Tambaran, near Madras, in 1938. The conference was dominated by the influence of Hendrik Kraemer, whose *The Christian Message in a Non-Christian World* (1938) was written for the conference; and Farmer accepted wholeheartedly the Kraemer line, itself deeply influenced by Karl Barth. Reporting on the conference, Farmer said,

> We came increasingly to see that the great non-Christian religions ... are in a very real sense all wrong: that is wrong as 'alls', as totalities – and must be all wrong, despite incidental and isolated rightnesses, for the reason that they leave, not having Christ, the absolutely basic problem of man's situation unresolved. Built upon another foundation, organised around another centre, they are radically and totally different; and if Christianity be right, they must be in a radical and total way wrong.'[6]

Although he spoke of genuine occasional rightnesses within other faiths, Farmer never, so far as I know, had any first-hand encounter with people of those faiths sufficient to take him beyond the letter, found in books, to the living spirit, found in people.

Having published his first set of Giffords Farmer decided not to publish the second. He was conscious at the time that they were not up to the standard of the first. He did not assume that everything he wrote must be published – he had both a genuine humility and a very clear critical judgment. He once said to me that when I came to give my own Gifford lectures – an encouraging remark, since I was still then a student at Westminster – I should beware of putting all my efforts into the first set and not having enough to say in the second; and clearly this was what had happened to him. (By the time that I did my Giffording, at Edinburgh, they had long been reduced to one year, so that I did not have to face Farmer's dilemma.) He initially intended to work on the second set when he retired, with a view to making them suitable for publication. But when he took them up again he soon decided that the project was hopeless. This was not because he had lost his intellectual energy, for he published another book (*The Word of Reconciliation*, 1966) and several smaller pieces in his retirement. It was because he had lost confidence in the programme and the quality of his second set of Giffords. However, nearly fifty years later, in 1998, long after Farmer's death, Christopher Partridge published the second set of Giffords, having obtained the family's permission. Partridge himself says that 'as time went on [Farmer] became very unsatisfied with the material, and eventually gave up the idea of revising it for publication. This needs to be borne in mind when reading the lectures. This is material with which Farmer was unhappy.'[7]

I read the newly published volume, and Partridge's own book, *H.H. Farmer's Theological Interpretation of Religion: Towards a Personalist Theology of Religions*, 1998, for a review, pointing out some of the weaknesses of Farmer's second set of Giffords and questioning whether it was right to overrule his own judgment and wishes by publishing them. However the two books were so expensive – £59.95 ($99.95) and £69.95 ($109.95) – that not many people or even libraries were likely to buy them. They do however have a use for anyone studying the history of English theology in the twentieth century.

On New Year's Day 1951 I asked myself

What will the world be like in the year 2000, a year which I hope to see? What do I hope to do myself during the next fifty years? Marry & bring up a family; be minister of a church; probably teach theology. I also want to write some books:- the philosophy of faith, the moral problem of war, a volume of sermons, a popular account & defence of Xian belief for the non-Christian; a book about the problems facing the church today.

I did write the first of these, but the others remain on 'the road not taken'. However life would be much less interesting if it held no surprises.

NOTES

1. See Michael Whitehorn, *Roy Whitehorn: A Servant of the Word*, 1991 (privately printed).
2. W.N. Leak, *Westminster College in the Life of the Church*, London: Presbyterian Historical Society, 1959, p. 3.
3. H.H. Farmer, *The World and God*, London: Nisbet, 1936, p. 28.
4. H.H. Farmer, *Revelation and Religion*, London: Nisbet, 1954, p. 35.
5. Ibid., p. 30.
6. Quoted by C.H. Partridge in *H.H. Farmer's Theological Interpretation of Religion*, New York, and Lampeter: Edwin Mellen Press, 1998, p. 3.
7. Introduction to H.H. Farmer, *Reconciliation and Religion: Some Aspects of Christianity as a Reconciling Faith*, New York and Lampeter: Edwin Mellen Press, 1998, p. xvi.

9

Minister at Belford

Belford is a village in Northumberland about fifteen miles south of Berwick-on-Tweed on the Scottish border. Early in August 1953 I was inducted as minister of the Belford Presbyterian church and at the end of the month Hazel and I were married in the church, with the congregation generously providing the reception. We spent our honeymoon at a village near Innsbruck, enjoying the Austrian mountains, the clear air, the sun, the food, the relaxation and one another. I had sent a recently published article to the Catholic philosopher Ivo Hollhuber who lived in Innsbruck and had written on the same topic, and we decided to see if we could meet him. His wife, who opened the door, told us that he was reading on top of the Hungerberg and that there was a mountain rail to the top, where we found him dozing under a tree but delighted to greet us. He gave us a conducted tour of Innsbruck and has remained in touch by friendly correspondence ever since, although his conservative Catholicism was later distressed by my views on religious pluralism and on Christology, on which he has published several critical discussions. In his last book, *Philosophie als Prae-eschatologie*, the third edition, which includes a critical chapter about my religious pluralism, he has written, 'The last book of my life I dedicate to my dear friend John Hick. God bless you, Yours, Ivo, Innsbruck, 30th Sept. 2000.'

Returning to Belford, in those days the A1, the Great North Road – though far from great – passed through the village. Now it passes a few miles further east and Belford is even more of a backwater then it was then. But the surrounding country is magnificent with the Cheviot hills, Wooler perched on top, to the west and the sea to the east with Holy Island and Bamburgh castle. In the early 1950s the area was socially barely out of the Victorian era. People could remember the time when the whole village had been owned by the local landlord, who had lived in the now empty Belford Hall, and as he rode through the village the men doffed their caps and the women curtsied. The Hall was later bought by Mr McLaren, the owner of the nearby quarry, a rough and tough but basically friendly character. The church bought a bit of land from him for the manse garden – but pinched eighteen inches extra when putting up the fence, which McLaren noticed and made a fuss about but finally very decently let it be.

The Belford area had its own distinctive accent and many of the villagers had never been further away than Berwick to the north or Alnwick to the south. Electricity had only recently come to most of the area and some of the bigger farms still had their own generators. When we were there the farm workers were still called hinds and were hired each year at an annual gathering in the market place. They lived in a row of tied cottages on the farms, so that not to be rehired was to lose your home as well as your job. The farmers were then in a prosperous phase with the bigger ones often able to buy other farms for their sons, and it was the farmers who ruled the land.

The church and manse are up a lane off the main street.[1] The church is a plain squareish building which had dark wood pews and a high pulpit built from the time when the balcony was in regular use. Before I left we were able to get the pulpit cut down to a lower level and the wood throughout lightened. Next door was the Ferguson Memorial Hall, another squareish building, and before I left we were able to get men's and women's lavatories installed. On the other side of the church was the manse. This is a nice house. As you enter through the front door – as things were arranged then – the study is on your left, a spare room which we used for guests on the right, and a good sized sitting room ahead. Off this is the kitchen, with a door out into a small yard. When we arrived cooking had to be done on an open coal fire which also heated an oven beside it. The fire consumed coal at an appalling rate and after a while the church, at the insistence of some of its leading ladies, installed a Raeburn stove. The house was heated by coal fires in each room and those in the sitting room and study had dampers so that they could smoulder through the night and be revived in the morning. The whole business of fetching buckets of coal from the coal shed, cleaning out the ashes, feeding the fire, clearing up the mess, took the better part of an hour a day. Upstairs are two bedrooms and the bathroom, where we also had an old-fashioned washing machine with a hand-operated mangle to squeeze the water out of the clothes. A village woman came in once a week to help Hazel with the weekly washing, which was then hung out in the yard. During the winter we kept a lighted oil lamp under the water tank in the attic to prevent it freezing up.

We were very lucky that at this time Gran (my mother's mother) gave up her home to live and be looked after at Athol House, and we were given the furniture that she could not take with her. So we had a virtually full set of furniture, though of course far from new.

Our nearest neighbour, in a big house with large gardens, was one of the two village doctors, David Macdonald, who was also the Session Clerk or leading layman in the church, then in his early sixties. David was also a JP, though he never sat lest he should have to sentence some of his patients. He had a wonderful fund of stories about local people and local history and was utterly devoted to the Belford area, where he had been born, his father having started the practice. He loved telling, for example, about the Holy Islanders and their superstitions – for example, they would never use the word 'pig' but always referred to one as 'the article'. He knew everyone in the district and everyone knew and respected him. There was a sense in which he was the real minister, for he had brought many of the people into the world, had known them throughout their lives, understood their way of life and their way of thinking. In a small settled community, such as Belford then was, anyone had to be there for many years before they were fully part of it. I as a newcomer was accepted and apparently well liked and the congregation flourished greatly during the short time that Hazel and I were there, but I am sure that it was Dr David to whom people would go to discuss intimate family problems. David had also served on the doctors' negotiating committee while the National Health Service was being created by Aneurin Bevan.

David's brother, Dr Willie, the other doctor in the region, was equally well liked, David covering the area to the south and Willie to the north.

I suggested when I arrived, and David agreed, that I would be Mr rather than Dr Hick because hardly anyone would understand the difference between a medical and an academic doctor. David himself, incidentally, had the advanced degree of MD for research on child health in a rural area.

My predecessor had been at Belford for twenty years having entered the ministry after retiring as a naval commander. He had been part of the life of the area, serving as a Conservative county councillor as well as minister. One of the stories about him was that once when he went to baptise a baby in the parents' cottage (a practice which I ended, insisting on church baptisms in the presence of the congregation) the father came home late, and as soon as he came through the door the minister, being now in 'bad fettle' at having been kept waiting so long, shoved the baby into his arms, dipped his finger in what he assumed to be the bowl of water and dabbed the baby's forehead with it – only he had put his finger into an ink pot! He stayed until he was about seventy and the people were then ready for a change. From my point of view it was of course a great benefit to come after someone who had evidently been there too long.

Northumberland was then still a fairly strongly Presbyterian area. It is a sign of the church's place in society at that time that *The Berwick Journal* printed in full my sermon at an Armistice Day united service in the parish church. There had once been three Presbyterian churches in Belford, as well as the Anglican parish church and a small Methodist church. Relations between my predecessor and the parish priest, the Rev. Herbert Pestle, had apparently been distant. But whilst I had not got anywhere near to a world ecumenical outlook, I was keen on the Christian ecumenical movement and established friendly relations with Mr Pestle and to a lesser extent with the small rather defensive Methodist group, and this was warmly welcomed in the village as a whole as overdue. Pestle was a bachelor, looked after by his sister in the large run-down vicarage. He was a deeply devout and faithful priest but very shy and uncommunicative and with a small congregation. I invited him to preach in our church, and he came but asked his brother, who was like him but more articulate, to preach the sermon; and Pestle asked me to preach in the parish church. We held some meetings about the World Council of Churches' Assembly at Evanston, and several other events, in the vicarage, and generally we established an atmosphere of colleagueship rather than rivalry. When we left for America, Mr Pestle graciously said of me to the local paper, 'He has concealed his learning with great modesty, and Church people especially will remember gratefully his concern for the unity of Christendom and the initiative he took in Belford to bring us more together in act and prayer.' When Herbert Pestle died his sister sent me a photo of him with her regards.

The Belford congregation with its 296 members on the roll was then the largest rural congregation in the denomination. Most of the members lived on the farms in an area stretching about ten miles in each direction from Belford. Hardly anyone except the farmers had a car and weekday meetings were rare. My job apart from the two Sunday services was mainly to go out and visit in the cottages and farms. There were not many telephones in the village so that I was not much interrupted by phone calls. The pattern of life was quite different from that of a minister today. I spent the morning in my study, and having written my two sermons and prepared the rest of the services I was able to devote the rest of the mornings to converting my Oxford thesis into a book. At first the sermons took a lot of time, but soon I was writing them quicker and I think better. I had to produce some ninety new sermons a year, each written by hand and then typed. They are biblically based and directed to a rural congregation few of whom had much education. I still have them and recently re-read one or two after nearly fifty years, and I have to say that I think they are quite good of their kind – though it is not the kind that I would preach today. And then after lunch I went out, at first on a bike but presently in the second-hand car that we bought in Newcastle, called 'Sin' after the letters on its number plate. Sin was started by vigorously turning a handle at the front, which you rapidly withdrew as soon as the engine fired before it could swing round and break your arm. During the winter we put a lighted oil lamp in the engine to prevent it from getting too cold to start – this sounds horrific today but it was necessary. And when driving in cold weather, there being no heater in the car, we had the lighted oil lamp under the rug covering our knees.

I fairly soon started a monthly congregational newsletter, duplicated on an old machine lent by Tommy Pringle, the church organist, who owned a clothes shop in the village and another at Seahouses on the coast, and the newsletter helped to keep the congregation interested. But although this picture of life sounds fairly leisurely our joint diary reminds me that life was actually often quite busy.

During our two and a half years the congregation flourished, and although my successor also did well this was only a blip in the long-term decline of church life throughout Northumberland, where new farm machinery needed fewer hands and a drift to the towns and cities had begun. And of course throughout the country as a whole church life had already long been in the decline which still continues. Today Belford is one of several congregations served by the same minister and the manse is no longer a manse.

The Presbytery of Berwick included some admirable characters. The interim moderator who had looked after Belford during the vacancy was David Holt Roberts, minister of a large congregation in Berwick, and he and his wife became good friends to Hazel and I. Another minister, who had long presided over a small congregation in the area and was approaching retirement, Mr Punch (as we called him) lived in the kitchen of his crumbling manse. The Moderator of the Presbytery, during my first year, was Gilbert Porteous, a fine man, then very keen on the Moral Rearmament movement. He was plagued by an unreliable car which he parked on top of a hill so as to be able to start it down the slope. But even then it sometimes let him down. When someone once asked him at a Presbytery meeting if he would be sure to get to a meeting in two days' time, he said, 'Yes, if I keep the engine going in the meantime.'

The ministers' basic stipend was £300 a year, and some better off congregations paid an additional £50. Belford did this when I was inducted there. This had not been necessary before because my predecessor had his naval pension and must have been quite reasonably off. But we had only the £350 a year, just under £1 a day. This was about the same, one of them told me, as the wages of a farm steward or foreman – though of course a minister also had a rent-free house. Although £1 a day then could buy much more than today, every penny counted. We usually had meat once or twice a week. We had fresh coffee for breakfast every other day, reusing the grounds the next day. Monday breakfast, the day off, was very special with fresh baps from one of the village shops. We bought very few clothes and hardly any luxuries, but did manage to save enough for a week in Austria each summer. Hazel was very good at making the money go as far as possible. But in spite of all this we did not in fact *feel* poor. Today, on that income, one would; but ministerial salaries have increased considerably in real terms since then. After about a year Hazel got a three days a week teaching job at the Duchess School, a girls' secondary school in Alnwick, where she went by bus each morning along with a number of Belford children, there being no local secondary school. In a diary entry she said, 'The Duchess's is a very good school – so good that H. has to work harder than she would like. Lots of VIth form work. A very pro-Catholic textbook in the form which does the Reformation is difficult. Special subject on the French Revolution.' Her job increased our income considerably, until she became pregnant with Ele, when the school thought it would be shocking for the girls to see a pregnant teacher!

The church treasurer was the gentle, shy and kindly Thos. Hunter (as he always signed himself) of Outchester farm. The strongest language I ever heard from him was when someone else had to do the accounts for a while and when Thomas took them over again he described them as 'a bubbly mess'. The auditor was James Henderson. He and his wife, who lived in a wooden bungalow in the country, were also very good to us. James looked after most of the farmers' accounts. He told me that they stuffed all documents into a suitcase during the year and then gave it to him to sort out; and the only way they knew how they were doing was by their current bank balance.

When we got married we decided to keep a joint diary, each (in theory) writing it up on alternate days though increasingly Hazel left it mostly to me. I still have the large volume which sheds its leather binding when handled. There is a lot of 'in' language. For example, Hazel's Nicking Irons were a small trowel and fork for collecting stray plants in the countryside as we drove around; the Chapel of Ease was the lavatory; fushing a sermon or a chapter was going through it again to improve it, and so on. I shall omit more esoteric terms in copying some extracts to recover the flavour of our life at Belford. It starts with an entry from me.

September 25/53. J: Yesterday was a Pestle and Pringle day. We had invited the Vicar to tea. He was the one authorised interruption, unauthorised ones being the man 'rumping' the hedge, a bread man from Wooler, Davidson trying to sell me an Austin 7, the Old Corpse digging in the jungle, and Tommy Pringle with Mr Kirby. These last two dropped in for coffee after lunch, and talked choirs and music, and photos and Austria; then we all went into the church and considered some five different ways of re-seating the choir if we get a communion table. Soon after they had gone, old Pestle arrived for tea. We started a row of subjects, hoping to hit upon something to interest him, but found none ... Today H. has cleaned the sitting room, and J. written half a communion sermon and read Boys Smith's Dissertation – the first piece of philosophical reading since we came here. So far there's nothing new in it. J. visited the George Thomsons at the station. He took me to meet a neighbour, but had first to 'dress properly', sallying forth in clean shirt (no collar) and bedroom slippers.

Out of diary: The Old Corpse was the church caretaker. Years ago he had been a Bible porteur, travelling the district selling religious tracts etc. Now he always walked leaning on a bike which he never rode. He divided those of the congregation of whom he approved into Grand Attenders and Grand Supporters. I remember his looking up at the sky one day and pronouncing that it would take it all its time to keep up. Another familiar Belford phrase was 'nearly almost'.

Tuesday, Oct. 6/53. J: Hazel's turn to write, but she insists on sewing curtains instead. Much too much happens every day to remember a week back. But Sunday was a busy day. Baptism of Hindmarsh infant in the morning. Session at 5.30 (Mac and Henderson and Tom Hunter in tails) to hear Janet Heatley's 'profession of faith' and meet those joining by transfer, six in all. Then my first Communion service. Session efficient and well drilled. Very good congregation, 174 members plus five visitors, the biggest communion congregation for 27 years. Then immediately afterwards a congregational meeting.

Thursday Oct. 8/53. H: Day of few interruptions and no mean achievements. J. got on with sermon in the morning. FLUE Day!

UGH! Did them less well and cleaned up less and so was quicker. H. finds the Belford shops maddening in the things they just don't stock. Lunch slightly more punctual than usual. In the afternoon J. sits in his study till tea. (What doing?) After tea H. planned J's sermon for him ... Memo. J. not to be a prig.

Sunday, Oct.11/53. J: On Friday we went with Mr Punch to Holy Island for me to take the harvest thanksgiving service there. We crossed from Beal sands in one of the ancient island taxis. It sounded from inside like being in an aeroplane. On the island we saw the parish church, strolled around Lindisfarne, which gave J. a more intense sense of its period than anywhere else, and were shown round the castle, which is fascinating, being still lived in. Four hundred year old four-poster bed, complete with sword cupboard. At the service the people sang with tremendous gusto. We brought a lobster back with us, but during the night a cat or someone else hoiked it out of the safe outside the kitchen door and chewed it, and our week's meat as well. We kept accounts last week for the first time, and were horrified to add the total to £5-8-6d.

Monday Oct. 19/53. H: Day of numberless interruptions. It began with a hangover from Harvest Sunday and the young people in here. J. still got up at the appalling hour of 7.45. We ran out of milk and had to wait for coffee till 9.15 when it arrived. Hardly had we drunk the coffee when Henderson arrived. The Syd Bells dropped in at lunch time. Some Berwick crooks tried to sell J. a car, but were staved off by the Purvoi [Purvis's]. The Women's Thing took place – about 40 females of low intelligence and little interest were present. Obviously it would be a mistake to change the present committee, they are greatly superior to anyone else who might be elected. (J:) H. chaired the Women's Thing brilliantly, 60 women present [!]. At the evening Harvest service there were 110 people, and the gallery had to be used. Afterwards we had about 25 under thirties into the Manse to discuss having a discussion group. Decided for them that it would be a good idea.

Monday, November 2/53. H: Last Sunday was the final of the congregational socials after the evening service, quite pleasant, but these people always tend to sit in serried ranks. At the eleventh hour J. has been asked to preach the Legion sermon. We were annoyed to be asked so late, but as a matter of fact J. has already written it in anticipation ... Happy [the local cat] has caught 5 mice.

Sunday, Nov. 8/53. J: Monday, 'Young Womens', and Mrs Farmer [wife of H.H. Farmer's brother, L.J. Farmer, minister at nearby Chatton] to supper. About fifty old women at the Young Womens ... Goodish attendance today, 44 this morning and 65 this evening. This week's funny thing. J. visiting Mrs Athey but going into wrong house and talking for half an hour with its occupants without their realising either that he hadn't intended to call or that he had no idea who they were.

Moving out of the diary for a moment, one day the chairman of the local Conservative party came to see me and explained that it was possible to make a donation to the party without this being publicly known. He was shocked when I told him that we were Labour voters, but later he and his wife invited us to dinner and were very friendly and we visited them several times.

Belford had an Old People's Home which I visited once a week. After a few visits, instead of holding a service, I truncated this into one prayer and then read instalments of George and Weedon Grossmith's comic classic *The Diary of a Nobody*, about life in England at about the time when they were young. This was a great success. They roared with laughter over the simple little jokes, and were very serious over the mock-serious parts. I am sure that their laughter did them more good than a church service.

I took over from I.J. Farmer of Chatton the idea of a Postal Sunday School for children whose parents did not often come to church and this proved quite useful. Even one or two Anglican families heard of it and joined.

We had a number of visitors to stay in the manse – relatives, fellow Westminster College students who were now ministers in various places, and Peter Heath, who was a lecturer in philosophy at Edinburgh when I was a student there and whom we have kept in touch with ever since. More about him later in the States. He gave us a copper coal scuttle as a wedding present, now used as a waste paper basket in the sitting room. The only other wedding present that I still have is Professor Jessop's fine pair of silver candlesticks, still on the sideboard in the dining room.

Saturday, Dec. 26/53. J: Our first Christmas in our own home, and a very lovely and memorable one ... Last Friday John Murray [a New Zealand student at Westminster College and later a very

successful minister back home] arrived from Cambridge. We all
went to the Male Voice Choir concert on the Saturday – it was
good as a village effort. John M. prat the 'Plea' [on behalf of the
College] in the morning, and in the evening we had a Festival of
Eight Lessons and Carols, with the lessons read by different
people. It was a great success. About 180 people present. Then 21
Young Things in the Manse to hear John M. talk about New
Zealand. George Purves launched the Camera Club. Some time
the week before last Charlie Dickson painted the sitting room
floor ... Great cookery and decorating last week. Door rings.
Holly. Red candles. Innumerable Christmas cards. Making of
fudge and peppermint creams for presents. On Christmas Eve we
went on a carol party of the three Belford churches. Quite
successful, though cold. Got up late on Christmas Day.
Continental breakfast with real coffee. Then J. painted study
floor, whilst H. cooked a wonderful Christmas dinner. Tomato
soup. Chicken, with bacon & stuffing, roast potatoes, and greens.
White wine, brought by John Murray. Christmas pud. with rum
butter. Then we sank deep into armchairs. In the evening the
Roundthwaites came to drink punch. A first-rate Christmas Day.
Only thing lacking, a service ...

Sunday, Jan.10/54. J: Harry Grunter comes to choir practice but
shirks sitting in choir at services ... Mild winter continuing. Trees
in front of the kitchen long since bare. Sheep in our field instead
of cows. Eating turnips. Saw strange animal – mole? – in field the
other day. Shelves painted today.

Tuesday, Jan.19/54. J: Full moon last night, and this evening,
having closed down all activities, we went for a moon-and-star-lit
walk along the road towards Middleton. Lovely night. Last
Thursday we had Belford's first post-war Soiree. It was a great
success. Wonderful response to the appeal for food, nearly every
family contributing. About 250 present. Holt Roberts and John
Hucker spoke well – H.R. had everyone in continuous laughter –
and the choir and imported singers did well. J. read Wittgenstein
and Paul Tillich this morning, interrupted by 3 tefelumps [phone
calls] and a newspaper reporter. J now getting 3 mornings a week
for reading – and later, writing. Good! Have read [Henry] Price's
new book [*Belief*], which is extremely good, and am now in the
midst of the curious posthumous Wittgenstein work [*Philosophical
Investigations*]. Keep meeting familiar ideas and ways of putting
them – which shows how much the book, which has long
circulated in typescript in Cambridge, has soaked in and become

influential. A book full of occasional lights and sidelights. Don't greatly like Tillich's 'Systematic Theology'.

Saturday, Jan 23/54. H: The trouble with J. is he is just so rational – a strange principle in everyday life. Wednesday was a Day Off. Shopping in Berwick. We find we are getting known there, sad to say; explored another café & thought none of it; ordered a pelmet. Tea with the Stenhice on Thursday, a gentle echo of Cranford ... J. has painted the study book cases.

Sunday Feb. 14/54. H: Last Thursday morning we were shattered to hear that David Macdonald was seriously, even dangerously, ill with heart & blood complications, and has been in a critical state since. Daphne does not want any visitors. This evening James [their son] came in with the news that he is definitely better & we are all much relieved.

Sunday March 14/54. J: The Play. This has been rehearsed once a week for a couple of months. The last rehearsal, on Wednesday, was good – surprisingly so. Cast of about 20 (including J. in two small parts), produced by Mrs Burn [Fred and Graham Burn of Fenham-le-Moor farm were good friends]. Colourful costumes and scenery. But tonight's performance was appalling (though the audience probably didn't notice!). George Purves, as Peter, failed to be on the stage when Thelma Lee rushed over to recognise him as a follower of Jesus. Then Thelma and Helen Anderson failed to make an entry in another scene, so that half of it had to be missed out. And Tommy, at the organ, lost his list of songs by the soloist, and had to have messengers flying to and fro. However the folk will undoubtedly want to do another play ... H's innocent enquiry about how farmers knew when the lambing would begin has gone round the district and become a famous joke.

Sunday Dec.12/54. J: Last Monday night seven corn stacks were burnt down at Plantation Farm. Margaret says they were deliberately set alight. Another account is that the stuff was stacked too wet and generated its own heat. Harry Wood's [the shepherd] comment on this was that a stack will smoulder in that way but not burst into flames. He also told me about the tramps who used to roam the Cheviot hills half a century ago. They were well-known characters, walking a definite round, and were welcomed as carrying the news & as being company for a lonely shepherd's household. There was one, an old Frenchman, who used to arrive in the district at about the same time each year, when a dance was held in his aid, called French's Ball.

Friday Dec. 31/54. H:

CERTIFICATE

This is to Certify that the Reverend
Doctor John Harwood Hick has
Passed an Examination in
the Art of Folding
Shirts.
Collar-less shirt class only.
(Signed) J. Hazel Hick
Date: Old Year's Night 1954.

Monday March 21/55. J: The first day of Spring, which is being celebrated by a fall of snow. Also Hazel's birthday, bringing a delightful black-and-white fush-pot [can't now remember what that was]; an unironable nighty; a bottle of scent; a large box full of tins of coffee, peaches, etc; a little pair of socklets, which J. thought were meant for the baby, but which expand to fit H's hoofkins; and an elegant glove-holder.

A lot has happened in the last two months. H. is now a Lady in Waiting, the infant being expected in mid-June. Harry Wood & his wife, & Douglas Tully have all had strokes. Jack Wood died suddenly a week ago. As we could not have the funeral service in the Wood's house [as was the custom], Pestle kindly let us use the parish church. Congregational meeting went OK a week ago. Tommy Pringle agitated for an electronic organ.

Finally,

Sunday July 17/55. J: Eleanor [born June 21st] is growing rapidly, and beginning to look around & take an interest in the world. So far she has not usually slept through the night, but sleeps soundly all day in the pram in the garden. Hot summer weather. H. copes with her magnificently, but J. is still a little frightened of handling her.

Out of the diary now, all parents will know what a moving and joyful event it is when your first child is born, a new life for which you are responsible. Ele was a fairly, but only fairly, 'good baby'. There were days when she did not sleep at all soundly during the day and we had to take her out in the car, whose uneven motion lulled her to sleep. But as soon as we got back she started crying again!

Sometime in 1954 I was approached by the philosophy department at Cornell University about applying for a job there as assistant professor to teach philosophy of religion that Fall. Price and others in Oxford must have recommended me. The final letter of invitation came on Christmas Day 1954, I having asked to postpone beginning there from September '55 until January '56 so as not to leave Belford so precipitately. It did not take us long to decide to go. We had tremendously enjoyed Belford and were in many ways sorry to leave. It was a wonderful period in our life. But on the other hand this was an ideal opportunity to enter the academic world, and the longer I stayed at Belford the less likely this would become. If I had stayed, say, ten years I would have been too rusty academically to be considered, even if I had managed to publish the book coming out of my thesis, *Faith and Knowledge*. But I tried several British publishers without success. This shows what a chancy business it is to catch a publisher's eye, for the book was published in 1957 by the Cornell University Press and has since been quite influential.

When many years later, 1983, I took daughter Ele on a 'Roots' tour we spent several days in the Blue Bell at Belford and visited a number of people. One day we visited a farm and knocked on a cottage door, which was opened by a women who greeted us with 'Good morning, Mr Hick' as though I had only been away for a week or two! And indeed writing this chapter with the aid of the diary and the old sermons and printed Soiree notices and old photos have made it seem like that.

NOTES

1. The history of the congregation begins in 1793 and is extremely interesting to anyone who knows the area. It is chronicled by the Rev. David Clarke in *The History of Belford United Reformed Church, 1776–1976*.

10

Philosopher at Cornell

In order to get the right visas for me to work in the USA we all – Hazel, three-month-old Eleanor and I – had to travel to London to be interviewed by a large formidably serious lady consul with a huge American flag behind her and swear that we were not communists – baby Ele expressing what Hazel and I were also thinking by a timely burp. This was the time of the McCarthy communist witch hunts during Eisenhower's presidency. We sailed in the *Queen Elizabeth* in January 1956 to New York where we were met by Chuck Schwartz, one of the Americans at Westminster College, who was soon to become Presbyterian minister in a small town quite near Cornell, so that we kept in touch with him and indeed he visited me here in Birmingham on an English trip only two years ago. We travelled to Ithaca by overnight train and were met by one of the ministers of the Presbyterian church, who took us to his house for a magnificent breakfast. The country was under deep snow, unfamiliar large bright red robins visible outside, the house luxuriously warm. We were in a new world.

Impressions recorded at the time are better than distant memories, and I shall be quoting from carbon copies of some of our letters home and our annual Christmas round-robin letters, it often being impossible now to tell which of us was writing. One of the things that first struck us as newcomers to the States was the universal presence of advertising. It seemed absurd, for example, that it was a great selling point for some brand of cigarettes, worth millions of dollars to get across to the public, that it came in 'a flip top box'.

And generally we seemed to be in a pervasively materialistic culture in which dollars were the most frequent topic of conversation. But on the other hand everyone was friendly, talking freely without any need for introductions, using first names instantly, and with no class distinctions – though of course behind this social equality were huge differences of wealth.

Cornell, a private university founded as a Land Grant college in 1862 at Ithaca in up-state New York and endowed as a university by Ezra Cornell in 1868, has one of the most beautiful campuses in the United States, on a hill overlooking Lake Cayuga, one of the five Finger Lakes. It was founded as a secular institution, and its first President, Andrew White, wrote a once famous *History of The Warfare of Science with Theology in Christendom* (1896). Cornell was the first major university to admit women and was in general an academically liberal institution. It had some 10,000 students, large by then UK standards but small in comparison with many other US universities. It was in general of high quality, being a member of the select Ivy League along with Harvard, Yale, Pennsylvania, Princeton, Columbia, Brown, and Dartmouth. In 1956 only twenty-four per cent of applicants were admitted. It was also a wealthy institution, with four million dollars worth of new buildings then under way on the campus. The students paid $1,100 a year fees – it will be a lot more now – and thus came from well-off families. They mostly lived in the fraternity and sorority houses. Although long established and accepted, these were divisive, with very expensive ones, less expensive ones, sporty ones, scholarly ones, Jewish ones, and so on.

Among the present generation of students here there is enormous general liveliness and vitality, but combined with a regrettable uniformity (no eccentrics) and intellectual docility (no heretics). The student population is much more colourful than in England – bright multicoloured sweaters, vivid slang, and large fast cars. But most of them conform very markedly to a pattern, and it is part of this pattern to be much more concerned with their own careers than with the state of their country or the world at large.

As soon as we arrived we found ourselves welcomed with warmth and friendliness to the university and the philosophy department. In the first hectic and confusing month or two J. had much help in the details of teaching, and H. had loans of baby equipment and lifts to the shops from faculty wives. The kindness of J's senior colleagues is unfailing, and the intellectual atmosphere of the place, and in particular of the Sage School of Philosophy, is stimulating.

We did not know when we first committed ourselves to go there that Cornell then had one of the strongest philosophy departments in the country, with a distinctive character as the leading US centre for the study of Wittgenstein, who had visited there not long before his death in 1951. The two dominant figures were Max Black and Norman Malcolm. Max had one of the most efficient and lucid, though narrowly focused, minds I have encountered. He was not a system builder and his writings consisted mostly of articles later collected into books. His central concern was language, and he wrote classic discussions of such topics as meaning, rules, metaphor. He was an expert on Wittgenstein's earlier logical work, whilst Norman was an authority on the later work. Norman had studied as a graduate student with both Wittgenstein and G.E. Moore at Cambridge, and although these two were very different in everything except their passionate search for truth, Norman had been deeply influenced by both. Whereas Max was always precise and lucid, in appearance as well as speech, Norman was more ruminative and exploratory in discussions, and was a large shambling, sometimes explosive figure. His writings however are beautifully clear. I attended some of Max's and Norman's graduate seminars, as well as those of the visiting professor von Wright from Finland, another great authority on Wittgenstein and one of his literary executors.

The other assistant professors included Jack Rawls, author later of the influential *A Theory of Justice* (1971), a subject on which he was already working in the 1950s; and Rogers Albritton. There were also several Instructors, this being then the lowest grade of university teacher, now no longer found. Some of the then graduate students have later become well known, including Sydney Shoemaker, Keith Lehrer and others. There was thus a very strong and active ethos of philosophical discussion. The senior professor who had been teaching the philosophy of religion, and whom I was replacing, was E.A. Burtt, author of *The Metaphysical Foundations of Modern Science*, and later a writer on the world religions and himself half a Buddhist. He was extremely helpful to me, although I was then a conservative Christian, my mind alas closed to his wider vision. Today I have a much greater affinity with his point of view. Fortunately we live and learn.

When I entered the large auditorium for my first philosophy of religion lecture I was on a stage confronted by a class of just over three hundred students – Burtt's legacy. I was delighted that during the first week or two they were listening intently – and then it dawned on me that they were savouring my English accent! However they stayed with me after this had ceased to be a novelty. I had one graduate assistant, and between us we had to read more than three hundred students' papers several times during the semester of about fifteen teaching weeks. It was impossible to read all these papers properly and the only thing to do was to read a few and then pass everyone, grading on a standard curve. Very shocking. But most of my time between lectures had to be spent in preparing the next one. I also took a section of the introductory philosophical classics course, studying Hume's *Dialogues on Natural Religion*, Hobbes' *De Cive*, and Berkeley's *Three Dialogues*, or in other years some of Plato's shorter *Dialogues*, Mill's *Utilitarianism*, and the Berkeley, all excellent choices which gave rise to good discussion in a class of about thirty. In my second semester I had two of these sections and also an elective course on Christian theology, which drew about a hundred and sixty students at first and went up next year to about two hundred. I also later did a course on Christian Ethics which drew an interested bunch. One spring semester I gave an advanced course entitled 'Problems in the philosophy of religion' dealing with essays by contemporary philosophers, which was attended mainly by graduate students. This was conducted by discussion, seminar-fashion, and was very profitable to me as well, I think, as the students.

The department's teaching was on Mondays, Wednesdays and Fridays. In my first semester I was given a light load. But thereafter I had a ten minute drive up to the campus for a 9 o'clock philosophical classics class, then after a ten minutes break, the senior problems class or one on Christian ethics. Between 11 and 12, coffee, chatting with colleagues, reading the campus newspaper, and looking over my notes for the big lecture at 12, on philosophy of religion or Christian theology, depending on the semester. On Thursday afternoons I also had a voluntary discussion group from the large lecture course; and three office hours during the week when students could drop in to talk about anything. On Fridays at the end of the morning there was a department meeting to which we took our own sandwiches and made coffee. Upstairs in a small room at Goldwin Smith Hall, among the Instructors, was an older tenured full professor, left over from the pre-Black and Malcolm period, who was despised (as a philosopher) by the leading figures in the department, and who was largely ignored and did not even attend department meetings. I went up sometimes to chat with him. He said that he had written a book on logic years ago but failed to get it published and had been in professional obscurity ever since. I think that the departmental judgment about him was right but could nevertheless only feel sorry for him.

I learned an enormous amount during these three and a half years at Cornell, about Wittgenstein, about Moore, about how to teach, and I appreciated the rigorous standard of argument in the philosophy club and in the smaller purely faculty discussion group, even though many of the topics were, to my mind, extremely trivial. The focus was always microscopic and no one except me (and Burtt) was interested in the big questions with which philosophy traditionally dealt. I was never drawn into the Wittgensteinian thought world, and retained the kind of independence from the dominant school of thought and the wider range of interests that I had seen in Price at Oxford. I would not have wanted to remain at Cornell permanently, nor would the department have wanted me to. Towards the end of my initial three years contract I tested the water by applying to become an associate professor with tenure. I was given an extension of an extra semester, to see if I was moving into the Wittgensteinian fold, but at this point began to make it known in wider circles that I was available. But more about the next move later.

The Presbyterian church, knowing that I was a minister, embraced us, not only meeting us on arrival but providing an apartment in its block of Missionary Apartments for our first semester – 114 Catherine Street, conveniently on the edge of the campus. To us this was palatially warm and comfortable. As spring came we explored outside a bit. One day

> we had lunch by the lakeside and then stopped at an orchard where you can pick your own cherries at about half the price of already picked ones. We picked 13 pounds, and they are now

stoned and bottled. Then we stopped at another orchard for a last picking of strawberries before the season ends. Mrs Myers had warned us that American strawberries are very inferior to English ones, and this is true. The ones we picked were about a quarter the size of those we grew at Belford last summer. And also they are not quite so tasty.

The Inf. can walk as much as she likes, though still unsteadily and with occasional sudden sits. She can also climb upstairs quite quickly, and downstairs slowly. There is a new family with children downstairs with whom she likes playing ... She has discovered a mirror standing on the floor and keeps going up to it to smile at herself. This evening we went to a diner for supper, and Eleanor walked round to each table and laughed at everyone. She is a great success in society.

There is only one Presbyterian church in town, but it has 1,800 members and seems to us unbelievably, and almost indecently, large and prosperous. There are three ministers (not counting the Presbyterian chaplain on the campus), three full-time ministers' wives!, a full-time church secretary, two paid organists, two adult choirs, two paid choir-masters. Fortunately there is only one organ, because this plays all the time and only holds itself in check during the sermon. Its sentimental, but supposedly holy, chimes tinkling in the background during the period of 'silent prayer', evoke thoughts of sabotage and a longing for the devotional atmosphere of the congregation at Belford. There are two identical morning services, at 9.30 and 11 o'clock, both generally crowded. This leaves the rest of the day free for youth organisations and all sorts of other church activities. The church school, as it is called, is taken very seriously, there being no religious teaching in the state schools. A very much larger proportion of the population are regular churchgoers here than in England and almost everyone brings their children to church school. Eleanor thoroughly enjoys the church nursery for toddlers, run by a rota of mothers, and we find it a great blessing to be able to go to church together. The USA is experiencing a religious boom in which it is fashionable to belong to and to attend a church. This is partly a religious and partly a sociological phenomenon, partly Christian and partly American ...

The senior minister, Dr Dodds, well known in Presbyterian circles, was very hospitable to us. His preaching however was devoid of theological content, consisting in sensible psychological counselling from the pulpit. But the main alternative on offer within American

Presbyterianism was infinitely worse, intolerant right-wing fundamentalism – as I was later to discover at Princeton.

Ithaca is on about the same latitude as Rome. It is extremely hot in the summer, sometimes over 90 degrees, and extremely cold in the winter, often with snow deep enough to bury a car, and with a wonderful spring and a brilliant Fall, the trees being far more colourful than in England. The surrounding countryside is very beautiful. There were picnics on the shore of Lake Cayuga, swimming in the lake, drives around the countryside, tobogganing in the winter.

When a second baby, Mark, was on the way we bought the first home that we had ever owned, a small wooden house (most US houses being of wood), 305 East Lincoln Street, in town but near the foot of the hill on which the campus stood. You entered up some steps, through the front door into the smallish living room, with a corridor beyond leading to two small bedrooms, small dining room, bathroom, and then the kitchen, with a small yard (garden, in British English) beyond. Up some narrow stairs there was attic space, half of which we partitioned off as my study. It was a novel luxury for us to have central heating, hot air blown through grills in the floor. There was also a useful basement rumpus room; and a garage for the car, Mr Pontiac. We bought the house for $10,000 and were able to pay the necessary deposit with the aid of Aunt Marg in Hutton Buscel. Her husband Norman, Mark's brother, had left capital which provided her with an income for life but with the capital to come to Pem, Shirley and me at her death, Norman and Marjorie having no children of their own. She allowed me to take my future share, paying her until her death the income that she would have received from it, and we had a local bank mortgage to make up the total. Although my dollar salary was the equivalent of about £1,000 (as compared with £350 at Belford) everything was more expensive, we had no free house, and we started with no furniture or household items of any kind.

> *August 9, 1956.* As you see, we are now in our new house. We 'completed' and moved in on Tuesday and are still settling in. During the last two days Hazel has spent most of the time cleaning the apartment in Catherine Street, and I have been painting the front porch and steps here, mowing the lawn, and

putting up a wire fence to make the garden Inf. proof. The house is in our names jointly. We pay $56 a month to the Bank which gave the mortgage, of which about $20 is interest and $36 amortisation. The interest is at 5%. We also pay to the Bank $22 a month for payment of the various taxes to the city and State.

Being only very moderately well off we supplemented our income by my sometimes taking services in Presbyterian and Congregational churches in the surrounding villages, by teaching a course at a Cornell summer school and by Hazel finding paid work. Out of the proceeds 'we have largely completed the furnishing of the house, which was previously rather bare. We have acquired curtains, crockery, an automatic washing machine, a sitting room carpet, and finally TV, mostly second hand.' This was our first TV. At that time the programmes were half-hour items, constantly interrupted by ads, and showing virtually nothing of any substance. The only programme that I particularly remember was *Gunsmoke* with Marshall Dillon, Chester, Doc, Kitty, and assorted bad men. Apart from that American TV was then a crime against humanity, except for Public Service programmes imported from the BBC.

A year after our move to the States, number two, Mark arrived.

In appearance Mark and Eleanor are rather alike, but he is the more hefty, and is less forward in the various baby accomplishments, and more placid than Eleanor. By now they are constant and happy companions. Eleanor never stops talking, and Mark listens with apparent adoration to all her remarks. She has begged to have him beside her on the floor so much that by now he considers the play-pen rather an insult. Eleanor hails with delight every achievement of 'my brother'. J. has had latterly to develop a line in fairy stories, the current one being The Story of the Three Sisters – Globula, who was very round, Gladys who was very flat, and Cinderella, who was very nice and very pretty. Fortunately, repetition is more important than invention

Hazel's full time job [I can't now remember what it was] has ended and after a week's holiday she is taking a part-time job in the University administration building, with a slightly higher pay. She will be part of the organization which hounds alumni to get them to give money to the University. She makes potted biographies of selected wealthy alumni, ferreting out their hobbies and interests, so that if some millionaire is, say, a tennis enthusiast, he can be invited to donate the Homer Z. Rumplemeier memorial tennis courts.

We have had some nice Belford letters lately, about how Grandma Tully got a shock when she saw the street flooded, and how it is a long way to write to America, and how the Misses Hunter have bought a car but find it difficult to get it out of the garage and prefer to take a bus, etc.

We gather that our voices are obviously British, but in many ways we have changed over to American habits of eating, when we can afford them. Most people get up earlier here than their English counterparts; we have the light American lunch of soup and a sandwich and our main meal in the evening. Our lunch is usually later than the standard time of 12 because J. is often not back from the campus by then. We have a salad as an accompaniment to most main meals, though J. is not always fond of this. Many Americans dispense with desert even at dinner for family meals, but needless to say J. and the infant feel very cheated by such a practice ...

We are doing a great deal of entertaining now of a rather low order; we shall have to leave returning all the hospitality we owe to faculty members till we have some more plates, preferably china not plastic, and some sort of dining room furniture. We have regular sessions with J's students on alternate Wednesdays and Thursdays. We have had 12 to 25 sitting on the floor for these, but the rest come in smaller numbers which we can get to know better. Tonight we had a rather pathetic English graduate student in philosophy who at the moment finds it difficult to enjoy any social life in the American style and can only talk nostalgically about Oxford which he is convinced is superior to anything America can offer. He thinks J. must be all right having heard about him from various Oxford people but doesn't think he has any right to be so much enjoying himself here.

Shopping I still find a bit confusing in these enormous supermarkets. Food is always hygenically wrapped and vegetables are sold scrubbed and in plastic bags on refrigerated stalls – wonderfully muck-saving but not a patch on muddy vegetables straight from the garden for flavour. We are able to buy apples straight from the University orchards and very good they are; and also buy dry skim milk from the Dairy department as a useful cheap supplement for cooking, and are trying as an experiment collecting our milk from the University farms at much less cost than having it delivered, but rather a fag. During the summer we very much enjoyed the semi-tropical fruits which are readily found here.

Whilst I was at Cornell there were two major academic visitors to the university. One was Paul Tillich, one of the two best known theologians in the country, the other being Reinhold Niebuhr. Tillich came to give a series of lectures over a couple of weeks. I had recently written a generally appreciative review article of the first volume of his *Systematic Theology* for the *Scottish Journal of Theology* and gave him an advance copy; and he was interested to meet me. We met at his hotel, and I then invited him to our house for an evening of discussion over the white wine which I was told he liked. He very graciously accepted, we bought a bottle of the wine, and I fetched him from the hotel. I asked him a series of critical questions, which he answered fully in his usual manner of enveloping the questioner's point of view in his own system. Tillich had an impressive presence; he was a bold original thinker; and I felt it a privilege to have this evening with him. When he later visited the Princeton Theological Seminary I was the only person he knew on the faculty and had more conversation with him. Although I never adopted his complex theological system, I saw him as a major force in opening up a new range of possibilities and thus as a wholly positive influence, today alas largely neglected. In his later years he visited Japan, held extensive dialogues with Zen philosophers in Kyoto, and opened his mind to an even more radical range of possibilities. Indeed he said in one of his last public lectures that if he had his time over again he would re-think his entire system on a multi-faith basis. At that time he was far ahead of me in this, though I have since caught up, at least on that issue.

The other academic visitor was Robert Calhoun, professor of the history of Christian thought at Yale. His lectures were famous, and although he had published very little the lectures had been taped and he now had a sabbatical in which to turn them into a book. He was provided with an office, a machine on which to play the tapes, a typewriter and a recording machine, and no teaching duties – though he did very kindly speak to one of my classes. I refer to him here because he illustrates very well one type of academic mind, one which I admire but which is quite foreign to me. He was a brilliant extempore speaker who lectured without notes and could express the same thoughts in endlessly different ways, giving what is essentially the same lecture many times and yet always as a fresh utterance. This is what made him such a scintillating and influential teacher. But he could never settle upon one particular way of saying it as the best way; next time there was always something else to be added or said in a new way. So he started out with his book in AD 1, exploring the origins and development of Christian thought, and by the end of the semester he had reached 55 BC and the projected book never came to be. In contrast, those of us who have no extempore gift have to work hard to find a form of words that satisfies us and we then stick with it, thus having something for publication. The overall result is that our sort probably publish much too much and the other sort much too little.

I am sure that the individual psychology of philosophers and theologians must affect significantly their manner of thinking. For example, I like order and clarity and dislike chaos, vagueness and cloudiness. I tend to be fairly well organised and prefer to leave my desk empty rather than littered with unfinished business. And so am I, in my metaphysical speculations, trying to tidy up the universe in my own mind by creating a systematic picture of it? More generally, are systematic thinkers generally also tidier in other aspects of their lives? Certainly Kant, with his elaborate and orderly philosophical architectonic, was famously tidy. But are unsystematic thinkers generally untidy and disorganised in their daily lives? I don't know. It is in any case important to see that if there are such correlations, this in no way invalidates either kind of work. It just means that it requires different kinds of mind to do different kinds of intellectual job. But the whole subject deserves more research.

Towards the end of our time in Ithaca number three was born.

We have not yet decided who he looks like, but have named him Peter Pentland. He has been received enthusiastically by Eleanor and Mark, who sit on either side of Hazel whilst she is feeding him, and want to take turns in holding him. The two older children resemble nothing so much as a duplex tribe of cave men. Noisy, grubby and jolly, they like above all to chase one another yelling Bang, Bang, or to join up as a train, with appropriate noises. Mark is nearly two, and nearly as big as Eleanor, who is three and a half; at any rate they are well matched for fighting purposes. They have occasional civilised periods, sufficient to impress visitors, and Eleanor is highly clothes-conscious, rushing down each morning to ask, 'Can I have a very pretty dress today?' They are of course acquiring American vocabulary and accent.

I had brought my completed manuscript of *Faith and Knowledge* with me, it having been turned down by several – I forget how many – UK publishers, and now submitted it to the Cornell University Press. It was read for the Press by an anonymous reader whom I could easily identify as the department chairman, Stuart Brown, who recommended that it should be accepted but with the first two chapters, on knowledge and on belief, omitted. At the time I refused to do this and asked the director of the Press to get a second opinion. This came from George Thomas, professor of the philosophy of religion at Princeton, and was strongly favourable and the book was published in full in 1957. However when I prepared a second edition nine years later I realised that those first two chapters ought after all to have been omitted, though with parts of them incorporated elsewhere, and as I wanted to add several new chapters the deletions caused no problem. But even in its first form the book was well received, except by the reviewer in the *Philosophical Review*, edited by the philosophy department, which was a hatchet job commissioned to distance the department from the book.

That apart, the book received good reviews and was fairly widely read, before long requiring a second printing and later a second and revised edition. The last reprinting was by Macmillan in 1988, thirty-one years after its first publication, and in between (in 1978) there was an inexpensive version in Collins' Fount Paperbacks. My style in this book was rather like Farmer's and a little old-fashioned in comparison with that of later books. But to give something of its flavour:

> We become conscious of other objects in the universe, whether things or persons, either by experiencing them for ourselves or by inferring their existence from evidences within our experience. The awareness of God reported by the ordinary religious believer [today I would say by the first-hand religious believer] is of the former kind. He [for this was before the coming of inclusive language] professes, not to have inferred that there is a God, but that God as a living being [or, better, as a living presence] has entered into his experience. He claims to enjoy something which

he describes as an experience of God. The ordinary [first-hand] believer does not, however, report an awareness of God as existing in isolation from all other objects of experience. His consciousness of the divine does not involve a cessation of his consciousness of a material and social environment. It is not a vision of God in solitary glory, filling the believer's entire mind and blotting out his normal field of perception.

He claims instead an apprehension of God meeting him in and through the material and social environments. He finds that in his dealings with the world of men and things he is somehow having to do with God, and God with him. The moments of ordinary life possess, or may possess, for him in varying degrees a religious significance ... I shall try to show, in various fields, that 'mediated' knowledge, such as is postulated by this religious claim, is ... a common and accepted feature of our cognitive experience. To this end we must study a basic characteristic of human experience, which I shall call 'significance', together with the correlative mental activity by which it is apprehended, which I shall call 'interpretation'. We shall find that interpretation takes place in relation to each of the three mains types of existence, or orders of significance, recognized by human thought – the natural, the human, and the divine; and that in order to relate ourselves appropriately to each a primary and unevidenceable act of interpretation is required which, when directed toward God, has traditionally been termed 'faith'. Thus I shall try to show that while the object of religious knowledge is unique, its basic epistemological pattern is that of all our knowing ... The significance for us of the physical world, nature, is that of an objective environment whose character and 'laws' we must learn, and toward which we have continually to relate ourselves aright if we are to survive.

The significance for us of the human world, man, is that of a realm of relationships in which we are responsible agents, subject to moral obligation. This world of moral significance is, so to speak, superimposed upon the natural world, so that relating ourselves to the moral world is not distinct from the business of relating ourselves to the natural world but is rather a particular manner of so doing. And likewise the more ultimately fateful and momentous matter of relating ourselves to the divine, to God, is not distinct from the task of directing ourselves within the natural and ethical spheres; on the contrary, it entails (without being reducible to) a way of so directing ourselves.

The book also introduced the concepts of 'eschatological verification', about which a number of articles have been published, of 'experiencing-as' (in the second edition), about which a number of articles have also appeared, and (likewise in the second edition) of Christian ethics as the dispositional aspect of Christian belief.

The philosophical reader can see in *Faith and Knowledge* the influence of Kant, received through Kemp Smith at Edinburgh; the influence of John Oman, particularly his *The Natural and the Supernatural* (1931), received through H.H. Farmer; a trace of John Macmurray of Edinburgh in his distinguishing of the natural, the ethical, and the divine; and (in the 2nd edition) of Wittgenstein's discussion of 'seeing as', received through John Wisdom. We are none of us – unless it be a Kant or a Wittgenstein – as original as we may be tempted to think. We live at a time and in a place which feed us with formative influences and any originality we may have is largely in the use that we make of them. And any long-term influence we may have is not in gaining disciples but in offering ideas which are later taken up in new ways into the thinking of others.

When reading the galley proofs, each perhaps two feet long, in my little attic study in East Lincoln Street, I met a curious phenomenon which I have never encountered since in the page proofs (which have superseded galleys) of subsequent books. This was the extraordinary number of times that two successive lines either began or ended with the same word. This looked to me anomalous and I usually felt that I had to alter the wording to avoid it.

I still feel a fondness for this, my first book. I was particularly pleased to learn that William Alston was strongly influenced by it. Approval of one's work is proportionate in value to the stature of the person making it. Bill Alston, of my own generation, has been highly influential, educating a whole generation of now distinguished American philosophers of religion, and I value greatly both the basic agreement between our approaches and his friendship over the years. We first met at a conference at the University of Minnesota shortly after the publication of *Faith and Knowledge* and discovered that we had much in common. He says of that occasion,

> I was slightly ahead of John at that time on the academic ladder, but that book made it abundantly clear that he was light years ahead of me in thinking about philosophical theology ... From

the first edition, the book made a profound impression on me, primarily for its insistence on the point that theistic faith, when live and fully-formed, rests on the experience of the presence and activity of God in our lives.[1]

And in his magnum opus, *Perceiving God*, he again speaks of his thought as having been 'strongly influenced by John Hick's treatment in *Faith and Knowledge*'.[2] We differ however in that he is much more orthodox in his theology than I have become. In connection with this, I have criticised his response to what he accepts as 'the most difficult problem for [his] position',[3] the problem of religious diversity. I have pointed out that his defense of experience-based religious belief applies as much to Muslim, Jewish, Hindu, Buddhist etc. as to Christian beliefs, so that in holding that Christian beliefs are true, but the others false in so far as they are incompatible with these, he has really propounded the principle that the Christian belief-system is the sole exception to the general rule that religious experience produces false beliefs![4] Bill has vigorously defended himself, and most recently has contributed a new piece in defense of his position in my *Dialogues in the Philosophy of Religion*.[5] We remain apart on this issue; but this does not affect in the least our basic epistemological agreement or our mutual regard and friendship.

The only other thing of any significance that I published whilst at Cornell was an article in the *Scottish Journal of Theology*[6] criticising the Scottish theologian Donald Baillie's Christology, in his justly famous book, *God Was in Christ*, as departing from Chalcedonian orthodoxy. I later however, in a theological U-turn, came to agree with him. I think I was right in pointing out that, whereas he believed that his 'paradox of grace' suggestion was in line with traditional orthodoxy, it was really a radical departure from it. But I also came to think that this radical departure was a right move! However, at the time, my article expressed my still traditionally orthodox version of Christian faith.

The American academic world is much quicker to recognise new talent and to be interested in new ideas than its British counterpart. In Britain a young newcomer, having published only his first book, could not at that time have become known and accepted in the space of a couple of years. But in the US, although it is so much bigger, I was soon invited to join the American Theological Society in New

York, of which most of the senior figures – Tillich, the Niebuhrs, etc. – were members. I was invited to lecture at Rochester University, Wells College, Colgate–Rochester Divinity School, Vassar College, the University of Minnesota, as well as McGill University and Union Theological Seminary, and spoke at a number of conferences.

In 1956 Farmer wrote to me that Union in New York had its eye on me.

> I very much hope that you will get into seminary work before long, for whilst I do not doubt that the opportunity for Christian work at Cornell is very great and that you are making good use of it, the training of future ministers, particularly in America, is strategically more important. I hope a really worth-while opportunity will not come too soon and plunge you into a quandary in relation to Cornell. On the other hand I find myself hoping that an American seminary appointment, if it is to come, will not be so long delayed that the acceptance of it would put you out of the running for a certain vacancy here, which I need not specify further [i.e. as his successor at Westminster College].

As Farmer had predicted, Union in New York did indeed invite me to visit, to give a lecture and a chapel sermon, to meet and be scrutinised by the faculty. I stayed for a few days in the palatial apartment of Dr Henry van Deusen, the president, attended one of Reinhold Niebuhr's lectures – Tillich had already moved to Harvard, and had many conversations and discussions with his colleagues. They were amused, I think, rather than annoyed to find that I had never heard of process theology, which was strongly represented there, particularly by Daniel Williams. But their interest in me was as a representative of the analytical school of philosophy who was also a committed Christian. In due course I was offered the post of assistant professor, but with the salary of an associate professor. I bargained about this. My position was that if I was worth an associate's salary I was worth an associate's status. Their equally reasonable position was that they never gave tenure, which went with associateship, without a trial period as assistant professor.

It was while I was on this or some other trip to New York that Hazel wrote a letter which I still have:

> I have been waiting in vain for anything to happen to relate to you, but the Lord has given no sign, so I had better assure you

that we continue to flush along, though without signs and portents ... I hope you are having a pleasant time in the intervals of being clever, distinguished, hardworking, nervous and so on ... Posty and Eleanor have both put very little into their respective pots, alas. Baby [Mark] has been very cross by day lately, perhaps because of the heat, but I doubt if the title 'Good Baby' can be won only by night work, some effort in the day is expected ... Eleanor has several times picked up her basket and departed for 'York' today ... Darling John, I miss you horribly and am longing for your return, infinities of love, Hazel.

If I had wanted enough to go to Union I would have accepted their offer. But whilst this was going on two other invitations came in. I was invited to McGill University at Montreal to give a lecture and meet people. I spoke about the parallels between Tillich's system and ancient Gnosticism, with the implication: so much the worse for Tillich. But the response from several of the faculty was, so much the better for Gnosticism! I am now more inclined to agree with them than with myself. However I was nevertheless offered the chair which George Caird was vacating to move to Oxford. It was on this visit to McGill that I first met Wilfred Cantwell Smith, who had created an Institute for the study of world religions. He later became a mentor and friend, and more about him later.

In competition with McGill, Princeton Theological Seminary was also interested in me. President John Mackay, a great Presbyterian figure then in his final year before retiring, invited me to visit. Mackay was probably the last of a generation of (usually) benevolent dictator academic presidents. He often did business purely by word of mouth, and a member of the Seminary faculty who claimed that Mackay had promised him a promotion which never occurred had complained to the academic accreditation authority; and Mackay and the Seminary were under censure for not having proper written contracts. I presume that I had one though I don't now remember. Mackay spoke at first of an associate professorship but then raised the offer to the Stuart chair of Christian philosophy, succeeding Emile Caillet.

It is evident from all these negotiations that I was taking a fairly cheerful view of my own abilities. I had now met many of the leading older people as well as contemporaries in my field and felt – however justifiably or unjustifiably – that while the seniors had a much greater learning and experience, and the younger often a good deal of promise, yet in analytic and constructive thinking none of them belonged to a different and higher species than myself. The Seminary regarded me as soundly conservative in my theology, as indeed I thought I was – otherwise I would have opted without hesitation for Union or McGill, both of which were much better environments for free thinkers. However it turned out before long that I was not conservative enough. But this was the largest and leading Presbyterian seminary in the country with a number of first-rate scholars on its faculty; Princeton was a very attractive town with a great university and excellent schools, the Seminary's offer was generous – and we went there.

NOTES

1. Arvind Sharma, ed., *God, Truth and Reality: Essays in Honour of John Hick*, London: Macmillan, 1993, pp. 24–5.
2. William Alston, *Perceiving God*, Ithaca and London: Cornell University Press, 1991, p. xi.
3. Ibid., p. 255.
4. John Hick, 'The Epistemological Challenge of Religious Pluralism', *Faith and Philosophy*, July 1997, and reprinted in my *Dialogues in the Philosophy of Religion*, London: Palgrave Press, 2001.
5. William Alston, 'Response' in ibid.
6. John Hick, 'The Christology of D.M. Baillie', the *Scottish Journal of Theology*, March 1958.

11

Heretic at Princeton Seminary

In the summer of 1959 we moved from Ithaca to Princeton where the Seminary gave us a lofty old red brick house, 60 Stockton Street, opposite the Governor of New Jersey's official residence. It had sixteen rooms and six bathrooms, and was heated by underground hot water pipes from a central campus boiler room.

John's large and pleasant study is his main place of business. The Infants enjoy the callers who come and go; they often play at visiting, and occasionally manage to open the door and receive real guests according to instructions. Eleanor, now four-and-a-half, goes to kindergarten, and has begun to pick up the school jokes, such as 'What is your middle name?' 'Eleanor Bubblegum Hick.' Mark is a little tough of nearly three, and Peter is just one'. The little tough was very active. The other day there was an agitated phone call from the Library to say that a little boy was sawing at a tree on the beautifully landscaped lawn. This was Mark, with a saw from the basement. Later the same morning he added insult to injury by using the tree as a public convenience in full view of a Library full of horrified spectators!

There was a cider (i.e. apple juice) factory outside town where we watched the apples being crushed and the juice flowing from the machine into quart bottles which we bought and took home – a delicious drink. There was also an ice-cream factory and parlour where we consumed wonderful many-flavoured concoctions.

The lighting of the Advent candle made Eleanor so excited about Christmas that she immediately announced that she and the boys and the dolls and bears are going to have a party in her room on Christmas Eve, and are going to get a lovely feast ready and have coca-cola to drink. She was quite overcome with joy when we offered to supply real coke – apparently she had assumed that it would be imaginary, as in most of their parties. She and Mark instantly rushed to her room to set out paper napkins and toy plates, ready for Christmas Eve. Such things as coca-cola and gum occupy a certain pedestal of glamour and rarity in the children's minds – the more rare we can keep them (particularly gum) the better ... Food habits die hard, and this brings to mind a major event in the life of the family – we have discovered American pancakes. They are like Scottish pancakes or drop scones, except that they are piled two or three together in a 'deck', and eaten with maple syrup for breakfast ...

Princeton Seminary, then in its 148th year, was the largest theological college in the American Presbyterian Church, with five hundred students, a hundred each in the three years of the BD course, about a hundred studying for the ThM, about twenty-five, all women, for the MRE (Master of Religious Education), about twenty five for the ThD and the rest taking special courses of various kinds. They were drawn from twenty-seven countries and included Lutherans, Baptists, Episcopalians, Methodists, Congregationalists and Greek Orthodox as well as Presbyterians. There was a faculty of more than fifty, my most immediate colleagues being George Hendry, from Scotland and Hugh Kerr (editor of the quarterly *Theology Today*). For them Karl Barth was the dominant influence, as the massive volumes of his *Church Dogmatics* continued to roll off the press. I blamed him for my 'slipped disk' since I first felt it after listening to his lectures when he visited the Seminary. (It became worse and was successfully operated on three years later.) There were two distinguished New Testament scholars, Otto Piper from Germany, and Bruce Metzger, both immensely conservative although Otto also had an unexpected radical streak in him. Various others were also well known in their own fields. My closest friend in the Seminary was Ed Dowey, professor of the history of Christian doctrine, author of an excellent book on Calvin, who was writing about another of the Swiss Reformers but alas never completed it before retiring with Parkinson's disease. I also came to know George Thomas in the University department of religion and Gregory Vlastos and Walter

Kaufman in the philosophy department. Walter was a militant atheist, an authority on Nietzsche (his understanding of whom revolutionised my own), and author of *The Faith of a Heretic*, but we got on well and he invited me to speak to his classes and I invited him to mine.

I was the Seminary's professor of Christian philosophy. But I had to explain in my inaugural lecture that there is no such subject! There are Christian philosophers but no Christian philosophy. What I actually taught was the philosophy of religion, including occasional seminars on the problem of evil and on Paul Tillich's thought. Several former students have since turned up in academic posts, including a good friend at Claremont, Steve Davis, professor of philosophy at McKenna College. He has remained a conservative evangelical, but untypical in that he is not politically right-wing. He will recur in chapter 22.

It was when I was at the Seminary that I gave a paper to some philosophical group in Philadelphia at which Elizabeth and Monroe Beardsley of Swarthmore college were present. They had been commissioned by Prentice-Hall, a big textbook publisher, to edit a new series of short books on all aspects of philosophy, the Foundations of Philosophy series. These were to be authoritative introductions by leading figures in the different fields, but written from the writers' own distinctive points of view. In most areas there were obvious top names and the series list included Roderick Chisholm on theory of knowledge, Joel Feinberg on political philosophy, William Frankena on ethics, Carl Hempel on philosophy of natural sciences, William Alston (already well established) on philosophy of language, Richard Taylor on metaphysics, Willard Van Orman Quine on philosophy of logic. But there was at that time no comparable figure in the philosophy of religion. There were the old guard – such as Paul Tillich, Charles Hartshorne, Paul Weiss, Brand Blanshard – but no outstanding individual within the new 'analytical' tradition. So they had to take a risk and I had the good fortune to be it. It was my easiest book to write because I had been teaching the subject long enough to know exactly what I wanted to say, and it was written in a summer. Prentice-Hall took great care with it, printing a pre-edition that was tested out in several colleges and which I also tested at the Seminary, before finally launching it. The book has sold some four hundred thousand copies in English and has thus been more widely read than any of my other books, although the fastest written. At one time it was bringing in well over $10,000 a year, paying for the education of the children – hence the dedication in the second edition, 'For Eleanor, Mark, Peter, and Michael, in the hope that this little book may assist in their education.' It was soon translated into a number of other languages (200,000 in Chinese) and has gone through revisions at roughly ten-year intervals reflecting the changing shape of a continuously developing subject. It is still being used today in its fourth edition nearly forty years later. A book of readings covering the same topics, *Classical and Contemporary Readings in the Philosophy of Religion* (1964, 1970, 1990), is also still selling. Whilst at Princeton I organised a conference and edited the papers as *Faith and the Philosophers* (1964), with contributions by Henry Price (then visiting at Berkeley in California), Charles Hartshorne, William Alston, Alasdair MacIntyre, Norris Clarke, Richard Brandt, Brand Blanshard, Alvin Plantinga, Kai Nielsen – many of both the established and the emerging American philosophers of religion of the day.

March 21, 1961: Last Monday, went to N.Y. to talk (in a Viennese restaurant) with Paul Edwards [professor of philosophy at New York University and a militant atheist] about the new three-and three-quarter-million word Encyclopedia of Philosophy which he is editing. He seems to have a good grasp of the immense problems involved. I am now a member of the Editorial Board, and have undertaken articles on 'Faith', 'Revelation', 'Evil', 'Teleological Argument', 'Oman' and 'Tennant', amounting to some 23,000 words. When I sent in my first article Paul's assistant made some stupid stylistic suggestions. I complained to Paul who told me to ignore them and soon sacked the offending interferer. Later, dissatisfied with the article on the ontological argument which someone had written he asked me to do one at fairly short notice, which I did. [The Encyclopedia, in eight volumes, was published in 1967 and served as the standard work until being superseded a generation later.] Lunched Friday with Richard Robinson [philosophy don at Oriel, then at the Princeton Institute for Advanced Study], soon returning to England. I mentioned his ferocious reviews, and he said he only attacked established men who were doing bad work, and so helped to keep standards up.

After a couple of years in 60 Stockton Street we bought our own house, 277 Hawthorne Avenue, a pleasant tree-lined road a walkable distance from the town centre and the Seminary. This is a two-storey house made of wood, like most private houses in the US, and is on a double lot with a large yard (garden) and many trees. A room had been built onto one side of the ground floor which became my study and another room, complete with its own bathroom, had been added between the house and the garage, which we let to a German research student in biology who kept a small crocodile in a tin bath, to the excitement of the infantry. There was a loggia at the back, with insect netting, from which we watched the fireflies after dark and where the children came down to help themselves to cereals in the morning before their parents were up. Hazel greatly enjoyed singing in several choirs. But I was a musical dunce. We bought a good record player for the new long-playing records, and the first one that I really appreciated was, appropriately, Dvorak's *New World Symphony*.

> *Diary*: Farmer has been staying with us for the past week. He is older and tireder, being in the midst of six hectic months of traveling and lecturing. But he has his usual humour, humility, and deeply Christian way of looking at things. He lectured twice in the University, once here, attended a faculty lunch in each place, and generally had a good week without being overworked.

But the biggest event in our time at Princeton was my, to my mind then and now, ridiculous 'Affair with the Virgin Mary', an anachronistic controversy that would have been more appropriate in the middle of the nineteenth than the twentieth century. I shall tell the story as it unfolded, as throwing light on American Presbyterianism, which has still today so far as I can tell barely progressed theologically since then.

When a Presbyterian minister settles in a new place he or she more or less automatically applies to become a member of the local Presbytery, which consists of ministers and lay elders, with authority over the congregations in its area. I made my application to join, complete with a letter from the Berwick Presbytery commending me to the Presbytery of New Brunswick. It happened that the chair of the committee which received such applications was one Clyde Henry, a disciple of J. Gresham Machen, author of *The Virgin Birth of Christ* (1930). Machen had been so much more conservative even than the

Princeton Seminary (one of whose nineteenth-century presidents had boasted that no new thoughts had emerged there under his rule) that in 1929 he had broken away to found his own Westminster seminary. Clyde Henry exercised his right to ask me, when I appeared before his committee, if there was anything in the *Westminster Confession* (1647) to which I took exception. I had in fact read the Confession and, although still theologically fairly conservative, regarded it as completely out of date. I mentioned the literal interpretation of the first two chapters of Genesis – the six days creation of the world, and Adam and Eve's eating of the forbidden fruit in the Garden of Eden, – and then the doctrine of double predestination to heaven and hell, and eventually arrived at the virgin birth of Jesus, which I did not deny but did not affirm and did not regard as essential to the central doctrine of incarnation, which I did affirm. There seem to have been two presbytery meetings at which this was discussed, at the second of which I made a speech expressing my generally very orthodox theology, and then saying:

> Now a word specifically about the virgin birth of our Lord. Left to myself I do not have anything to say about this at all – and in this, as the ministers here will certainly know, I am following the example of the majority of the New Testament writers: Paul, John, Mark, Peter, James and Jude all believe in Christ as the Word Incarnate, but none of them mentions the idea of a virgin birth; and I am content to follow them in this. However if I am specifically challenged to say something about it, I have to say simply that I do not affirm it; it plays no part in my personal faith. I do not assert that it is impossible, or that it may not be true; and I have no quarrel with those who do affirm it; but I am not myself able to affirm it.

Most members of the Presbytery evidently regarded this as satisfactory and, to quote an account which I later wrote in the third person, 'After prolonged discussion from the floor, and a strong affirmative vote, he was duly received as a member of presbytery.'[1]

However Clyde Henry and others then addressed a Complaint against the Presbytery's action to the next higher authority, the synod of New Jersey, and to the surprise of all of us in the Seminary this was sustained and my reception by the Presbytery rescinded. According to the Clerk of the Synod, failing an appeal this action would strip me of my professorship; for all professors in the Seminary must be ministers of the United Presbyterian Church. However a counter Complaint was promptly addressed to the supreme body of the Church, the General Assembly, due to meet the following May, nearly a year later.

Knowing that the press would be ringing me up for a comment I prepared one which was published in the *New York Times* and then repeated in other papers, saying that

> The theological question at issue is whether every Presbyterian minister must affirm a biological miracle in connection with the birth of Christ, or whether this is a secondary matter about which it is possible for some of us to be uncertain. I distinguish between the central Christian faith in the incarnation and the theologically peripheral story of the virgin birth. I anticipate that when this matter is finally decided by the general assembly of our church the broader view will prevail.

The 'Hick case' was widely reported in newspapers around the country.

The appeal to the General Assembly was signed by Benjamin Anderson and others, Ben being the minister of the Witherspoon church which we had joined some time before, having been totally uninspired by the complacent affluence of the First Presbyterian Church. Witherspoon was originally the slave church, founded in 1837, and now had several white families, we having been the second to join, in a predominantly black congregation with a black minister. Worship at Witherspoon was the most real, with an almost tangible atmosphere of reverence, that Hazel and I had experienced and Ben was a good minister and friend.

The Seminary's president, Jim McCord, was at first cautious but soon came down on the side of the Presbytery, and me, against the synod, and in general the Seminary can be said to have supported me, some individuals more wholeheartedly then others. From my diary:

> At faculty meeting yesterday [President Jim] McCord announced, 'I hope that all who are members of the New Brunswick Presbytery will be present at the meeting on April 18. The Seminary has a great deal at stake, and the Church has a great deal at stake, at that meeting. If you have classes, cancel them, for this meeting has higher priority.' Good for him!

A hundred or so of the students signed a letter to me saying that whilst they were not all agreed about the virgin birth they were all agreed that I should not be excluded for failing to affirm it. Whilst the matter was pending until the General Assembly the following year I received over a hundred letters. Some were from distinguished churchmen and theologians offering their support and encouragement. These included John Bennett, then dean of Union Theological Seminary in New York; John Mackay, the former president of the Princeton Seminary, by whom I had been appointed; the well-known theologian Nels Ferré, then visiting Beirut, Lebanon where, he said, the papers had been full of my case, and expressing his agreement with me; James Pike, episcopalian bishop of California, saying that 'We will be glad to have you' if the appeal fails; and Norman Pittenger, well-known liberal episcopalian theologian at General theological seminary in New York – I later came to know him well when he retired to Cambridge, England, and I like his response to heresy charges against himself, 'I deny the allegation, and defy the allegator.' One correspondent commended to me the motto, '*non illegitimati carborundum*', don't let the bastards grind you down. Another offered a position at Trinity University in Texas if I had to leave the Seminary.

I also of course had letters from militant fundamentalists, telling me that I was one heartbeat from hell, or 'warning, you are in great danger', etc. Others were several degrees calmer. 'You set yourself apart from the Divine Word and see fit to contradict this. If you deny the Virgin Birth, what do you have left? We would then be reduced to atheism.' Some of the ripest of these were honoured with a place in my psycho-ceramic (crack-pot) file.

But local Presbytery opinion soon began to move against Clyde Henry and Co.

> Since Presbytery, three interesting visits. First Rev. Good, first to announce support for the Complaint [against my acceptance], came to say he was withdrawing his name, after talking with Ed Dowey. He has since sent out a very good mimeographed letter about this. Then Russell Alnwick, the Stated Clerk, came to see if I would make a statement about accepting the V.B. 'as a mystery', in which case the Complaint would be withdrawn. Said politely, No. Then today the Minister of Plainfield (name not noted), who had spoken after Good in Presbytery, came to say that he was

withdrawing his name too. It seems that the opposite of a bandwagon is going on.

The appeal to the General Assembly was to be presented by Judge James H. Tunnell, a Presbyterian layman, and Lefferts Loetscher, professor of church history at the seminary, and one or two other ministers. I knew that it would succeed because one day when I was with Jim McCord in his office he was on the phone with Eugene Carson Blake, the powerful general secretary of the United Presbyterian Church, discussing strategy in presenting the appeal. Clearly Blake wanted to settle the matter on procedural grounds, thus avoiding splitting the church, and I was confident that he would succeed. But even before the outcome became predictable the episode was not one that gave me any serious anxiety. I was more inclined to see it as ridiculous. And I was confident that if I did have to leave the Seminary I would find somewhere else, in the States or in Britain.

As expected, the ecclesiastical establishment prevailed. The Judicial Commission of the General Assembly, meeting in Denver in May 1962, received our Complaint in the name of Benjamin J. Anderson, et al. v. Synod of New Jersey. To quote my own third person account,

The issue which was thus brought to the General Assembly was a constitutional one, lying in that branch of the law of the Church which deals with the doctrinal profession of ministers. The difference of interpretation between the two parties was clearly defined. The synod's Judicial Commission pointed to statements and actions of the General Assemblies between the years 1910 and 1925 which named the doctrine of the virgin birth as 'essential and necessary' to the system of Presbyterian doctrine, and it claimed that those pronouncements were still in force. The other side pointed to the work of the Special Commission appointed by the General Assembly in 1927. That Commission's task was to try to resolve deep differences and bitter controversies arising out of those same actions of 1910 to 1925 upon which the synod relied. In its findings the Commission discountenanced the designating of specified doctrines as essential and necessary, and placed upon each local presbytery the responsibility for forming its own judgement under the Constitution regarding the theological qualifications of any seeking to become ministers within its bounds. It was argued that the Assembly action of 1927, adopting the Commission's report, superseded the older actions and has been fruitful in securing the peace of the Church during the years which have followed. In endorsing and applying this view, the General Assembly of 1962 recalled the statement of the Special Commission that, 'The principle of toleration when rightly conceived and frankly and fairly applied is as truly a part of our constitution as are any of the doctrines stated in that instrument.'[2]

I think it is clear that this judgment was legally and theologically correct. At the same time the Judicial Commission pointed out several procedural errors committed by the synod, of the kind that are only of interest to lawyers. The result was, so far as I was concerned, that I remained beyond dispute a professor at the Seminary and, so far as the church as a whole was concerned that it became harder for people like Clyde Henry to pressure students seeking ordination to profess beliefs which they did not really hold. It was thus a good outcome. But the fundamentalist brethren neither forgave nor forgot, and were able to take their revenge many years later when I went to Claremont – on which see chapter 23.

When all this was over I had a very nice letter from Waley, now retired from his principalship of Westminster College, saying that he was aware that 'the fundamentalists (or Pre-Noachians) had cast you for the part of Robertson Smith. What damage those idiots do to the Bible and Christianity in the thoughts of myriads who live in the knowledge of our age, and turn on the television ...' On the other hand one of the said idiots wrote to the Seminary to say that 'if this trend away from the standards of our church is not reversed a vast number of Princeton alumni will feel the seminary's usefulness has ended'. And Clyde Henry published a twelve-page pamphlet, *Some Reflections on the Hick Case*, declaring that

> For the first time in its history, the Church has taken a deliberate step down the road that leads to apostasy by permitting, in effect, the word of man to be superior to the Word of God. The Church has declared officially that it is hospitable to heresy, and that error may stand on an equality with truth.

And even today there are a depressing number of people in the churches, proportionately as well as absolutely more numerous in the US than the UK, who still think like that.

Others of us, of course, thought that on the contrary the Presbyterian church had taken a tiny step in the direction of credibility in the modern world. But it was an interesting experience to be accused of heresy with the matter seriously pursued right up to the level of the General Assembly. If I had seen it as other than basically silly it would probably have been a worrying experience. But the tortuous maneuvers of the churches as they try to be relevant, although still lagging a generation or two behind the society around them, can be seen either as pathetic or as humorous but hardly as intellectually or morally serious.

But in the States there are still vast numbers of 'born again' Christians who respond to the fundamentalist televangelists, with their political as well as theological right-wing ideology, for whom such issues as the historicity of the miraculous conception of Jesus can be whipped up into matters of religious life and death.

NOTES

1. 'Theological Table-Talk' in *Theology Today*, October 1962, p. 410.
2. Ibid., pp. 410–11.

12

Cambridge interlude

When I told my colleagues that I was going to a lectureship in divinity at Cambridge University most of them, having no knowledge of the different academic setup in Britain, thought that I was moving down to the equivalent of being a lecturer in the States, which is usually a part-time position lower even than that of an Instructor, which is itself the lowest full-time position. They had no idea that in Oxford and Cambridge it was not uncommon for very eminent scholars to be university lecturers and college fellows rather than professors, since there were only a fixed number of chairs, to which a new appointment could only be made when the current occupant retired. Bertrand Russell, for example, was never a professor in Britain but when already famous, having published *The Principles of Mathematics* and the first volume of *Principia Mathematica*, was a lecturer at Cambridge, as also was the famous historian A.J.P. Taylor at Oxford. Indeed there were many Oxbridge lecturers who preferred to remain there, in their comfortable college fellowships, with distinguished colleagues and first-rate students, rather than move to a chair in one of the 'redbrick' universities – such as Birmingham where in due course I went!

The move from the Seminary to Cambridge happened through my receiving a Guggenheim Fellowship during the 1963–4 academic year to write about the philosophical/theological problem of evil and this, combined with a half year paid sabbatical from the Seminary, enabled us to spend that year plus the summers before and after it in Cambridge. I was also appointed to the S.A. Cooke Bye-Fellowship at Gonville and Caius College for that year. We rented a nice house on Huntingdon Road, and the children went to the excellent Newnham Croft primary school. Caius gave me a room in its new building (near the university library), where I worked each day, usually walking the half hour or so route from the house. I was entitled to one free college meal a day, and usually crossed the river to the main Caius building for lunch in the senior common room, but occasionally had dinner in the hall instead. Lunches were substantial but self-served and pleasantly informal. Dinners were formal, gowns worn, first sherry, then a march to the high table in hall, Latin grace, then being waited on with a magnificent meal with several wines, followed by coffee and port etc. in the common room again. The permanent fellows were friendly and interesting, though some of them extremely conservative in outlook. However the dean of chapel was Hugh Montefiore, who later became bishop of Birmingham, with whom I am still in friendly contact today. (In his autobiography Hugh misremembers me at Caius as having assisted him by giving supervisions – Cantab for tutorials – in philosophy of religion to some of his undergraduates.[1] In fact I did no teaching whilst at Caius, only my own writing.) The president, i.e. president of the senior common room, was the fascinating and delightful Joseph Needham, a socialist and a radical thinker on religion, as well as an FRS and author over many years of his multi-volume *History of Chinese Science*. The Master was the physicist Sir Nevill Mott, head of the Cavendish laboratory.

I am afraid that Hazel, like other fellows' wives in those days, was largely left out of college life, and was pretty much left on her own that year as my study was not at home as it has otherwise always been but at Caius. She did however teach classics in a local school. We had a very nice German au pair girl living with us. In those days an au pair from abroad came to England to live as part of the family, to attend English classes, and to help with the housework and the children. They are much less common, and perhaps almost non-existent, today. I remember that one night Hazel and I were woken by what sounded like a burglar entering one of the ground floor windows, but it turned out to be only Hilda being helped by her undergraduate boyfriend to get back in, having lost her key.

The University library was a great resource. I spent the summer before term started reading and writing on Augustine, producing what became chapters 3 and 4 of the book that grew during the year into *Evil and the God of Love* – a title suggested by a fellow passenger on the *Queen Mary* on our way back to the States. I got to know Dom Illtyd Trethowan of Downside Abbey and St Edmund's Hall in Cambridge, a generation older than myself, who was a useful critic of my views on the fourth/fifth century St Augustine, and after my book was published he wrote several articles disputing some of it, to which I replied, all in a courteous vein. Another Catholic whom I got to know at St Edmund's was Dom Mark Pontifex, two generations (as it seemed) older than I. One day, 'Tea with old Pontifex yesterday. He made the interesting and true remark that whilst people sometimes change their religion they hardly ever change their philosophy.'

Augustine's immense influence laid down the main lines of western or Latin Christian orthodoxy, within the Reformed as well as Catholic traditions, until it came under attack from the eighteenth century onwards, and indeed much of it still remains normative in doctrinally fundamentalist circles. The origin of moral evil was the fall of the rebellious angels issuing in the fall of Adam and Eve on earth, from whom every succeeding generation has inherited an inbuilt original sinfulness; and 'natural evil' (diseases, earthquakes, floods, droughts, etc.) was a punishment for the fall, the fallen angels having been allowed to cause havoc in the natural order. But evil of all kinds had the metaphysical status of a privation of good, a theme which Augustine received from the Neo-Platonists. Evil was not a reality in its own right but the going wrong of something good – as blindness is not anything positive but something negative, a lack of the proper functioning of the eye, which in itself is good. Thus evil has not been created by God who is therefore not responsible for it. The basic idea was taken up in a new way by Karl Barth in the twentieth century in his theory of evil as *das Nichtige*, nothingness, the negative, negation.

All this seemed to me a mistake, though an impressive, powerful and influential one which dominated the Christian imagination in the west for over a thousand years. I argued on philosophical grounds that the account of evil as a privation of good is not in the end defensible and that Barth's more modern version is internally incoherent; that the fall was not an historical reality but a mythic story; that natural evil could not have been a divinely permitted punishment for the fall of humanity, since we now know that it had existed for millions of years before the emergence of homo sapiens; and that the doctrine of original sin, in virtue of which we are guilty for being human quite apart from the particular wrong acts that we do is a piece of dark and destructive imagining. And more fundamentally, the basic idea of a wholly good creation going wrong was a self-contradiction. For wholly good creatures, though free to sin, never would. The idea thus amounted to the self-creation of evil *ex nihilo*! The creator of everything other than himself must ultimately be responsible for his creation and for its development, including the emergence of evil within it. Although I did not pursue this in *Evil and the God of Love*, in rejecting the idea of original sin we are on the way to rejecting the whole traditional picture of the economy of salvation in which the limitless evil of the fall requires the limitless sacrifice of Christ on the cross to cancel it.

The discovery of the second century St Irenaeus' very different kind of theology pointed to a better alternative. He and others of the early Greek speaking Fathers of the church (such as Clement of Alexandria), long before Augustine, had laid the groundwork for a more credible approach to the problem of evil. According to Irenaeus, humans were not created as finitely perfect beings but as immature creatures with a potentiality to grow eventually into what God intended for them. The fall was not the great cosmic disaster that Augustine made it but an understandable mistake by morally child-like creatures. In Irenaeus' terminology, humans were created in the 'image' of God but had yet to develop into the 'likeness' of God. They were already, in the first stage of creation, intelligent and basically ethical animals, with an innate capacity to respond to the divine presence, and they were to grow in the second stage through their own free responses to the circumstances of their lives into 'children of God'. Irenaeus did not apply this specifically to the problem of evil, which is what I now did, labelling the result the Irenaean theodicy, thus giving a respectable historical lineage and a patron saint to what was already in its general approach a familiar idea within modern liberal theology. The ideal state does not lie behind us in the distant past but before us in the distant future, and instead of our present life receiving its meaning from an original fall into sinfulness it receives it as a part of our long journey towards an ultimate limitless good. And because the creative process so obviously does not reach its goal for the great majority of people within this life we must take seriously the claim of the religions that our present life on earth is only a small part of a much larger existence.

Working this out further, I argued that this moral and spiritual growth could not take place in a paradise in which there were no problems, challenges, dangers, setbacks, possibility of real disasters and tragedies. On the contrary, the kind of environment in which the second stage of creation could occur would be basically like our present world. Here I deployed counter-factual considerations: if our actions could never harm anyone there would be no such thing as wrong actions, and therefore no such thing as right actions, and therefore no such thing as moral choice – and so on, developing the theme within different aspects of life. It is not that life's hard knocks are specifically designed or 'sent' for our good, but that ultimately, in the very long run, all that happens in the contingencies of time can be turned retrospectively into the particular, and often very difficult, path along which we shall each have arrived at 'the kingdom of heaven'. For the meaning of what is happening now depends on what comes out of it later. And the very fact that we cannot now see the 'soul making' (in Keats' phrase) character of our human existence, but have to live it in faith, is itself an aspect of its soul making potentiality. Likewise the fact that the sheer quantity and appalling intensity of much of the evil, both humanly inflicted and caused by the course of nature, seems so much more than is needed for human soul making, so that its existence can only be a mystery to the religious believer, is again a necessary aspect of the soul making potentiality of the world.[2]

This is of course a very compressed summary of an extended argument which can be found in *Evil and the God of Love*[3] The book was published by Macmillan in London and Harper & Row in the States in 1966 (with a second revised edition in 1977), and was very well received, with glowing reviews. Its subsequent wider spread was greatly assisted by a cheap paperback version in Collins' Fontana Library in 1968 and again in a new format in 1979, and there was a reissue by Macmillan in both hard and softback in 1985, reprinted in 2001. In connection with the Fontana version I had good meetings with Lady Priscilla Collins, who also put *Faith and Knowledge* and later *God and the Universe of Faiths* into the Fontana format, which helped considerably to make some of my work inexpensively available. At Macmillan the person with whom I dealt very agreeably over many years until his retirement was Tim Farmiloe, a gentle soul with an astute mind who was wholly dedicated to publishing.

Egol, as it became known to my students, has been the subject of considerable discussion in books and articles. In Barry Whitney's *Theodicy: An Annotated Bibliography on the Problem of Evil 1960–1990*[4] there is a twenty-six-page section on 'Hick's Irenaean Theodicy', listing sixty-six items (including my own replies to some of the critical articles) and there have been quite a few more since then. I was already on the philosophy of religion map through *Faith and Knowledge* and *Philosophy of Religion* (and also two books of readings, *The Existence of God* and *Classical and Contemporary Readings in the Philosophy of Religion*), but this book put me on the theological map as well. It was written from a liberal Christian perspective and was welcomed by the mainstream theological community on both sides of the Atlantic. I still think that its basic suggestion is sound, although I now put it in a different and larger context as a 'true myth'.[5]

In distinction from the theologians, interest in the problem of evil within the philosophical community, particularly in the States, has been largely dominated during the last twenty or so years by the work of Alvin Plantinga and others making a not very ambitious argument for the logical possibility of the coexistence of God and evil. The argument is confined to moral evil, made possible by human free will, and uses the concepts of possible worlds and trans-world depravity, according to which it is logically possible that humans make a morally wrong choice in every possible world. Given this, it is possible that God could not have created a world without moral evil, and it is therefore possible that God is not responsible for evil and that the divine goodness is thus not in any way diminished. For even God cannot do the logically impossible; and so it is logically possible, because of unpredictable human freedom, that it is logically impossible for God to have created a world without evil. The problem of natural evil is left aside, or subsumed under the problem of moral evil via the free wickedness of the fallen angels.

Plantinga's formulation (set out in a much more complicated form than this summary) is logically impressive but, in my opinion, of very little use to anyone who wants to go beyond bare logical possibility when confronting the appalling problem of evil. I have criticised it in the new chapter added to the second edition of *Egol*.

Egol was written almost entirely during the fifteen months of my Guggenheim supported sabbatical in Cambridge. During that time I also made a more serious attempt than before to learn to read academic German and got far enough to use some untranslated books and articles. In the Princeton Seminary German was the sacred language, replacing Latin and before that Greek. Anything said in German sounded much more impressive and much more true than when said in English. And the dominant theology was that of Karl Barth. However, although I was never anything remotely approaching a German-reading scholar, I found the language conducive to vast vague pronouncements to which it was very difficult to give any precise meaning. And I felt that some of my colleagues in the theological world confused the obscure and incomprehensible with the profound. In contrast English, and also French, seemed to me to encourage intellectual clarity. Indeed I still harbour this perhaps reprehensible prejudice. However I find that I am not alone in it. Bryan Magee remarks that

> In so-called Continental philosophy, however, the prevailing tradition remains the one established by Fichte, Schelling and Hegel. Obscurity prevails, even with those who have something to say; and for those who have nothing to say it provides a smoke-screen from behind which they make their advances in the world.[6]

Towards the end of my sabbatical year a University lectureship in the philosophy of religion became vacant, and Farmer, and also the kindly George Woods, one of the lecturers in the subject, encouraged me to apply and after some thought I did so. Hazel was not in favour but did not oppose, although she always had half a wish that we had never returned to England – until our later return to the States and our very happy Claremont years. I was in due course appointed and sent a telegram to Jim McCord to say that we would be returning to the Seminary for one more semester and then leaving for Cambridge. This caused consternation within the Seminary faculty. Some there and elsewhere thought that I must be leaving because of the Virgin Birth controversy, but this was not the case – that was to me basically a ridiculous episode. The reason was the attraction of beautiful Cambridge, with its excellent colleagues, students and schools, and the proximity of our two families.

So we returned to the Seminary for the Fall semester and then back to Cambridge at the end of the year. We sold the house in Hawthorne Avenue well, it having increased considerably in value even over five years. The only thing about our departure that I remember is that Ed Dowey drove us to New York to board the *Queen Elizabeth*, and in my agitation I paid a porter a tip with a $100 bill which Ed managed to recover for me. In England Michael Bowers met us at the port and drove us to Cambridge, where Caius rented us a flat in one of their large old houses in Harvey Road, conveniently central. The children went back to school and Hazel, who was always good at job hunting, taught classics. In the Divinity School, which was then in St John's Street where it had been more or less since time immemorial, I taught an introductory course on philosophical classics which included Descartes' *Meditations*, Berkeley's *Dialogues*, and Hume's *Dialogues*, and a more advanced course on philosophy of religion generally, together with supervisions usually with groups of two or at most three. The undergraduates were the best I have ever taught. These courses were for Tripos papers, but in the summer term I could give a course on anything I liked and chose 'Aspects, Onlooks, and Experiencing-as' which drew a number of graduate students.

In those days not all University lecturers were college fellows, though this is now no longer the case. It was almost impossible for me to become a fellow because theology lecturers were nearly always elected to fill at the same time the ecclesiastical post of dean of chapel (an academic position distinct from that of chaplain), and as such they then had to be ordained Anglicans. Thus Howard Root and George Woods were both deans. However in my last term at Cambridge, as I was applying for the H.G. Wood chair at Birmingham, the Catholic St Edmund's Hall invited me to become a fellow, explaining frankly that it would be very helpful to them to have among them the secretary of the committee which accepted or rejected applications to become graduate students within the faculty of Divinity. I do not know whether I would have accepted the offer if I had stayed in Cambridge. I had visited St Edmund's as Illtyd's Trethowan's guest and again as a guest when they were considering inviting me to become a fellow, and I found them all thoroughly friendly, and good in their respective subjects. But on the other hand most of their students then were preparing for the Catholic priesthood and I was far from sure that I could fit in.

The Divinity faculty was then at a lively moment of its history. The Regius (because appointed by the crown) professor was Dennis Nineham, the radical New Testament scholar. He was from the first very helpful and supportive, and remains a good friend. Maurice Wiles, a future Regius at Oxford, was a fellow lecturer. Don Cupitt was then dean of chapel at Emmanuel but not yet a lecturer. All these three were later close colleagues as contributors to *The Myth of God Incarnate*, about which more in chapter 20. George Woods was sound and thoughtful but not exciting. Charlie Moule was a revered conservative New Testament scholar. Geoffrey Lampe was the Ely professor, a New Testament scholar who looked so massively orthodox that no one could take exception to what he said but whose Spirit Christology was in fact very radical – so much so that I later came largely to agree with it. John Bowker was a lecturer, later succeeding John Robinson (of *Honest to God* fame) as dean of Trinity. Stephen Sykes (later Bishop of Ely) was dean of St John's. Dennis Nineham, Maurice Wiles, Don Cupitt, and John Bowker have continued as good friends over many years.

The Norris-Hulse professor succeeding Farmer was Donald MacKinnon. He was a man of enormous learning, a scholar of Latin and Greek as well as French and German, an authority on both Aristotle and Kant, an insightful but chaotic thinker. He was also a famous eccentric. Numerous stories are told about him, many of them true. I will stick here to a few minor incidents for which I can myself vouch. The first time I saw him was when he came to give a paper to the philosophy society at Edinburgh whilst I was a student there. He began sitting in an armchair and ended sitting on one of its arms holding one of his shoes in his hands, his suit crumpled, and sweating profusely. But this was a mild example. In Faculty Board meetings at Cambridge he regularly wrote letters and then walked out, his boots creaking loudly, to give them to the porter to post. On one occasion I was sitting on his left and he was writing a letter to someone whom he had not noticed happened to be sitting on his right – and then went out to post it. He would often take out a safety razor blade and sharpen a pencil until the lead grew to an inch or more in length. To the horror of all who were watching he would sometimes put the razor blade meditatively in his mouth, though I never saw him cut himself. But although he did not seem to be attending to the discussion he had in fact been listening, at least sometimes, and would unexpectedly intervene with a remark that was entirely pertinent. In his lectures he always seemed, from his intense manner, to be saying something profound and important, though it was often difficult to know what it was, and how what he was saying now related to what he had been saying a minute ago. He was one of those thinkers who circle round a subject and eventually stop without having reached any conclusion. Indeed to this kind of thinker it would seem shallow and immature to come to any conclusion. They may be right. But the reader or listener does not take away anything to analyse and criticise, to agree with or try to improve upon. However others with a similar cast of mind have found him much more profitable than I was able to do. The alternative kind, to which I belong myself, struggles for clarity and aims for a coherent hypothesis which can be examined and criticised, so that it can then be either developed and strengthened or rejected and a better hypothesis proposed. It is partly because I have always striven for clarity that my writings have drawn so much discussion and criticism, and even if my suggestions turn out to be entirely wrong they have at least contributed to on-going discussion and research in the philosophy of religion and theology.

The D Society (named I believe after a non-existent Tripos subject), a senior discussion group in the philosophy of religion, met at Donald's house and included Donald, Howard Root, who was appointed to the lectureship for which I had also applied when I was at Westminster, George Woods, the other lecturer in the subject, together with myself, one or two graduate students, and occasional visitors. One of these was an overweight, chain smoking, hand trembling American whose name I did not catch at the time but who turned out to be bishop James Pike of California, a notable liberal but battered by the church hostility around him, later to die alone in his car in the Palestinian desert.

After a term in the Harvey Road flat we bought a very nice house on Hills Road, beside the hospital. My diary has the usual notes of moments in the garden: 'Cloudy day, followed by a perfect evening – clear, bright, warm and seemingly endless. Sitting in the garden, almost nothing but nature visible – sky, grass, trees, bushes, flowers; & the birds' songs.' Again, 'A perfect summer day – "to live through its sun drenched hours is longevity enough" .' And 'Hot sunny days with long bright evenings. In garden. A thin veil of cloud like hazy diaphanous skeletons in the sky. Birds chirping all round'. We usually cycled everywhere, as so many people in Cambridge did. But early one morning each week we all went by car to the municipal swimming pool, returning via the 'Hog-Pape shop' where we bought a paper and some sweets (hoggery). Walks along the river to the Orchard at Grantchester were a favourite expedition, with lunch or tea in the orchard. We sometimes drove around the Cambridgeshire countryside, visiting the lovely old villages, once centres of a flourishing wool trade. We attended St Columba's Presbyterian Church, of which I became an Elder.

During these years in Cambridge I joined the Labour party, and discovered to my surprise and pleasure that the parliamentary candidate for the next general election was Robert Davies who with his wife had lived in the next door house in St John's Street, Oxford, when I was in digs there. He was then writing a thesis on Berkeley. I did a lot of canvassing for him, and often with him, and was one of the party's scrutineers at the count when he was elected with narrow majority of 991. Someone in our Labour group began to sing the Red Flag and we all tried to join in but soon realised that no one knew the words, and so we clapped heartily instead! Labour's majority in Parliament was a comfortable ninety-seven. I visited the House of Commons once as Robert's guest and heard him ask a Parliamentary Question. He explained how difficult it sometimes was to ask a supplementary question, because the answer to the initial question was often read out in a rapid low tone, barely audible. He found being a backbencher deeply frustrating, and alas died from a massive heart attack before the next election.

My initial appointment was for three years, which would have been followed by a tenure appointment until retirement at sixty-seven. But during the third year Ninian Smart moved from the H.G.

Wood chair at Birmingham to found the new department of Religious Studies, the first in Britain, at Lancaster, and I applied for his vacant chair. I had previously the same year applied for the chair of theology at Nottingham, but knew as soon as I got there for interview that I would not get it because the external advisors on the appointing committee were traditional biblical scholars who would, and did, appoint one of their own kind. The Nottingham Vice-Chancellor asked me if I would be interested instead in the chair of philosophy, because Ronald Hepburn was about to move to Edinburgh; but I declined – I wanted to stay specifically in the philosophy of religion and there would not have been enough of this within the small Nottingham department. But the Birmingham chair was in the philosophy of religion – at least until I left fifteen years later – and I was appointed to it. So a new, long and busy chapter of life began.

NOTES

1. Hugh Montefiore, *Oh God, What Next?* An Autobiography, London: Hodder & Stoughton, 1995, p. 89.
2. This rather crucial point has been the subject of considerable debate, particularly with my philosopher friend William Rowe – see Harold Hewett, ed., *Problems in the Philosophy of Religion*, London: Macmillan, 1991, chap. 5.
3. You can also find it in shorter form in my essay in Stephen Davis, ed., *Encountering Evil*, Louisville and London: Westminster John Knox Press, revised edition 2001.
4. New York and London: Garland Publishing, 1993.
5. See *An Interpretation of Religion*, the appendix on 'Theodicy as mythology'.
6. Bryan Magee, *Confessions of a Philosopher*, London: Phoenix, 1998, p. 468.

13

Birmingham University

During the tenure of its first holder, Ninian Smart, the H.G. Wood chair of theology at Birmingham was one of the few in England explicitly devoted to the philosophy of religion, the others being at Oxford, Cambridge and London. And so when Ninian moved to Lancaster I applied for the Birmingham post, wanting to move from a lectureship, even at Cambridge, to the greater freedom of a chair in which I would be able to pursue my own developing agenda. I was appointed and started in the 1967–8 academic year. We bought a large house with a big garden, 70 Arthur Road, a mile from the campus, a pleasant walk past the well landscaped Vale site of student halls. My diary records the usual remembered moments in the garden, this on a Sunday morning in May: 'Sitting in the garden. Sun, blue sky, daffodils out, dew still sparkling on the grass, many birds singing, church bells across the road (which I hear as the sound of faith) – much too good to leave to go to church!'

Here again we had an au pair, and for many years also a student lodger. We particularly wanted overseas students, partly to introduce the children to the wider world. The first was Lloyd from Jamaica, who got on so well with the family that he stayed through his three undergraduate years and then his two Master's years and now heads a management and systems consultancy in Kingston, Jamaica. Then there was Siva from the Punjab, now a doctor in Britain, and Prakash from another part of India, each staying several years. They had breakfasts and Sunday lunches with us but their other meals out. We enjoyed all of them and I think they enjoyed being with us.

Birmingham is a secular university, largely science oriented, but with a department of theology founded in 1940 with the creation of the Edward Cadbury chair with a donation from the Cadbury trust, the university later taking over most of the financial responsibility for it. The first professor was the Quaker theologian H.G. Wood. He had a much broader vision than was common in British theology at that time, or indeed still in some circles today, and in his inaugural lecture he looked forward to the time when there would be lectureships in each of the great world religions. Throughout Ninian's six years as H.G. Wood professor and my own fifteen years we tried to move the department in that direction but without success. Whenever there was an appointment to be made our colleagues insisted on filling it in the traditional biblical and historical mould. It was only much later that the successful centre for the study of Islam and of Christian–Muslim relations in the Selly Oak Colleges began to be used peripherally by the department, and also the short-lived centre for Jewish studies, which however collapsed for lack of financial support. But now, much later again, the Selly Oak colleges (other than the missionary colleges) have become the Selly Oak campus of Birmingham University, with the Islam centre as part of the theology department, and a new centre for the study of Asian religions established, and three new chairs created (with outside funds) in Global Ethics, Judaism and Inter-religious relations, and in Inter-religious relations as such. This reflects a trend throughout the country, in response to student demand, from the traditional purely Christian and biblical study to broader departments of religious studies.

The outlook of the department was determined by its head, Gordon Davies, with Old and New Testament studies and patristics as the core, but with Dan Hardy adding nineteenth- and twentieth-century theology. Philosophy of religion had a peripheral place as an elective course, though I also taught a required course in Christian ethics. Later I shared this with John Hapgood, then principal of the Queen's Theological College, I doing the ethical theory and he dealing with specific moral problems. John went to Durham as the most educated and intelligent of the bench of bishops, and later became archbishop of York but was too liberal to be made Archbishop of Canterbury by Margaret Thatcher. After he left I shared the ethics course with Anthony Bird, an innovative medical doctor, who succeeded John as principal of Queen's College.

Soon after I arrived the University went through the wave of student unrest which had swept the States and was now sweeping Britain. In my second year the vice-chancellor, Sir Robert Aitken, retired. He was a charming and brilliant man, one of the last of the old school of highly cultured vice-chancellors before the new generation of tough administrators whose central concern has to be the budget, and it was always a pleasure to hear his lucid and elegantly expressed reports to the Senate, of which all professors were then members. But in his first year the new vice-chancellor, Dr Robert Hunter (later Sir and then Lord) resolved to deal with the students firmly, hiring new security staff and taking a generally tough stance. The revolting students occupied the Great Hall and besieged the vice-chancellor in his office. When he emerged he was escorted to the Great Hall, packed with excited students, a microphone put in front of him, and engaged in debate. He naturally profoundly resented this humiliation and became even more alienated from the students. A number on the teaching staff, including myself, thought that the students' revolt was basically harmless and that the vice-chancellor's tough initial response had been counter productive. The students wanted more representation on university committees and we thought, cynically, that once they had got this they would soon lose interest and cease to attend – which is what eventually happened. But at the time for most of them it was the first occasion when they had been involved in a cause greater than themselves, and this was potentially a valuable experience. Without making any public statements we felt free to go occasionally into the occupied Great Hall and listen to the proceedings and chat with students.

Among my colleagues Gordon was one of the last of the 'monarchical' department heads. He was a patristic scholar and also a major authority on liturgy and church architecture, for the study of which he created an Institute within the department with Gilbert Cope as a full-time lecturer in the field. At first I got on well with Gordon but at some point he became distinctly anti-me. This was not however the reason why I retired from Birmingham early, at the age of sixty, to move to California – see chapter 22. Unfortunately the H.G. Wood chair was then 'frozen' – for thirteen years. It was revived with the appointment of Denys Turner, a great authority on medieval Christian mysticism. Although with a strong philosophical training, Denys did not teach the philosophy of religion, which thus remained largely off the department's map except for a course by Rex Ambler on the neighbouring subject of philosophical theology. Denys moved to Cambridge after three years, and his successor, Markus Vinzent, an extremely interesting and lively German theologian, is basically a patristic scholar and does not teach the philosophy of religion, although the Department accepts some graduate students in that field. But since I retired in 1982 Birmingham has not been a centre specifically to attract researchers in this subject.

Other members of the department included Rex Ambler who remains a good friend today. He is indeed one of the nicest human beings I know. He has had health problems over the years but after retiring early has found a new and fulfilling role as a Quaker thinker (rather than 'theologian', which is not a popular term among Friends), doing interesting new work on early Quaker practice and seeking to reproduce it in a modern setting through a combination of lectures and guided meditations. I have found the taped lecture valuable but do not see the guided meditation which I have practiced from the tape as reflecting it. This is a form of therapeutic self-healing in which the meditaters are led to face their troubled relationship with anyone else, to see it objectively from outside it, and thus be freed from it. And the same format is applied to other anxieties, fears, prejudices, etc. I have no doubt that this can be a valuable form of therapy in its own right, and for some a useful preparation for religious meditation. But whilst this does heal, purify, and ultimately transcend the ego, its therapeutic effects are (in my opinion) by-products rather than its central goal, which is openness to the Transcendent, the Divine, the Real. And whilst Rex points to some interesting analogies between Quaker themes and Zen, the kind of therapeutic meditation which Rex teaches is not at all like either zazen or satipatthana in which, so far from filling the mind with the individual's problems in order to resolve them, the mind is emptied of all ordinary concerns in order to become open to the ultimate reality which Buddhists variously refer to as nirvana, or sunyatta, or the universal Buddha nature. But Rex has been active in putting his viewpoint in Quaker circles and conducting workshops for Friends in several countries; and it is not for me as a non-Friend (although an attender at the local Meeting) to pronounce on Quaker matters. Hugh McLeod, author of important comparative studies of religion in the cities of several countries, is also both a friend and a Friend. Dan Hardy, a very English American, had insights which he found hard to communicate clearly to others. However this did not prevent him from being elected to the prestigious Van Mildert chair at Durham and then becoming an effective director of the Theological Institute at Princeton, attached to the seminary. Since retiring from there and returning to England he has played a leading part in the Society for the Study of Theology. I was once (1975–6) president of this Society in its more open days, but it has since become extremely conservative, with many of the more liberal members leaving. Dan has settled in Cambridge where his son-in-law David Ford, who was also in the Birmingham department, is now the Regius professor of divinity, playing an important leadership role in the development of the faculty and its move to splendid new premises, and supporting new developments such as the Hindujah Institute of Indic Research, initially directed by another good friend, Julius Lipner. As well as writing on his own, David has collaborated with Dan in some joint work in which he has managed to articulate and enlarge upon the somewhat inchoate insights of his father-in-law, who has latterly also written independently. Whilst recognising the sterling personal qualities of Dan, and the great intellectual abilities of David, I myself find their kind of theology, which is a new internal elaboration of traditional Christian concepts, of use only within the shrinking ecclesiastical world.

Indeed a great deal of contemporary British (and also German) theology continues to be depressingly inward looking, a continuation of traditional Church Dogmatics. Within the churches there is today a great concern and effort to contribute to solving the problems of British society and of the world. But theology itself remains basically as it was several generations ago. The more outward-looking theologians have grappled with the reality of secularism, have absorbed the insights of feminism, and are facing the challenge of modern science – in the latter area in particular much excellent work is being done – but few have faced more than superficially the issues raised by the fact that Christianity is only one of the great world faiths, and does not seem, when viewed throughout history and around the world, to be spiritually, intellectually or morally superior to all other religious traditions, as however its theology implicitly claims. And so the theologian whose head is not buried in the ecclesiastical sand has either to make a convincing case for Christianity's unique superiority, or prepare to rethink those of its dogmas which misleadingly imply such a superiority. A small minority are doing this – Professor Perry Schmidt-Leukel of Glasgow being the leading, but by no means only one, in Britain, with a number in the USA, and increasing forays into the problem among theologians in India, Sri Lanka, Japan and elsewhere, as well as very interesting parallel moves emerging within Islam, Judaism, Hinduism and Buddhism.

Frances Young was another notable member of the department, teaching patristics and NT – more about her in connection with *The Myth of God Incarnate*. John Eaton was our extraordinarily kindly, extremely learned, and surprisingly open-minded Old Testament scholar – surprisingly because OT scholars can often see no further than their ancient texts. Denise Newton came to teach the sociology of religion, but suffered from ill health and retired early and is now flourishing greatly in her retirement. With the aid of seed money from Cadbury a chair of mission was established and Walter Hollenweger from Switzerland, a world authority on Pentecostalism and himself a former Pentecostalist, was appointed. Mission does not mean, for the purposes of this chair, the history of the church's world-wide missions, or the ways in which to evangelise, but something more like Christianity and the world. Walter attracted numerous overseas students sent by their churches in Africa and Asia to acquire a British PhD, researching on a wide range of subjects often to do with their own home churches. Walter is a deeply sensitive and creative person who expresses himself most naturally in story and drama rather than in direct statement, although he always insisted on his students observing the high standards of German footnotery. I have to confess that I was not able to learn a great deal from him, except for fascinating information about such matters as the Kimbanguist movement in the Congo region of Africa. But his style of creative theological writing was so different from anything that I could either agree or disagree with that we had an unhappy breach when I mistakenly – my fault – invited him to join the *Myth of God Incarnate* team. He wrote something that was entirely unacceptable to the rest of us and felt that in rejecting it I had let him down by caving in to pressure from the Oxbridge members of the group (Dennis Nineham, Maurice Wiles, Leslie Houlden, Don Cupitt). In fact I entirely agreed with them, and with the others of the Birmingham group (Frances Young and Michael Goulder), that Walter's piece could not possibly fit into our projected book; but I did not want to insult him by saying this to him. So there was a period of estrangement. However after a few weeks I visited him and his wife in their flat and Walter's Christian charity enabled us to be fully reconciled. He presumably still felt that he had been unjustly excluded but nevertheless generously forgave me. Walter's replacement, Werner Ustorf, a good friend, has proved much more profitable as a colleague, being an extraordinarily interesting, stimulating and innovative thinker with remarkably challenging insights.

The pastoral studies section of the department was headed, first, by Bob Lambourne, and then Michael Wilson, and continued until recently as a successful training programme. I knew Michael, in particular, well and kept closely in touch with him and his wife, visiting them fairly regularly after their nearly fatal car crash shortly after his retirement. He later bore a painful cancer in the neck with extraordinary courage and cheerfulness until his death, nursed by his wife, Jean, a fully qualified nurse.

The Cadbury trusts, which encouraged a broader rather than a narrower religious outlook, offered with prompting from myself to provide seed money for a lectureship in Indian religions with the intention that after an initial three years it would be taken over by the university. I was then about to go to India and was to look out for a suitable Indian candidate. I found him at Santiniketan, Dr Sushanta Sen, who came for the first year. When he returned to India he was succeeded by Julius Lipner, who had taken his PhD under Hywel Lewis at London. But during that year Cambridge initiated a new lectureship in Indian religions and Julius was appointed there. We have kept well in touch over the years and I have had many happy Indian meals in Julius and Anita's house. Whereas Sushanta and Julius taught mainly about Hinduism, our third year appointee, Chris Gudmunsen, was a Buddhist and taught mainly about Buddhism. But at the end of the three years the University dropped the lectureship, and it remained only a brief episode until fairly recently.

With a number of exceptions the undergraduates were of medium academic quality. In contrast however to today, when the department has more graduate than undergraduate students, we then had only a sprinkling of post-grads. During my time there I had three excellent ones. Paul Badham, whose dissertation was published as *Christian Beliefs about Life after Death*, is now a professor in the University of Wales at Lampeter where he has developed a small into a large and successful department of religious studies. Bill (William Lane) Craig is a very bright and energetic American whose massive dissertation was published in two volumes as *The Cosmological Argument from Plato to Leibniz* and *The Kalam Cosmological Argument*. Bill is an evangelical Christian who later worked for the Campus Crusade for Christ and – or but – who has written philosophically first-rate articles on cosmology and on 'middle knowledge' (God's alleged knowledge of what everyone would freely do in all possible circumstances) and other topics, including the, to me, horrific theory that in virtue of the divine middle knowledge God knows of the hundreds of millions of unevangelised people outside Christianity that they would reject the gospel if it had been brought to them, so that it is not unjust for them to remain unsaved. But his extreme theological conservatism did not affect his purely philosophical work on the cosmological argument, and has not prevented us from remaining on good terms when we have since met occasionally in the States. The third is Alan Keightley, whose dissertation was published as *Wittgenstein, Grammar and God* and who became a Zen practitioner and a very successful religious studies teacher in a sixth form college, where I went several times as a visiting speaker.

To me discussion has always been important. Only very rare philosophical geniuses – like Kant – can do their work largely without the benefit of criticism from others. And so almost as soon as I arrived in Birmingham I founded a small discussion group which we called the Open End. We met in the evening once a month in one another's houses, starting with coffee, someone then reading a paper which was discussed at length, and ending with cheese, fruit and wine and academic gossip – often not getting home until nearly midnight. The meetings have continued to this day, with of course the membership changing over the years, the only two original members now left being Michael Goulder and myself. Regrettably, I never kept a record of our meetings, although I have occasional diary references to them. For example, 'Quite a good Open End here last night – Tim Moore [of the philosophy department] reading paper on divine action.' I have a Staff House dinner menu signed on the back by all of us who were present at the 100th meeting, on 24 April 1978: Rex Ambler, Alan Keightley, John Hick, John Hull, Chris Gudmunsen, Dan Hardy, Harry Stopes-Roe, Michael Goulder, David Ford. At one point a couple of meetings were devoted to the Turin Shroud, then much in the news. David Ford believed that it was genuinely the figure of Jesus, the rest of us not. Michael Goulder even did experiments to show how it could be faked. (It has since, in 1988, been carbon dated to the Middle Ages, not the first century, though in spite of that it still has its devotees.) But there has been a wide range of usually very interesting topics and often really excellent discussions. The informal setting, sitting round comfortably in armchairs and sofas, and the good personal relations between us all, is favourable to co-operative explorations as distinguished from academic combat. Recent topics have included Michael Goulder on the (according to him, vanishing) future of religion, and on the real Jesus, Werner Ustorf on the close relations between the German missionary societies and Nazism, Marius Felderhof on a Wittgensteinian understanding of religion, Markus Vinzent on the German academic refugees from Nazism, and a preview of his provocative inaugural lecture called 'Forget about God', myself on naturalism, the brain and religious experience, and another on 'Who or What is God?', Stephen Pattison on the idea of shame, Michael Snape on seventeenth-century folk religion. (It is interesting that both our German members are fascinated by the theological impact of Nazism.)

Many of the meetings during the first few years were dominated by responses to the aggressive atheism of Harry Stopes-Roe, whom I have known since we were both graduate students, he at Cambridge. He is the son of Marie Stopes, the famous and at the time very controversial advocate of birth control and founder of clinics for contraception which continue today in several countries. Harry, endowed with an undoubtedly first-class mind, was for several years an enormously energetic member of the Open End, sending one long single-spaced letters after a meeting and expecting a prompt reply. It was the same when he was involved as the humanist representative in the creation of the new Agreed Syllabus of Religious Education, about which more in the next chapter.

After a while we all, realising that we would be drawn into an endless, time-consuming and unprofitable correspondence, ceased to reply; and in due course when the Open End meetings no longer revolved around his concerns Harry ceased to come to them. He has since spent his energies, partly in an attempt which has been going on for a number of years to set forth a humanist foundation for ethics, and partly as an office bearer in the British Humanist Association. In the former endeavour he works alone without however being, in my opinion, one of the very few who can afford to forego the critical input of their peers. We remain on personally friendly terms, and he is very close to Michael whom he *may* perhaps be said to have converted from Christianity to Humanism. (The question mark signalled by the italics do not refer to Michael's rejection of Christian theism but to the degree of Harry's responsibility for this.)

I have a warm friendship with Michael which has developed (with one or two glitches) ever since we both arrived in Birmingham. We lunch together fairly regularly at the University and enjoy one another's conversation on a wide range of subjects. Michael has a first-class mind, a good classical education at Eton and Oxford, a great breadth of culture and interests, and a kindly disposition behind a sometimes acerbic speech. As a New Testament, and more recently also as an Old Testament scholar – a rare achievement – he has become prominent and internationally respected in both fields, having gradually overcome the opposition of the biblical establishment to his wealth of new theories. After many years as an Anglican priest, including serving as principal of Union Theological College in Hong Kong, Michael experienced rising doubts and in 1981, fifteen years after coming to Birmingham as tutor (and later as professor) in the department of extra-mural studies, declared himself to be an atheist and renounced his Anglican orders.[1]

He had been brought up on the 'red-blooded' theism of his Oxford mentor Austin Farrer. Our relationship with God was to be thought of like a human friendship: we found out what God was like by attending to his wishes. God acted in the world, sometimes in response to our prayers, though not by suspending natural law in any visible way. Farrer had supported his faith with subtle philosophical arguments which however Michael increasingly found to be inadequate – abetted in this by myself. I was not myself astonished by his atheism because it had long seemed to me that his Christian faith had been built on precarious foundations – the teachings of the church and philosophical arguments – without any element of first-hand religious experience. But the same applies to many churchmen, and if he had not come to see the inadequacy of this conventional churchianity he would very probably have gone far within the ecclesiastical world. As it is, he remains, paradoxically, an archetypal Anglican in every respect except for the detail (as it increasingly seems within the more liberal end of the Church of England) of his lack of belief in the God of Christian orthodoxy. But his avowal of atheism has not interrupted our friendship at all. However my basic criticism of his thinking about religion is that it does not go beyond a well-founded and elegantly expressed rejection of the anthropomorphic and interventionist God of his upbringing. His answering criticism of my own position is that in going beyond belief in an anthropomorphic deity to affirm an ultimate transcategorial reality that is manifested through our human religious concepts as the various god figures and non-personal 'absolutes' of the different religions, I have gone off into something too vague to be either believable or useful. Behind this difference there lies my basic conviction that human religious experience is not totally projection but is also at the same time, in very varying degrees, a response to reality, versus Michael's firm naturalistic assumption that it must all be purely imaginative projection.

We debated this at one of his then famous Saturday extra-mural courses at the university, which was published in our joint book *Why Believe in God?* (1983). One further observation about Michael, and something that I greatly admire, has been his courage after an almost fatal accident two years ago in coping with the serious damage, including the loss of sight in one eye, and in his determination to return, as he has done, to active and productive life.

John Hull is another good Birmingham University friend. At the age of about forty, when a lecturer in religious education, he became blind.[2] The way in which he has coped with this is astonishing, developing a range of electronic aids, continuing to research and becoming a professor, and dean of his faculty, and travelling all over the world to lecture. In his public lectures his rapport with the audience is better than that of most sighted speakers. He is a significant and original thinker, full of exciting insights. He is another with whom I lunch habitually in the university.

During the Birmingham years I gave many lectures and attended many conferences in many places. For example during 1977–9 for which I have an intermittent diary I lectured at Cambridge, Uppsala, London, Manchester, Ghana, Stirling, Toronto, Harvard, San Francisco, Los Angeles, Glasgow, Belfast, Colraine, Dublin, the Open University, Sheffield, and hosted a conference in Birmingham with Russian 'Scientific Atheists'. Out of all this at least one event is worth recalling here.

In 1977 Uppsala University in Sweden celebrated its 500th anniversary as one of the oldest universities in Europe and awarded a number of honorary degrees. Its faculty of theology very kindly invited me to receive one. There were various events over a period of several days, including my giving a public lecture. The degree ceremony itself was impressive, with several heads of state present including the king of Sweden before whom one bowed after receiving the gold ring which signified the degree, accompanied by the firing of a cannon outside the great hall. I also received a Swedish doctor's top hat which I still have but would never dream of wearing. Another theological recipient was the major Muslim scholar Hossein Seyyed Nasr of Iran, then regarded as the Shah's cultural ambassador in the west. This was the time when the Shah was under growing pressure leading to the revolution which toppled him in 1979. There were a number of Iranian students at Uppsala, political refugees from the Shah's dictatorial regime. They objected to the award of an honorary degree to Nasr as an unacceptable political act; and my sympathies were with them in this. There was the possibility of violent demonstrations, and security was strong, with an armed guard at night outside Nasr's room along the corridor at the hotel where we stayed, and some of the apparently student ushers at the degree ceremony being armed plain clothes police. I had nothing to do with all this except that I was to walk with Hossein Nasr in the procession. I hoped that if anyone did try to shoot him, they would have a good aim! In fact the event in the hall went off undisturbed although there were demonstrations outside. (A more recent ceremony of the same kind at Glasgow University was less dramatic – no cannon fire or assassinatables – but equally friendly and enjoyable.)

Years later when Hossein Nasr had disentangled himself from Iranian politics and was teaching in the States I met him again at several conferences, and again when he gave the Cadbury lectures at Birmingham. At that time we did a joint interview with a Turkish graduate student at Lancaster University who was writing his thesis on a comparison between our positions on the relations between religions.[3] Hossein Nasr is a Sufi scholar and the difference between us is that whilst we both hold that the world faiths are different ways to the same ultimate divine reality, I hold that this must have implications for the belief system of each religion. It implies that each should filter out its traditional claim to unique superiority by jettisoning or reinterpreting those doctrines which require this. He on the other hand denies this, believing that each system should remain unchanged, and so holding that I ought to affirm the traditional doctrines of trinity and incarnation, although the latter implies that Christianity alone among the religions of the world was founded by God in person. So at this point we remain in disagreement, although we are at one in the basic belief that, as he put it in his Cadbury lectures, the divine grace can be likened to water flowing down the many sides of a mountain and taking different shapes according to the different shapes of the ground on its different sides. There seems, incidentally, to be a growing interest among the younger generation of Muslim scholars in Turkey in the problems of religious plurality, including my own suggestions for dealing with them.

In 1968 Ian Ramsey was to leave the Nolloth chair of the philosophy of religion at Oxford to become bishop of Durham and I 'put in' for the chair. I was not appointed, the position going to the Oxford philosopher Basil Mitchell. This was an excellent appointment with which neither I nor anyone else could quarrel. Missing the Nolloth chair was not a great surprise nor a great disappointment. In 1977 I was invited to move to the chair being vacated by Hywel

Lewis at King's College, London. In January 1977,

> The London ad. has now appeared, and Hywel has rung up to ask
> if I have decided to apply. He is far too concerned to appoint his
> own successor, tho' I suppose I am the one person who shouldn't
> complain, since he wants me to be appointed ... [Feb. 13] The
> question of the King's College chair has now resolved itself. On
> my first Stanton visit [to give the Stanton lectures at Cambridge] I
> had a talk with Donald [Mackinnon], who said that he was
> definitely going to retire at the end of the 1977–8 academic year.
> That being so I am not applying for the London chair – much to
> Hywel's annoyance. Hazel doesn't want to live in London; the
> King's College situation seems to be a mess; commuting for a year
> or two whilst we are still involved in schools here would be very
> unattractive – expensive and tiring. I shall take my chance with
> Cambridge instead ... [Feb. 26] On Tuesday I lunched with Huw
> Parry Owen at the Liberal Club in London, when he asked – from,
> he said, the Principal & Dean & other members of the selection
> committee – how I would react to an invitation to the Kings'
> College chair. I discouraged the idea ... [May 3] Trip to London.
> Visited Lady Collins and agreed cover for Fontana edition of *God
> and the Universe of Faiths*. Dozed after lunch in Nat. Portrait Gallery,
> whilst it rained heavily outside. Then to King's College to give the
> second Younghusband lecture to quite a large audience of the
> World Congress of Faiths, Bp Appleton in the chair. Then invited
> to meet the Principal of King's who over drinks offered me the
> chair. Politely declined; but nice to be asked.

As I have indicated, I intended to and did apply next year for the
Norris-Hulse chair at Cambridge, in succession to Donald. But the
timing was bad in that *The Myth of God Incarnate* had come out the
previous year, infuriating the traditionally orthodox, of whom there
were many within the Cambridge establishment. But for this I might
perhaps have been appointed – although this can only be pure speculation. Nicholas Lash was appointed, a brilliant and subtle
Cambridge theologian, already in Cambridge as a Fellow of St
Edmund's Hall, but not a philosopher of religion. My diary (20
February 1978) notes, 'I am surprised to find how few minutes it
takes to become reconciled to this disappointment!'

In retrospect, my missing of these two possibilities of an Oxbridge
career has left me entirely content. The initial probability was not
great, for the Oxbridge electors did not then interview candidates but

relied on personal knowledge and reputation, and usually ended by making an internal appointment – at least this was the case in the 1970s. If I had gone to either place as they were then I would have had a continuous uphill task in pursuing my own much wider concerns, and would have missed the years in California where my own agenda was readily accepted, and would likewise have missed my encounters with far eastern Buddhism. I might well never have developed the ideas that came to me at Claremont, embodied in *An Interpretation of Religion*. And so the result is that, on the one hand, I was never associated with one of the world's top universities, with the wealth of graduate students that they attract, but on the other hand I was free from the then entrenched Anglican dominated traditionalism of Oxford and Cambridge and have been able to pursue my own agenda. On balance I think that I have had the better bargain.

Because of the peripheral status of the philosophy of religion within the syllabus my teaching duties at Birmingham were not very arduous, though tutorials were time consuming and, because they consisted of six or so students, rather than the one or two at Cambridge, not very profitable. (They have since been abandoned.) I was on the campus on Mondays, Wednesdays and Fridays, lecturing in the morning, lunch in the Staff House, 'ten minutes' on the sofa in my room with the door locked, and tutorials in the afternoon.

This 'ten minutes' as it is known in the family is a siesta after lunch, not of literal but notional minutes which often amount to an hour or, today, even more of ordinary mundane time. This is not of course always possible, but in general I have arranged my working days to include it and believe that I have benefited greatly. It fits the natural rhythm of the body and I feel no need to justify it. But for those who do, let me commend some words of Winston Churchill's (one of the few of his policies that I can agree with):

> You must sleep sometime between lunch and dinner, and no half-way measures. Take off your clothes and get into bed. That's what I always do. Don't think that you will be doing less work because you sleep during the day. That's a foolish notion held by people who have no imagination. You will be able to accomplish more.[4]

And some years ago I was at a conference with Charles Hartshorne, then in his late nineties (he has since died at the age of 101), and asked him one morning at breakfast what was the secret of his

longevity. He said, having a siesta after lunch every day.
Here is my diary for 26 February 1977:

A busy week. An Open End at the Goulders on Sunday, with
David Ford speaking about a contemporary French philosopher –
whose ideas seemed to some of us impossibly impressionistic &
rhetorical. Unusually intense disagreement. On Monday we had
25 students in for the evening from Intro. to Theol. Thinking ...
Gave a Stanton at Cambridge, returned to London, spent night at
Tavistock Hotel, caught 8.40 a.m. train to B'm & lectured to the
Xian Ethics class on race relations. Then home for '10 minutes' &
by car to Manchester to give a paper to the Theol. Soc. on life
after death – a pleasant meal and discussion. Stayed night at Leaks
& back to B'm in time to collect proofs of Nat. Front document at
AFFOR, & then speak to a lunch meeting at St Francis Hall on
Christ & world religions; followed by Cadbury Lect. Committee;
followed by first of a pair of Institute lectures on ritual & ethics ...
Tomorrow drive to Cambridge to preach in Gt St Mary's & stay
there until after Stanton on Tuesday.

During the fifteen years at Birmingham I published *Christianity at the
Centre* (in later versions *The Centre of Christianity* and then *The Second
Christianity*), *Arguments for the Existence of God*, *God and the Universe of
Faiths*, *Death and Eternal Life*, *God Has Many Names*, *Problems of
Religious Pluralism*, *Why Believe in God?* with Michael Goulder, and
edited and contributed to *The Myth of God Incarnate*, as well as
numerous articles and book reviews. Again, unrelated to my
university work, I became deeply involved in race and community
relations work, which will occupy the next three chapters, as well as
two extended visits to India and one to Sri Lanka.

NOTES

1. For Michael's account of all this, see his chapter 1 in our joint book,
   Why Believe in God?, London: SCM Press, 1983, reissued in 1994.
2. See his book *On Sight and Insight: A Journey into the World of Blindness*,
   Oxford: Oneworld, 1997.
3. Adnan Aslan, *Religious Pluralism in Christian and Islamic Philosophy: The
   Thought of John Hick and Seyyed Hossein Nasr*, Richmond: Curzon Press,
   1998.
4. Quoted by Martin Gilbert, *Never Despair: Winston Churchill 1945–
   1965*, London: Heinemann, 1988, p. 225.

14

Multi-faith work in Birmingham

Having arrived in Birmingham in 1967 I quickly became interested in the ethnic mix that had resulted from immigration from the Caribbean (then still called the West Indies) and from India and Pakistan, with East Pakistan becoming independent as Bangladesh in 1971. The biggest ethnic group were the Afro-Caribbeans, who were Christians, usually in the Pentecostal traditions; and the main non-Christian communities were the Muslims, the Sikhs and the Hindus, – and the same is true today, with Buddhists, Taoists, Jains and Bahai's now added. And there was already a small but long established but now, with a shift to Manchester and London, slowly declining Jewish community.

There was an official Birmingham Community Relations Committee (CRC), chaired by the Quaker (former Labour councillor and Lord Mayor) Corbyn Barrow, with an excellent full-time community relations officer, Peter Hutchinson, who invited me to chair a new religious education panel which was to be formed. This first met in March 1969 in a grand room in the Council House and included representatives of the Muslim, Sikh and Hindu communities, soon joined by Sydney Gold, chief minister of the Singers Hill Hebrew Congregation, and a Catholic priest, the remarkable Patrick O'Mahoney of Our Lady of the Wayside in Shirley, together with Canon Leonard Schiff, the Anglican bishop's race relations chaplain, who was also a prominent member of the parent CRC.

I thought it important to get to know personally as many of these people as possible and accepted all invitations from within the other faiths. My diary records going soon after the first meeting of the committee to the festival of Ram Naumi in a house in Handsworth used by the Hindus, who were then in process of buying a redundant Presbyterian church which they converted into a colourful temple serving both Vaishnavites and Shaivites, and later to Diwali celebrations there; to prayers and discussion with Muslims at their Islamic Culture Centre then in a small upstairs room in Aston, and presently to a Walima (after-marriage dinner) at the Centre where I also met the headmaster of a local primary school where Abdul Aziz, whose wedding party it was, went in to give Islamic instruction to Muslim children during the RI period (this was still pre-RE and even more pre-RS), and I also met the Pakistani Assistant High Commissioner; and to the Overseas Teachers' Circle at the Sikh Gurudwara, a converted former church in the High Street of Smethwick; later a huge celebration of the 500th anniversary of Guru Nanak's birth in the Town Hall, where I made a brief speech in ill-pronounced Punjabi (written by our then student lodger, Seva Singh Lyall), also organising messages from the Anglican bishop, Catholic archbishop, and Free Church president of the Birmingham Council of Churches; and over the years to weddings, funerals, Diwali celebrations, dinner parties, seders, etc. of every kind. Twenty years later, when we returned to Birmingham from Claremont Hazel began teaching English as a second language to Asian ladies in their homes, and was herself learning Urdu, and we came to know some Asian families, having meals in their houses and they in ours.

As I spent time in the mosques, synagogues, gurudwaras and temples as well as churches something very important dawned on me. On the one hand all the externals were different. In a Hindu temple, for example, the sights, the sounds, the smells, the colours were those of India and I could imagine myself (after I had been in India) back there. And not only the externals, but also the languages, the concepts, the scriptures, the traditions are all different and distinctive. But at a deeper level it seemed evident to me that essentially the same thing was going on in all these different places of worship, namely men and women were coming together under the auspices of some ancient, highly developed tradition which enables them to open their minds and hearts 'upwards' towards a higher divine reality which makes a claim on the living of their lives. They are called, in the words of a Hebrew prophet, 'to do justly, to love mercy, and to walk humbly before their God'. At this basic level the religions are at one. In my favourite words of the Sufi Jalaluldin Rumi, 'The lamps are different, but the Light is the same: it comes from Beyond.'

Among those who shared this insight Father Patrick O'Mahoney became a friend whom I admired greatly and with whom I often shared meals until his premature death from cancer many years later. This unimpressive looking little Catholic priest was in fact one of the more remarkable people whom I have known. He was utterly dedicated to the service of humanity. He had educated his congregation into a world outlook. Indeed the architecture of his church (which he had guided) and the liturgy both express involvement in the world, and the congregation was sending a quarter of a million pounds worth of medicines a year to Calcutta (where they were distributed by a Salvation Army officer) and to parts of Africa. The church was a centre for collecting medical supplies, many from Birmingham doctors who donated the samples given to them by the pharmaceutical companies. He was also actively involved in Amnesty International, and by careful research into the records of arms manufacturers and other companies, and the effects of apartheid, got his archdiocese to disinvest from South Africa; and he also gave leadership in several other areas. Leonard Schiff, a former missionary in India who had been a follower of Gandhi and for a while secretary to Nehru, likewise became a long-time friend. And among the other-faiths' representatives on the panel several likewise became friends and colleagues in AFFOR (about which more later) – Darshan Singh Bhogal (later deputy chairman of the Birmingham CRC), Bashir Awan, Bashir Waraich.

Our major recommendation to the City, expressed in official documents, letters to the press, meetings with Council officials, was for provision for the new religious communities within the religious education programmes of the LEA schools; and we suggested a pattern which eventually became that of the new Birmingham Agreed Syllabus. Under the 1944 Education Act religious instruction, later called religious education and now more often religious studies, took place according to an Agreed Syllabus adopted by each Local Education Authority. At that time they were all, including the

Birmingham one, exclusively Christian, consisting mostly of traditional Bible study. There had long been Catholic and Jewish schools, but the presence of substantial numbers of Muslim, Sikh and Hindu children had not then been envisaged and we had to look for ways of catering for them within the existing legal framework. This was already being stretched in practice by some schools allowing representatives of these other faiths to come in to teach separated groups during the RI, and sometimes the assembly, periods. But this met the need only very partially and haphazardly. However we sought the approval of the Chief Education Officer for this, and also sought out suitable teachers within the other-faiths communities to expand the practice. The Chief Education Officer was at first cautious and therefore negative, as officials of all kinds normally are, and a delegation of us went to see him. We were later told that whilst he could not issue any directive, nevertheless anything that could be done on the basis of goodwill and personal contact could proceed. In other words, a blind eye to expanding the existing practice.

However there was a growing mood in educational circles throughout the country for a new start in RE, led by Ninian Smart and the SHAP conferences, and the next thing that happened was that a big official car with the Birmingham coat of arms on it, with uniformed chauffeur, turned up at 20 Arthur Road bringing the Chief Education Officer's assistant, Mr C.C. Tipple. The Education Committee had decided in principle to commission a new Agreed Syllabus, and he hoped that it would agree to include a Muslim, a Sikh, a Hindu, a Jewish and a Catholic member and invited me to oversee its work as chair of its co-ordinating committee. I gladly agreed, providing the other-faiths members were included as planned and that I was to suggest who these should be. I later had a lunch at the university with the Chief Education Officer, Mr K. Brooksbank, and Mr Tipple, to confirm all this. In due course, when the new Syllabus was launched, it superseded what we had been doing in the Community Relations panel which we then turned into a Religious and Cultural panel.

Under the 1944 Act a Statutory Conference to produce an Agreed Syllabus must consist of four groups consisting of representatives of the teachers, of the Local Education Authority, of the Church of England, and of the other churches; and by a kind of legal fiction the other-faiths members were included in this last group. The Birmingham City Council then had a Conservative majority and our first meeting, in March 1970, was chaired by a Conservative Alderman (steered by Tipple). I and others stressed the need for a multi-faith syllabus and the need for it to be genuinely educational rather than an extension of the work of the churches and other religious organisations into the schools. It was agreed that the new syllabus should be multi-faith and should also take account of secular world-views. The nearly forty members of the Conference were then organised into working parties on syllabuses for the different age-levels, their work co-ordinated by the small central committee which I chaired, and eventually produced both a brief official Syllabus and a much more substantial Handbook for Teachers. At the younger ages the teaching was to be largely thematic. For older pupils the basic principle was that each should major in one religion (normally their own), and minor in one or more others, with Christianity, as the religion integral to the history of Britain, having to be either a major or a minor. And as well as the religions we included some study of the secular faiths of communism and humanism.

As the meetings got fully under way an experienced RE teacher, Cecil Knight (later head of a large ethnically mixed school), was seconded to work full time on the project. The whole exercise took almost five years, with innumerable meetings – I attended many of the working party meetings as well as regular meetings of the steering committee, meetings with members of the city's education committee, etc., etc., and have a stack of minutes, drafts and correspondence to remind me of it all. It so happened that what had been launched under a Conservative Council reported several years later under a Labour Council, which adopted our proposals in their entirety. Some of the Conservatives and the Anglican bishop attacked the inclusion of communism and humanism as 'non-religious stances for living' (a term invented by Harry Stopes-Roe) as part of the total scene today and there was a mighty row in Council and in the press. The National Society for Promoting Religious Education in accordance with the Principles of the Church of England declared that the proposed new Syllabus was illegal, and its publication was held up whilst this challenge was examined, the Chief Education Officer seeking the city counsel's opinion. Counsel said that the form in which the Syllabus was presented did not constitute a syllabus according to the OED's definition but that it could be expanded so as to come within this definition. He saw no objection to including teaching about other religions and non-religious stances for living, so long as the latter were introduced to support the study of religion; and it was agreed to set up a small committee to bring the Syllabus into good legal order.

The result was finally agreed in November 1974,

> Meeting at 10.30 a.m. of Agreed Syllabus Conference, chaired by [Labour councillor] Moira Symons. Very full attendance. Chief Education Officer reported on legal situation ... Councillor Dawes (Conservative) then raised the question of the 'non-religious stances for living', arguing that communism, in particular, should be excluded. A number of us spoke, all saying that the study of the great secular faiths does contribute to an understanding of the religious situation today, & should be included. Dawes formally moved the deletion of the reference to non-religious stances, and Sydney Gold seconded. These two voted for the motion & everyone else against. It was then moved to reaffirm the principles accepted at an early meeting, in 1970, including the principle of including some study of non-religious stances; and this was voted by everyone, except Dawes who voted against and Sydney who abstained. Thus the result of all the controversy & discussion has been a clarification of this issue and a considerable unanimity in the conference. A most successful meeting, very ably chaired by Moira. At the weekend I had wondered whether she had a clear plan and knew what she was doing: but she knows exactly what she is doing, and does it very effectively.

Another councillor, Sheila Wright (later Labour MP) was also a very helpful influence.

> *February 14,1975*: Dramatic, but very satisfactory, final meeting of Agreed Syllabus Conference in Council House. After accepting two small amendments from the Anglican group we divided into the four committees. The Free Churches, Anglicans, and Teachers committees each voted unanimously for the Syllabus, and the LEA committee by a majority of three to one – the one being Alderman Sydney Dawes. It was then decided to hold a news conference next Friday, by which time the Council's finance and general purposes committee will have received the Syllabus. But

Dawes said that he felt free to criticise the Syllabus publicly immediately. So it was decided to bring the news conference forward to Tuesday. I am to chair it with two members of each committee. Word came of disapproval of Chief Education Officer – for not waiting until next Friday, – so we have arranged (with much telephoning last night) to hold the conference at Carrs Lane and to duplicate copies of the Syllabus & Introduction privately. Sunday's *Birmingham Post* has an encouraging headline: 'Big vote of confidence for controversial R.I. syllabus', with an article which includes part of a statement which John Hull drafted after the Conference meeting & which Peter Davies gave to the paper.

March 14, 1975: In Cambridge (for last of first series of Stantons) & read in *Guardian* that Agreed Syllabus adopted by City's Education Committee yesterday ... So ends five years of work, including one year of political and ecclesiastical maneuvering. The B'm Humanists (or rather Harry using them) have now protested that the Syllabus is too preponderantly religious, and want to wreck it as illegal – a bad mistake, I think, on their part. [Later, *May 8*, 'Reconciling coffee with Harry Stopes-Roe. I infer that humanist legal action against the Agreed Syllabus, as threatened, is now not on.] And the Conservatives are complaining that communism has forced its way into the B'm schools. But it looks as though now the Syllabus will be printed and used; and in a few years people will wonder what the fuss was all about.

During the long process I had to write several times to the *Birmingham Post* – for example:

As the correspondence about Birmingham's new Religious Education syllabus has continued in your columns, a myth has been developing which ought to be exploded before it becomes mistaken for fact. This is the myth that the inclusion of a section on Communism in the handbook was the result of a political rather than an educational judgement, and was foisted on the statutory conference by Communist or other Left-wing influences. The myth lacks even a grain of truth. The conference, consisting of experienced local heads and R.E. teachers, official representatives of all the churches, educational and theological experts, and members of the local education authority, included no Communists or fellow-travellers. Until becoming, unhappily, politicised in the period of the February 1974 General Election and since, the new syllabus was regarded by all as a purely educational matter. It has happened that the conference completed its work and reported at a time when the education committee and council were Labour dominated. But the conference was originally convened under a Conservative dominated education committee and council, and the basic decision that the syllabus should treat of 'several faiths' and of 'other major ideologies', as well as Christianity, was taken at a full meeting of the conference in June 1970, under the chairmanship of a Conservative alderman ... The principles which the statutory conference adopted in 1970 are those on which the more successful R.E. teachers have been working for a number of years. The new Agreed Syllabus represents a major advance, not in the sense of proposing something new, but in the sense of giving legal recognition to what most of the teachers have long known to be educationally desirable and in many cases long practicing ...

For our new Syllabus was part of a nationwide move to multi-faith religious education. In the whole revision process John Hull, then lecturer (now professor) in religious education at the university, was a major force. He knew, needless to say, far more than me about religious education and its problems and had been a pioneer in the move from religious indoctrination to RE as an important aspect of education. Nationally, the SHAP working party, co-chaired by Ninian Smart, led the way in this development.

Whilst I strongly supported the inclusion of some teaching about communism and humanism I was even more concerned to get the basic multi-faith character of the Syllabus accepted, and the attacks on the other issue served as a lightning conductor to divert Conservative attention from this. As soon as the syllabus was adopted eight thousand copies of it and the handbook were distributed within the Birmingham schools. The Syllabus has, as intended, been under continuous revision ever since in the light of teaching experience by the Standing Advisory Council on Religious Education (SACRE), of which I was for a while a member. The main problem encountered has not been its content but the lack of enough qualified teachers to deliver it fully, though today virtually all specialist RE or RS teachers are trained in multi-faith teaching.

In the meantime the Religious and Cultural Panel of the CRC continued its work, turning to other issues. The first was the problems faced by Asian patients in the hospitals, arising from their special cultural or religious backgrounds. We held a series of meetings with nurses, doctors and hospital administrators, discussing such topics as diet, the language barrier, special beliefs and customs connected with birth and death, hospital visiting by priests etc. of the different faiths, and the attitudes of some Asian women to male doctors and of some Asian men to women doctors. Out of all this we produced a leaflet for the use of hospital administrators, nurses and doctors, about fifteen thousand copies being distributed.

Other issues with which we dealt included the treatment of Asians in the local Winson Green prison, whose governor met with us. (When we invited someone from outside to meet with the committee I usually took them out for a meal beforehand and found that this often oiled the wheels of discussion.) We also discussed sex education in the schools; the uniforms which had to be worn by Muslim nurses, who wanted to be allowed to wear trousers instead of skirts; the use of helmets by Sikh motor cyclists – eventually allowed to wear their turbans instead; provision for the other faiths in local religious broadcasting; the requirement, eventually dropped, for Muslim dead to be placed in coffins contrary to their custom. Another issue was the conditions in which halal meat was slaughtered, which often needed improvement. A lot of discussion took place, and I find from a letter that I sent to Mr Traxson, the then community relations officer, in July 1973, that I was annoyed to find that my report to the Community Relations Committee had been censored to remove my statement that

> a more vigorous approach would be necessary for the CRC to constitute an effective 'pressure group' on such matters ... I was in fact picking up a phrase used by the Commission's Chairman on one of his visits to Birmingham ... The omitting of what I had written ... was done without consulting me, presumably in the interests of a bland universal inoffensiveness ... I want you to know that I do not appreciate being censored and that I trust such a thing will not happen again.

This minor incident flags the difference between the official Birmingham CRC with its largely establishment point of view and the independent and much more activist AFFOR, about which more in the next chapter. But our religious and cultural panel nevertheless did much useful work, though with some items more successfully carried through than others.

I also proposed the creation of a Birmingham Inter-Faiths Council, and this was created in January 1975. I was elected its first chairman, and I have a note of a meeting in the Graham Street gurudwara at which the five initial constituting faiths, Hinduism, Christianity, Islam, Judaism and Sikhism were represented. 'Agreed a series of meetings to explain each faith in turn.' In July that year we had a party for the Council members in our garden at 70 Arthur Road attended by a number of members, including the bishop, Laurence Brown, and his wife. I cannot claim that the Council became very active in my time, though it did hold some useful meetings. I am glad to say that it still exists, though its full potential has still yet to be realised. But it did at least get started back in 1975. I was also in on the early discussions which led to the building of what became the Central Mosque in Belgrave Road, intended to be common to Pakistani, Bangladeshi, Indian, Arab and other Muslims. Its chairman is Dr Naseem with whom I worked in the 70s on the issue of Muslim nurses' uniforms. He is a remarkable man whom the Birmingham Muslim community is fortunate to have in a leadership role.

So the late '60s and '70s were a busy time for me, chairing the Agreed Syllabus work, the Inter-Faiths Council, serving on SACRE, on Radio Birmingham's religious advisory panel, being a Governor of the Queen's College and a member of the Council of the Selly Oak Colleges, as well as my teaching and research at the University, and – the most time consuming and productive of all – chairing AFFOR, about which more in the next chapter. I hope the family did not suffer from all this. It meant for Hazel that I was often out in the evening at meetings. But on the other hand she enjoyed making friendships with people of the other faiths. And I think that the children benefited from another side of it all, the people of other faiths and cultures and colours who were familiar visitors at home.

15

All Faiths for One Race

In 1970 an all-white cricket team from apartheid South Africa was to visit England and protests against the tour, led by Peter Hain and others, erupted around the country. To host the tour would be a tacit endorsement of the apartheid regime, which was firmly established in its full brutality with all protests disregarded and Nelson Mandela imprisoned on Robben Island. One of the games was to be played at the Edgbaston ground in Birmingham. A young businessman of whom I had not previously heard, John Plummer, who turned out to be a highly dynamic, charismatic figure, convened a meeting of individuals from all denominations in the University's Catholic Chaplaincy to arrange a demonstration against the match. In retrospect it seems curious that he looked initially to the churches because, or so I understood, he was himself a Marxist, of the Trotskyist as distinguished from the Stalinist camp. But his initiative was successful, with others soon joining in.

It was decided to hold a march from the city centre to the cricket ground. A pamphlet by Plummer, *Time is Running Out*, packed with information about apartheid was widely distributed, the Anglican bishop encouraged his clergy to support the march, student stewards were recruited, the police kept informed, and all prepared for a large march on Friday 25 March, two days before the beginning of play on Sunday 27th. (The march was not on the Saturday because the Jewish contingent would then have been unable to come.) Forty-two local church leaders, starting with myself and Gordon Davies, Leslie Mitton, principal of Handsworth Methodist college, John Hapgood, principal of Queen's College, Charles Buckmaster, principal of St Peter's College, Leonard Schiff and many others, but not the anglican bishop or Catholic archbishop themselves, sent 'A reasoned protest against the matches with South Africa at Edgbaston' to the County Cricket Club. The Club secretary replied that it was better to influence South Africa by playing it at cricket than by ostracising it and revealed the Club's real sympathies by enclosing a letter from 'Briton Backs South Africa' saying that South Africa fought for this country in two world wars, that many people wanted to see the game, that apartheid is rooted way back in history and is not the invention of present-day South Africans, and that demonstrations inevitably become violent. *The Evening Mail* announced the shock news that the police would have to field 1500 men to protect the game for eight days and that most of the cost would fall on the local taxpayers. The Conservative leader of the city council said, 'I do not feel that the tour should be called off but the root cause, the threat of violence, should be attacked on a national scale.' I received the first of many anonymous racist letters often with an implied threat:

> Don't you know that coloureds have been written off by mother nature, they are doomed to extinction by the law of natural selection. They cannot survive in their own countries by their own efforts, so they spread throughout the world like a verminous plague, preying like the parasites they are on the living body of white society. You know today, we have Nazi criminals on trial. Tomorrow – white renegades.

In May, 'Carrs Lane Church meeting at which I introduced motion supporting the march. Passed by 42 to 6 with some 14 abstaining. But a strong element of the negative – what about other evils than apartheid, & shouldn't we prevent salacious plays in London before we presume to condemn South Africa?'

Shortly before the all-white South African team was due to arrive in England the nation-wide protests caused the tour to be cancelled. John Plummer now proposed a continuing organisation, which became All Faiths for One Race, i.e. the human race. (Later, when the organisation was established, the name was of course reversed by conservative Christian critics as One faith for all races!) It was decided to go ahead with the march, now without reference to the cancelled cricket tour but to promote better community relations in the city. A small group of us, John Plummer, his partner Sylvia, Leonard Schiff, Darshan Singh Bhogal, Dr Naseem and myself met the press and launched the new body, later bringing in Bashir Awan and Bashir Waraich (Muslims), Sydney Gold (Jewish), Ben Sharma (Hindu) and others.

Eric Fenn, a leading Presbyterian (living at 144 Oak Tree Lane, where I now live) told me that he thought the bishop, the RC archbishop, and himself as moderator of the Free Church Council should all be present at the march; but in the end only Eric himself came. The Salvation Army band declined to attend on orders from London. However the march was a great success.

> Some nine hundred people formed a procession a quarter of a mile long, walking from the Bull Ring market place round the city centre to the Cathedral grounds. Banners saying 'All Faiths for One Race', 'Islam Teaches Unity of Mankind', etc. Good sprinkling of non-Christian immigrants. Brief speeches (but not as brief as intended!) outside Cathedral by bishop Sinker as provost of Cathedral; Sant Singh Shattar (who insisted on representing the Sikhs as well as their official representative!), Bashir Awan, Richard White (RC layman), Bashir Waraich of the Speedwell Road mosque, Eric Fenn (for the Free Churches), Dr Sen and Ben Sharma (for the Hindus), Eric Tucker (Quaker), Mehar Singh (President of the Sikh Temple at Smethwick), Reuben Brooks (for the Jews), and the bishop of Aston. There were no hostile signs except for a speaker from outside the crowd who tried to shout but made no headway against the microphone and gave up. Finally songs by a W. Indian group, a Sikh group, Ben Sharma, and a girl singing protest songs.

So the final meeting was over-loaded, but the event as a whole was a great success so long as it could prove to be the beginning of a continuing endeavour.

During the next fifteen years AFFOR did an enormous amount of work, but I shall only describe some parts of it in which I was directly involved. Throughout, the organisation depended entirely on the dedication and enthusiasm of a growing number of like-minded people – far more than I can mention here – for work made possible by grants from several public-spirited charities. No one benefited financially, except in the sense that some were employed, on basic salaries, most of them having qualifications which could have earned them much more elsewhere; many were attacked in speech or print by implicit racists; a few were physically assaulted by violent racist groups.

After the march John Plummer continued actively – pro-actively is the term today – approaching the Barrow and Edward Cadbury trusts, which both made grants, time limited but renewable. I was to get to know Anthony Wilson in the Cadbury office well during the following years, his support and experienced advice, and also that of his wife Anne, being key factors in the success of AFFOR. With the Cadbury money we were able to hire a full-time director, the first being John, and a secretary. John is one of the more remarkable people whom I have known, highly intelligent and talented, totally committed to social justice from a very left-wing perspective, very effective in getting results. A mystery surrounded his previous career. Some said that he had been an extreme right-winger who had been dramatically converted, but he was reticent about his past and I never tried to prise out the full story. But he was the creator of AFFOR. Without him it would never have existed and without his dynamic leadership it would never have grown and flourished as it did. But in the course of it he made many enemies, including at the local police headquarters – on one occasion we lodged a formal complaint about threats made against him but, as was normal in such cases, the complaint was internally investigated and dismissed. Nor was John popular with many within the establishment. Even Corbyn Barrow, chair of the Community Relations Committee, once invited me to lunch at his Club with John Traxson, his then community relations officer, hoping to define and limit the scope of AFFOR – and in particular of John. Traxson thought that being too forceful could be counter-productive. I expressed no sympathy with this point of view. On another occasion I was asked if John 'stepped on too many toes'? I thought not: just about the right number. For the attitude of both church and state to the widespread British racism of the time was cautious to the point of being almost entirely ineffective and needed the uncompromising challenge embodied in people like John Plummer. AFFOR was dismissed by one public figure as 'angry young men intent on stirring up trouble'. Not all were men, almost as many were women, and some of the men, including myself, were middle aged. But it is true that we were angry – about the injustices of racism. But it is also true that AFFOR's work was carried on with considerable professionalism and on the basis of accurate firsthand information.

I served as chair of AFFOR's management committee for several years, being succeeded by Trevor Rowe, a lecturer at Queen's Theological College who believed deeply in the cause of social justice, and then by Arthur McHugh, a brilliant administrator who worked in the city's education department, and then by Bon Bartlett, an experienced company director who was committed to the work of AFFOR. Whilst I lived in white and leafy Edgbaston, John Plummer, and subsequent directors, Geoff Wilkins, Clare Short, David Jennings, Marilyn Phillips-Bell, Anil Bhalla, lived in multi-racial Handsworth in the midst of its excitements and turmoil. My own function was partly that of one who strongly supported the work of AFFOR and gave a lot of time to it, and partly as someone who could act as a link with the political and ecclesiastical establishment. For the Community Relations Committee, including the religious and cultural panel which I chaired, was government sponsored whilst AFFOR was an independent activist and campaigning organisation. The Birmingham CRC tried to avoid controversy, and may have been right to some extent to do so; AFFOR on the other hand did not need to avoid controversy and did not hesitate to challenge prevailing attitudes.

We had very simple upstairs offices, originally at 165 Heathfield Road in Handsworth and later within the Lozells Social Development Centre at 1 Finch Road in neighbouring Lozells. Before we had our own premises we met in various places, such as sitting on the floor of a Hindu temple or a Sikh gurudwara, or on chairs in the vestry of St Martins in the Bull Ring, or in the British Council offices, or the Bournville Friends' Meeting. The committee included Christians, Jews, Muslims, Sikhs, Hindus, Marxists and Humanists. One key member was Richard White, Catholic layman, a solicitor and lecturer in law at the University, a first-rate mind, who was our invaluable legal adviser. He later moved to London as a solicitor in the Lord Chancellor's office, and was succeeded in AFFOR by a law faculty colleague, Philip Morrell. Another key member was Trevor Rowe of the Queen's College, who invented the AFFOR name. Another, Arthur McHugh, was a forceful down-to-earth character who was also, paradoxically, a mystic and poet. Another colleague was Ranjit Sondhi, who continues today to be a good friend, together with his wife Anita, known professionally in the BBC as Anita Bhalla. Ranjit created the very successful Asian Resources Centre, about which more presently, and was later deputy-chairman of the national Commission for Racial Equality, a member of various government committees, a Governor of the BBC and chair of the Heart of Birmingham Primary Care Trust in the NHS. Ranjit and Anita are two alpha plus human beings! Chris Wadham had very valuable experience as director of the Shape housing association. Councillor Dick Knowles (later Labour leader of the city Council and later again, as Sir Richard, Lord Mayor), though not on the AFFOR committee, was actively helpful on several occasions. One of the Muslim members, Bashir Waraich, had been an officer in the Indian army and then emigrated to Britain and worked for many years in the Post Office. One of his sons went to Oxford and became an accountant, the other being a dentist within the National Health Service, and his daughter marrying another professional. The family is a good example of the long-term benefit that can come to Britain from immigration.

A small excitement involving one of the committee occurred in 1972 when Bashir Awan was arrested and charged with attempted murder. His seventeen-year-old daughter had run away with a young Pakistani man. Under the Pathan code of family honour blood must be shed, and Bashir shot the young man, deliberately inflicting only a flesh wound and then rang the police. Knowing him, I was sure that if he had intended to kill him he would have succeeded – the Pathans are known as formidable fighters. I visited him in Winson Green prison, and at his trial several months later was a character witness, with Leonard Schiff (who did much better than I), and the judge accepted the code of honour explanation, plus the fact that Bashir had no more daughters, and gave him a conditional discharge. According to my diary, at one time, after an earlier hearing at which bail was refused, 'Pleasant scene afterwards of Awan's sons, the "victim", the girl, the detective in charge of the case, Chief Inspector Wilson, Leonard Schiff, Patel, myself, & sundry other Pakistanis, all chatting amicably together in the court house lobby!'

One of the first problems that we took up was that faced by the

Muslim community in using houses as prayer houses and places for
Qur'anic instruction of their children. When they first arrived they
had known nothing about planning permission and were getting into
trouble with the city planning authorities, who were closing some of
them down. In a 1974 AFFOR Newsletter I reported:

> There have been various meetings with leaders of the Muslim
> community and with City officials and councillors; expeditions
> through the streets of Small Heath and Balsall Heath in search of
> suitable buildings; visits to prayer-houses in different parts of the
> city; conferences with an expert on town planning; the provision
> of legal advice ... Two memories: First, an afternoon spent with
> Councillor Dick Knowles attending worship at the Speedwell
> Road mosque and discussing planning problems with the leaders
> of the congregation. Dick has devoted considerable time and
> energy over more than a year to working for a solution to the
> prayer-houses problem, and the partial solution so far achieved
> owes much to his efforts. Second, in company with Bashir
> Waraich and Imam Farooqi knocking on doors in a street in Small
> Heath inviting people to sign a petition saying that as neighbours
> they have no objection to a nearby house being used as a place of
> Muslim worship. Another Muslim-Christian team was at work
> further up the street. We wondered apprehensively whether we
> were going to meet with colour prejudice or religious prejudice
> and were delighted to find practically none. Almost everyone,
> amounting in two different streets and in connection with two
> different houses – to nearly a hundred people, expressed a
> straight-forwardly human reaction and said that the Muslims were
> welcome to hold their worship here.

When some of us went to talk to the city's Planning Committee to
explain that most Muslims usually had to walk to a local centre for
their communal prayers, so that such places were needed in many
parts of the city, we found that the civil servants were more helpful
than the councillors. In this case the relevant official offered to be
consulted about prospective properties that we found. When
planning permissions were given they originally came with a
prohibition of any use between 11 p.m. and 8 a.m.

> *July 28, 1975*: Meeting, lasting 2 hours, at Planning Dept. office
> with Councillor J.H. Sowton, chairman, Councillor J.M. Bailey,
> Mr C.W. Rodgers, divisional planning officer, and another officer
> who took notes. I was present, with Darshan Bhogal, now vice-

chairman of the Community Relations Committee, and Michael Waters, secretary of B'm Council of Christian Churches. We were asked to speak first, and I put the case for exception to clause 2 of Code to allow Muslim pre-dawn prayers. Very small numbers involved, have been practising this for years, would be harsh now to declare it illegal. Sowton let off at length his resentments & grievances against the Muslims – have not observed the law, buy houses & use them as mosques & then later ask for planning permission. Against any change in the Code of Practice. Possibility however emerged of 'no objection' note about early prayers; and proposal to set up small Muslim committee to confer with planning officers. So, largely negative attitude, but slight hints of possible way forward.

We also tried to be helpful to the Ramgharia Sikh group wanting to buy a redundant church building in Graham Street from an Elim congregation which tried to get out of the contract when they learned who the buyer was. But the gurudwara was established and held a great opening ceremony, attended by the Lord Mayor, at which a few of us were presented with Sikh swords, mine being still on the wall above the study door.

As AFFOR became more widely known it attracted further grants which enabled the work to expand. There was a small membership subscription but this could never have been anything like enough. As well as Cadbury which, with Anthony Wilson's support, remained the core financial resource throughout, AFFOR was also helped by the Committee on Society, Development and Peace of the World Council of Churches and the Pontifical Commission on Justice and Peace (Sodepax – 'not a detergent, but still it helps'), represented by Christophe von Wachter of Taize, who visited us; and from the Wates Foundation, the British Council of Churches' Race Relations Unit, and the Joseph Rowntree Foundation, the Gulbenkian Foundation, and the Hilden Charitable Fund – though not all at the same time. But nevertheless, with the work always expanding, we were nearly always functioning on the verge of financial crisis.

However as time went on we were able to employ more people, and there was also a changing population of student volunteers giving some time to the work. Our first full-time education worker, speaking in schools, to teachers' conferences, city education department officials, running adult literacy classes etc., was Philip

Nanton (later, lecturer in the Institute for Local Government at the University). Anil Bhalla (later a director of AFFOR) was the research worker producing a well-based factual report on the needs of 'ethnic elderlies', which was supported by a grant from the Commission for Racial Equality, and later developing sheltered housing for Asian elderlies in Handsworth; and another report on the local sweatshops in which immigrant workers were often being badly exploited. Another report was on Wednesday's Children, published for us by the Community Relations Committee, concerning the acute needs of under-five children in the area. There were about thirty playgrounds for an under-five population of sixteen hundred and we pressed for more. AFFOR also acted in a 'managing-editor' capacity, with the aid of a student placement from the university, for the Trapeze community newspaper delivered to some 5500 households in Handsworth. Other areas of research, to which different people contributed and on which we published reports were *Read All About It*, a study of race reporting in newspapers; *Tip of the Iceberg*, on the role of organised racist groups in British society, *What Are You Going to Do about the National Front?* by Tony Holden; *Racist Movements, West Midlands '74*, by John Plummer and Geoff Wilkins, *The New Nazism of the National Front and National Party* by myself; *Brick Lane 1978, The Events and their Significance*, by Kenneth Leech; *Here Today and Here Tomorrow*, as a resource for teachers about immigration; and *Christianity and Race in Britain Today* and *Apartheid Observed* by myself, and the widely read *Talking Blues*, produced by Clare Short.

AFFOR helped Ranjit Sondhi and his team to set up the Asian Resources Centre on Soho Road, Handsworth, supported once again by Cadbury money. This proved a tremendous success and continues today, now supported by the City Council. There were teams of trained workers giving advice in Urdu, Punjabi, and Hindi on how to find one's way through the complexities of the welfare state, what individuals were entitled to, how to make a claim, immigration applications and appeals, what the law was on birth, death, marriage etc., etc., and the people coming into the Centre at any given time included Muslims, Sikhs and Hindus meeting on common ground and often helping one another out of their own experiences. The Asian Resources Centre was soon able to take over much of the case-work load that AFFOR had been handling.

With funds from the Wates Foundation AFFOR created the Wates Library, initially directed by Ivan Henry, a Caribbean teacher. This proved an increasingly widely used resource on ethnic, racial and religious matters by teachers, not only in Handsworth. And following the publication of a report, *Babel in Birmingham*, about the need for help for non-English speakers, we created an interpreting and translating agency, staffed by well-qualified people and maintained by charging fees to courts, social services, law centres, the probation service, hospitals, solicitors, immigration appeal tribunals, etc.

We also carried through a survey of multi-faith education in theological colleges, headed by David Jennings and Kenneth Cracknell, who were supported in this by the Committee on Other Faiths of the British Council of Churches. The conclusion was that practically nothing was being done in this area and so the published report was appropriately called *Blind Leaders of the Blind*. A lot more is being done today, but still (in my opinion) without any adequately thought-through theological basis.

We organised speakers to schools and churches about the needs and problems of the immigrant populations, and on multicultural studies; tried to stir up the church leaders on this; supported such public events as People to People week; designed, printed and sold multi-faith greeting cards; produced a pamphlet on Sikhism by Darshan Bhogal, briefly describing the origin, history, beliefs and practices of the Sikhs, with similar pamphlets planned for the other faiths; organised a conference on 'Power, Prejudice and People'; lobbied for an Urdu as well as the Punjabi and Hindi translations of the official 'rights on arrest' card; arranged with Radio Birmingham to broadcast special events from other-faiths centres, beginning with a forty-five minute live broadcast from the Sikh gurudwara in Smethwick on Basaki Day in 1972, with a subsequent one from one of the mosques; helped with the reception of the Uganda Asians coming to this country after their expulsion by Idi Amin; helped with the arrangements for the celebration of Bangladesh Independence Day in 1972; published in a press release a report on racial discrimination at the Longbridge car factory; and much more.

The 1975–6 annual report lists under 'Miscellaneous', support for Uhuru, a food co-operative operating from the Lozells Social Development Centre; talks with the police on the increasing numbers of apparently racist attacks on black people in Birmingham; a small project on testing racial discrimination in employment by postal applications to selected employers; fund-raising for under-fives childminders' playgroup and playbus; and the usual very varied and time-consuming caseload of advice work and referral on a multitude of individuals' problems – people confused, frustrated and often angry at the lack of response they so often meet when they sought help from the official agencies. It was this experience that prompted our report *Strangled by the Safety Net*, on the failure of the social services to reach many Asian and black clients.

I think it can be said that AFFOR did a great deal of good work, initially in the face of establishment suspicion and opposition, but progressively with official acquiescence and eventually support. Indeed its success led in the 1980s to its gradual transformation from an independent to an establishment-dependent organisation (although the establishment itself changed considerably during the same period), and then eventually to its end.

16

AFFOR – racial issues

The religious issues became less prominent as the new faith communities became more established and organised and able to look after their own interests and AFFOR's focus moved more fully to its other initial concern, the needs of the ethnic minorities. We had of course from the start been actively combating racism – this was the original issue raised by the South African cricket tour – and its powerful embodiment in the National Front and National Party, which were active in the West Midlands. Racism was rife in the 1970s and showed itself in many ways. As a typical small example, '*Dec. 7, 1972*: 18 Speedwell Rd, Balsall Heath. Imam: Khalid Mahmoud. Brick thrown through front window that morning & Mahmoud badly cut on hands and was at hospital this morning.' At a National Front march during a by-election at nearby Stechford some of the slogans chanted were, 'If they're black send them back', 'If you want a nigger for a neighbour, vote Labour'.

One pressing concern was the 1971 Immigration Bill before Parliament, much of it highly objectionable. We collaborated with the West Indian Standing Conference on this and published a leaflet by John Plummer, *How to Encourage Racial Prejudice*. Already in 1968 Enoch Powell, Conservative MP for nearby Wolverhampton, had given his famous 'rivers of blood' speech in which he said that immigrants were flooding into the country and would cause conflicts such that he foresaw (in Latin) rivers flowing with blood. The reality however was that in 1964 60,000 more people emigrated out of Britain than immigrated into it; in 1965, 74,000 more leaving than entering; in 1966, 82,000 more leaving than entering; in 1967, 84,000 more, and in 1968, 56,000 more. Thus the problem for Powell was clearly not numbers but colour. Whenever Powell made his racist speeches local violence ensued, there was an outbreak of 'Paki-bashing', and the Neo-Nazi National Front and National Party took heart and held big demonstrations. Locally, we lobbied successfully against their attempt to hire a hall in Digbeth, Birmingham, owned by the City Council.

We supported Maurice Ludmer in launching the journal *Searchlight* to monitor the activities of the racist organisations. Maurice's background was trades unionism and one year in the 1970s he was chairman of the Birmingham Trades Council, the joint trades unions body. He was a brave man, both hated and feared by the racists. His address and phone number were known to as few people as possible, and his extensive records were kept in several safe houses in the city. But the violent racist groups would have loved to silence him and on one occasion, at a demonstration in London, he was set upon by a group of violent racist thugs and severely knifed. Maurice, who died several years ago now, deserves to be remembered as a significant figure in the fight against racism in Britain.

John Plummer worked closely with the Black Community Workers organisation, led by Maurice Andrews, to establish Harambee (Swahili for working together). There were frequent cases of young black men who had been in trouble with the law and were rejected or alienated from their families. Under such circumstances more was needed than a bed and basic shelter. Harambee aimed to provide such support and reinforcement and the first house opened in Handsworth and was soon full. I sometimes used my VW caravette to take groups from Haramabee to visit their friends in the Brockhill Remand Centre at Redditch.

The widespread racism in society as a whole was present in concentrated form within the police, and AFFOR worked with young blacks in their relations with the local police. Needless to say, not all coppers were racially prejudiced, but far too many were. John Plummer was often, and I very occasionally, in court monitoring cases. One was that of Dave Butchere, a community youth worker supported by the Cadbury Trust. Dave was well over six feet tall and strongly built, just the sort of young black man whom some of the police saw as a dangerous enemy though he was in fact, as one friend put it, a gentle giant. They were out to get him and one day stopped him – for no reason that they could explain – and searched him and his car, where they found in his tool kit something that could have been used as a cosh. They arrested him and charged him with carrying an offensive weapon and he was tried by a judge and jury. There was a skilful prosecuting barrister and a very weak defending barrister. But Dave won the case for himself from the witness box, explaining how he used the cosh-like thing to tap something in the engine that was always going wrong. It was evident from the look on one of the juror's face that his car had the same problem. This, plus character evidence from Anthony Wilson of the Cadbury trust, won the day. The jury was unable to agree, and the police did not renew the prosecution.

In 1972 John Plummer was in the large lobby of the old Victoria Law Courts having observed a hearing at which two black men were bailed, having to report daily to the local police station. Some two minutes after those concerned had left the courtroom a group, consisting of a number of friends and relatives who had been listening to the hearing, were approached by four police officers. They addressed themselves to the two bailed men and pulled them away from the remainder of the group who became increasingly resentful but not violent. The pair were angry but did not resist. At this moment a large number of police officers with a police dog entered the lobby and started pushing the group towards the exit. The dog barked continually and jumped up against many of the black people as they were hustled out of the Court house. While this was happening a member of the police Drugs Squad remarked to John, 'This is what happens when the Thornhill Road [the Handsworth police station] heavies move in.' The action was completely out of order, and we sent in an official complaint. There followed a two-hour meeting of John Plummer and Richard White with a Superintendent and a Chief Inspector at which the latter failed to persuade them to withdraw the complaint. David Lane MP, the Home Office minister responsible for community relations in the Conservative government, visited Birmingham and I was one of those invited to meet with him. I handed him a letter, drafted by Richard White, about the importance of this case and asking the

Home Office to interest itself in it, and we were then invited to meet the Chief Constable.

Jn Plummer, Richard White & I had an interview at 10 a.m. with the Chief Constable, Sir Derek Capper, & the Deputy Chief Constable, Mr Knight [who later became the Birmingham CC][1] about our complaint arising out of the incident in the Law Court lobby on August 18th. After trying a different tack they agreed with our criticisms, & said that if they (either of them) had been the officer in charge they would have acted differently, and that judgment had been exercised wrongly. Also that a police dog should not have been used. The CC said that he would use the incident as an example in a training session which would include the officers concerned. There were however no grounds for disciplinary charges. They also said that they had learned something from this case; & that it was difficult to change police attitudes quickly; and that they would be ready to move a policeman from one area to another if he showed a persistently prejudiced attitude. We stressed that what got back to the officers involved in this case should be such as to make an impact & leave no doubt as to the CC's attitude. I asked him to send me a letter confirming what he and the Deputy CC had said. After leaving we felt on balance that our complaint had served a constructive purpose.

We did not feel that Capper or Knight themselves were tainted by racism, but we realised that the police force was a huge organisation with its own trades union and that racism was part of its prevailing culture. That this is still so nearly thirty years later was evident from the 1999 Macpherson report (chap. 46, para.1) on the police response to the Stephen Lawrence murder, describing the Metropolitan police force as institutionally racist.

But although our meeting with the Chief Constable seemed satisfactory the matter then took a different turn. When his letter came it went back on all the constructive points which he had made at the meeting. He said that 'having studied the investigating officer's report, I am bound to support the officers in their decision to arrest the two men on the 18 August', and 'I understand that the dog was not in fact used on this occasion', and made no reference whatever to his statements that the action of the police could have been more positively controlled on that morning; that he and the Deputy CC would have handled the situation differently; that he intended to increase the number of officers with responsibility for community relations in the future; that he was including this case in future training sessions, at which the officers concerned were likely to be present; and that if any individual officer showed racial prejudice he would be transferred to a less sensitive area. I wrote again (again drafted by Richard White) expressing disappointment and saying that the CC's letter, if known within the police force, would only have the effect of hardening the attitudes that had led to the incident. At this point we let it be rumoured that we were planning a Parliamentary question about the matter. I don't know whether we would in fact have been able to do this, but a Parliamentary question is the last thing that a Chief Constable wants. In due course another letter from the CC arrived in which he confirmed all the points that we had made. I then wrote again to the Minister, enclosing a copy of the CC's second letter, and hoping that he would support the Chief Constable in these positive measures. My suspicion however, which may or may not have been justified, was that the CC's first letter was made known within the local force and his second was not.

In 1973 a Handsworth Teach-In on Police Power and Community Relations was held with a packed audience in the New Trinity Hall. It was attended by the new Deputy CC, the Handsworth police community relations officer, and a large mainly black audience. I chaired the first part, when Mike Townsend (senior area officer for social services), Maurice Andrews (black community worker), Chris Wood (a senior probation officer), Gus John (author of *Race in the Inner City*, etc.) and Monica Savage spoke. The question and discussion period was spotty. In the second part, the new Deputy Chief Constable, Chief Inspector Wilson, John Plummer, John Lambert (author of *Crime, Police and Race Relations*) and Rudi Narayan (controversial Indian barrister) spoke. The Deputy CC was strongly heckled by black members of the audience and must have been left in no doubt that the police had a community relations problem. Stuart Hall of the Centre for Contemporary Cultural Studies in the University attended the event, strongly concerned about police racial prejudice, and was helpful to AFFOR on several occasions.

The same year John Plummer was arrested at a counter-demonstration against a British Movement rally, led by Colin Jordan, in Wolverhampton. John had been walking alongside the British Movement march, handing out anti-racist leaflets, when he was jumped on by several people and beaten up, all being arrested together. He was bailed to appear in court in Wolverhampton charged with conduct liable to cause a breach of the peace. 'Put strongly to John case for his being represented by a solicitor next Wednesday. More likely to be found not guilty. Verdict of guilty would give him an undeserved "record" & would frighten some AFFOR supporters.' Several of us went over to Wolverhampton with him, David Morris, who was a sympathetic solicitor and skilled magistrates' court advocate, Richard White and another law lecturer specializing in magistrates court cases, and the mysterious figure of 'the Professor' in the background – presumed by the police and court officials to be a professor of law! When we arrived the police added a second charge against John. At the hearing

> Direct conflict between police evidence & John's. John an excellent witness, and David Morris presented his case very well. After whispering together the three magistrates found him not guilty on both charges and (to the apparent disgust of the Clerk) required no contribution to expenses. Reassuring as regards Wolverhampton JPs, but alarming as regards police perjury.

In 1976, when Clare Short was director of AFFOR, I wrote a pamphlet, *The New Nazism of the National Front and National Party: A Warning to Christians*, designed to be commended by the local church leaders. Their failure to support it is a sad story. I included in the pamphlet details of the previous convictions for violent crimes of the British neo-Nazi leaders. They were literally neo-Nazis, members of the British National Socialist Movement in the 1950s, celebrating the anniversaries of Hitler's birthday, photographed wearing Nazi-style uniforms and giving the Nazi salute. They organised a para-military group, Spearhead, armed with coshes, and John Tyndall, chairman of the National Front, was sentenced as one of his four convictions to six-months' imprisonment for illegally possessing a firearm and ammunition. Martin Webster, the Front's Activities Organiser, had received a two-month sentence and Dennis Pirie of the National Party a three-month sentence. Their propaganda was full of hatred of Jews and black immigrants, blaming them for the country's problems of poverty and unemployment, thus provoking attacks on black people, 'Paki-bashing', attacks on synagogues and mosques, the creation of an atmosphere of prejudice and fear. Further, in a time of unemployment and economic recession they were having an alarming degree of success in turning working-class voters into racists: in 1976 the National Front polled 23% in the Leicester by-election and the National Party 38% in Blackburn. Many of us felt it imperative that the churches should not only issue general statements against racism, which they did, but that Christian people should very positively reject and condemn these specific movements.

My pamphlet was discussed and some changes made by the AFFOR committee, checked for accuracy by Maurice Ludmer from whom most of the information had originally come (and out of scholarly habit double checked by myself from the original newspaper reports in the city's reference library), plus an exchange of information with Martin Walker of the *Guardian*, checked from a legal point of view by Phillip Morrell; and Clare approached Cadbury for funds for publication. We sent copies to the Anglican bishop, the Catholic archbishop, and the then Methodist president of the Free Church Council inviting them to sign a joint Preface commending the pamphlet to the churches. The latter, Chris Hughes-Smith, was in favour of the three doing so. Basil Moss, provost of the Anglican cathedral, wrote to the bishop recommending him to sign and there were indications that he was sympathetic to the idea. The archbishop on the other hand was very doubtful. The bishop then received advice from the diocesan Registrar, or legal adviser, who strongly advised against signing. He referred to the Rehabilitation of Offenders Act, 1974, and said that if the bishop did sign he must 'insist on all personal references to individuals and their convictions being expunged'. It was not illegal to refer to spent convictions, but the question was whether the authors of the pamphlet and of the preface would be liable for defamation. Phillip Morrell in the law faculty had already assured us that these references were perfectly safe, and we also obtained counsel's opinion from a barrister, Alex Lyon, MP, whom Clare knew well and later married, who as a Home Office minister had steered the Act through Parliament and was thus obviously an expert on its contents and their implications. He wrote that

> the civil law was changed very slightly in relation to defamation. Section 8 applies the Act to defamation but section 8 (3) makes it

clear that all the former defences apply, save that if the defence of justification is raised it may be defeated by proving malice. The effect of these changes is that none of those named in your pamphlet could sue for defamation on the grounds that you had published spent convictions unless they could show that you had some personal interest in hurting them. Clearly that does not apply in your case. If it is correct therefore that they were convicted as you allege, the chances of an action for defamation are non-existent. Other comments in the document could clearly be defamatory but in my view are either true or fair comment. I do not think that anyone need worry about a civil action arising from this pamphlet.

We sent a copy of this to the bishop who however maintained his refusal to endorse the pamphlet but suggested two editions of it, one without the convictions, which the church leaders would support, and one in AFFOR's name and including the convictions. We rejected this compromise, feeling that the convictions were an integral part of the case against these neo Nazi organisations and feeling certain that the real problem for the bishop, and also for the archbishop, was not any legal issue but the fact that there were racists within the churches, mainly among the laity, and that for the leadership to take a public stand of this kind would be divisive within their own flocks, this taking priority over their concerns about the National Front and National Party.

To my surprise they were even joined in this by Lesslie Newbigin, who was then moderator-elect of the United Reformed Church and a very senior and influential Birmingham churchman. He had previously been a missionary in India, playing a major part in the union which created the Church of South India, and I had first met him in Madras when he was bishop there. When a minister at Belford I had been thrilled by his *South India Diary*. He now taught in the Selly Oak Colleges in Birmingham. I knew that he was theologically very conservative, but had thought that he was socially and politically liberal; he was certainly in no sense and no degree a racist. However he took a high view of the church and on this issue sided with the ecclesiastical establishment. He wrote to me to say that in his view the pamphlet would be counter-productive. On its title page there was a quotation from Lord Justice Salmon, 'This despicable band of neo-nazis masquerading under the name of the

National Front and the National Party, whose aim is to stir up race hatred', and Lesslie said that

> this immediately warns the reader that this is going to be an essay in character assassination, and therefore puts him on his guard ... I gather that the officers of the Birmingham Council of Churches and the British Council of Churches would be willing to sponsor the paper if these passages were cut out ... There is clear evidence of growing racism in the Conservative party, and a personal attack on the leadership of the NF/NP does nothing at all to expose this.

Some may consider this a defensible reason for not publicising the violent records of the National Front and National Party leaders. My own view remains that it was a deplorable misjudgement. Anthony Wilson at Cadbury, who strongly supported the document, advised us not to spend any more time on the local church leaders but to go ahead on our own with publication and this was the unanimous view of our committee. We now turned to Dr Colin Morris, a highly respected Methodist minister, known for his anti-racist views, who was that year's president of the Methodist Conference. He replied that in order to sign the Preface in his capacity as conference president he would have to get the agreement of the church's Division of Social Responsibility, which would take some time, but that he would be very happy to provide one immediately in his personal capacity. I had mentioned that if the NF/NP sued for defamation those who signed the Preface would only be responsible for the contents of that Preface; to which he replied, 'I really couldn't care a damn if the entire membership of the National Front sue me'. He enclosed his own Preface, which became part of the pamphlet, which was published in 1977.

Clare pointed out that if the NF/NP did sue, they would lose, and would only succeed in making the information about themselves more widely known. We hoped that they would sue but they evidently received the same legal advice as us and did not. I received a card from 'Wally Wogwolloper': 'Race traitors like you had better keep away from us wog killers in Lewisham Saturday', which I did not take very seriously (to attack me at this time would have been too obvious) though Hazel did; and in any case I would be in the United States on that day. But the racist movements liked to let their enemies know that they knew where they lived, hoping that this would frighten them off. *The New Nazism* pamphlet seemed to come at a strategic moment when many clergy and lay people were looking for some leadership and encouragement on this issue, and the pamphlet sold twelve thousand copies (including five hundred to the Bishop of Southwark, Mervyn Stockwood), and many sermons were based on it.

All this was part of a growing wave of opposition to the racist activities not only of the National Front and National Party but also of smaller groups and of such politicians as Enoch Powell. In February 1978 Colin Barker, organiser of the newly formed Anti-Nazi League invited me to become one of the League's Sponsors – prompted, he said, by a suggestion from my colleague Rodney Hilton, the Birmingham medieval historian, and by the New Nazism pamphlet – and I gladly accepted. The following year I wrote another AFFOR pamphlet, *Christianity and Race in Britain Today*, which was reviewed in some of the newspapers and also provoked some angry responses: 'To hell with a multi-racial society ... You are a traitor to us ...'

> Why should [the British people] allow you and your kind to give away their country to overcrowd still further their overcrowded country? ... When you and your allies, the left-wing rent-a-mobs, go on the rampage under the guise of promoting human rights, meaning black racism, they are really trying to destroy the good old-fashioned decencies and standards of the British, all in favour of creating a mongrel society called Communism.

I felt it better to reply rather than to ignore such letters when they came with a name and address: thus, for example,

> Thank you for writing about my recent pamphlet, *Christianity and Race in Britain Today*. I expect you will agree with me that, whether you welcome their presence or not, the black citizens of this country are mostly here to stay – more than 40% of them were, after all, born here and have no other homeland. That being so, I would invite you to consider whether your attitude of hostility and rejection is more likely to contribute to the creation of a successful future for the new pluralistic Britain, or to work against that end.

Laurence Brown had become bishop of Birmingham shortly after I came to the University, and apart from his refusal to support *The New*

Nazism pamphlet I had good relations with him. He invited me to take part in planning the New Initiative, a name which I suggested for the diocese's attempt at evangelical outreach, and I wrote two leaflets for it, one on racism and one on the minority religious communities. He also invited me to address a meeting of the clergy of the diocese on inter-faith matters, and when some of them haggled about whether we should call Muslims etc. God's children or children of God, one (I forget which) being regarded as a lesser and therefore more appropriate status, he told them not to be absurd. And in 1994 he spoke publicly against the Immigration Bill. He was a good and decent man, and on this matter of *The New Nazism* pamphlet I think he felt torn between a personal readiness to take a strong anti-racist stance and a fear of causing controversy within the church – which church leaders so often regard as something to be avoided at any cost. However, in retrospect, the pamphlet was spread at least as widely with Colin Morris' Preface than it would have been with the local church leaders. But this was the late 1970s and the practical attitude of the churches to racial prejudice and discrimination is now happily very different.

This is not however, unhappily, true today of the population as a whole. Within our society the same racist movement is still active, now under the name of the British National Party as its more respectable-seeming face, and the National Front as its frankly neo-Nazi side, with Combat 18 as its violent thugs. The BNP fastens upon the very real problems of deprived areas, the poverty, unemployment, lack of facilities, and directs public anger for all this against the Asians and Afro-Caribbeans, who in fact usually suffer from the same multiple deprivations even more than their white neighbours. *Searchlight* continues to monitor the racist movements and the Anti-Nazi League, a broad coalition of people in the trades unions, political parties, churches, and others, presents an organized opposition to them. Pete, living in greater Manchester and working (as an educational psychologist) in an area which includes Oldham, one of the places where the BNP received an alarmingly high vote in the 2001 Council elections, is an active member of the Anti-Nazi League. He is doing work (sometimes dangerous, because some of the NF members are violent people) in organising opposition to the racists and in supporting those who are working for a peaceful multi-racial, multi-faith society. He is in fact doing what we were doing in AFFOR a generation ago, though he is more in the directly activist role of a John Plummer than in my much easier role as chairman of AFFOR. I am extremely proud of him for his (Marxist rather than Christian) dedication to work based on the worth and potential of all, a dedication which shames that of most church people to their own professed faith. He also has, incidentally, a remarkable capacity for the sympathetic understanding of people facing problems, and considerable skill and experience as a trades union organiser and negotiator.

Returning to the Birmingham of a generation ago, bishop Brown was succeeded by Hugh Montefiore, whom I had known when he was dean of Caius where I was for one year a Bye-Fellow, and also later as fellow members of Caps and Mitres, an annual meeting in London of theologians and bishops. In Birmingham Hugh was at first slow on the inter-faith front, but strong on other social issues, but later an AFFOR fund-raising leaflet went out with a photo of him and a message of support under his signature. We have kept in touch ever since and often corresponded about our respective writings. I have long had a great respect for him and value his friendship. We have long conversations on the phone from time to time. We have each lost a wife, his lingering through a long and sad period of Altzheimer's disease, mine dying suddenly from a massive stroke – more about which in chapter 26. We discuss all sorts of current issues and ideas; and Hugh and I are among the very few Christian theologians who take parapsychology seriously and who also hold some form of reincarnation belief.

Each director of AFFOR had his or her own individual emphasis. When John Plummer left to take a law degree at the university, and then to work for the Joint Committee for the Welfare of Immigrants in London, he was succeeded by Geoff Wilkins, known as the man with frizzy hair and flip-flop shoes, a social worker with a First in Classics from Cambridge who did the *Times* crossword most days in fifteen minutes. Geoff worked specially with the Uganda Asians who arrived in the area having been expelled by Idi Amin. He was succeeded by Clare Short, then a community social worker, later MP for Ladywood, later member of Tony Blair's Labour cabinet as Secretary of State for International Development, and widely popular in the country because of her straightforward plain speaking. She is obviously much the most famous of the succession of AFFOR directors. Clare spent a lot of time on immigration issues, doing a great deal of much needed case work as well as lobbying. In another area she produced *Talking Blues*, a widely read and widely influential study of young West Indians' views of policing based on interviews in the Handsworth area. (More about Clare in chapter 26). Then David Jennings, Anglican priest active on behalf of minority communities, and later a busy and successful rector in Leicestershire, was an 'all rounder', developing the whole AFFOR programme and also taking a lead in CARAF (Christians against Racism and Fascism); and in the 1980s, after I had moved to California (remaining on the books only as president of AFFOR), there were Anil Bhalla, who has done so much for Asian elderlies, who had been neglected by the social services, and Marilyn Phillips-Bell, previously the youth opportunities worker, and briefly Betty Hanks, former head of the large, multi-ethnic Mount Pleasant comprehensive school.

By the mid-1980s AFFOR had become large, well-established, and in danger of becoming too respectable! Since then the organisation has been wound up, having done a great deal of positive work, in very sensitive areas, for the people of Birmingham.

NOTES

1. And whom I happened to meet again last year at a social gathering, when I found him to be a charming old gentleman who had had a very successful career in the police service and has now been made a life peer.

17

With Hindus in India

My first visit to India did not happen until I was forty-eight. Of the only other two British philosophers of religion then interested in the other world faiths, H. D. Lewis was older than me and Ninian Smart younger but already knew India well. My going happened by serendipitous chance. I was at a meal at some conference in London, sitting between Hywel Lewis of King's College and Jehangir Chubb, a Parsee philosopher and devotee of Sri Aurobindo (whom I had been reading recently) and we were discussing the Hindu concept of reincarnation. Hywel mentioned a conference he was looking forward to in Madras that winter and Chubb on the spot offered to get me invited also; and I accepted with alacrity. This was an 'International Seminar on World Philosophy' to be hosted by Madras University for ten days in December 1970, the British Council paying my fare. What follows comes mostly from my letters home. Remember that they express my own experience of visiting India thirty years ago and that since then the country has seen huge developments.

> We landed here at 4.30 a.m. Bombay time. Guess who was the first person I met – Dr Prem! [an Indian doctor who took part in some of the AFFOR events], who I last saw in Birmingham a week or two ago. Then I went as a guest of BOAC to a hotel for the five hours until my plane to Madras. When I woke at 7 a.m. it was obviously the beginning of a hot summer day – blue sky, bright sun, tall palm trees, multi-coloured birds singing, breakfast in the open air. Even in the early morning my 'thin' suit was obviously too heavy and has been getting heavier all the time.

In the taxi between airport and hotel I have already seen sights galore – little shanties, cattle wandering all over the road, beggars in rags. There is dust, confusion, dogs, hens, cattle, children and an enormous variety of kinds of people. Cars rush about murderously, sounding horns at full screech. People walk in front of them and emerge miraculously in one piece on the other side.

Later, in Patiala, my host's chauffeur was ill and he asked me if I would drive us both to a function, which I did. But it was a horrendous experience. There seems to be a telepathic connection between Indian drivers and the crowds through whom they drive at speed, such that the crowd parts just in time for the car to rush through. But I was 'out of the loop' of that telepathic system and could only make my way through by driving painfully slowly.

Arrived in Madras:

I was met at the airport by a British Council rep, who drove me to the hotel. There was a letter waiting for me from Lesslie Newbigin, bishop in Madras in the United Church of South India, and I shall be meeting him sometime whilst I am here. I am sitting out sunbathing on the balcony of my room at the hotel. The sun is very hot by English standards – in fact hotter than it ever is in England, so one does not do this for long at a time. The hotel is a great mixture of comfort and inconvenience. My room is large, and has a great fan in the ceiling, a balcony, a bathroom the fittings of which were probably imported from England in the 1920s. The lighting is dim, but on the whole everything works even though it has an air of being about to break down. This is a land of abundant cheap labour, so there are dozens of hotel servants, most of whom seem to have no specific duties but just hang about until wanted ...

Unfortunately all the Indian participants in the Seminar are in another hotel and only Europeans and Americans here, and we are given western food. The only meals we will all have together will be lunches at the university. Proceedings begin this evening with a very formal opening, and then continue at a great rate. There are sessions each morning from 9–12.30, followed by lunch and then another session from 2–4.30, and an evening event at 6 p.m. before returning for dinner. During the ten days I have to give a paper, and be a critic of three other papers, chair a session, and give a 6 p.m. public lecture. (I noticed after a day or two that most of the Indian participants were absent from the afternoon session having a siesta, and I then did the same, taking one of the innumerable three-wheeled taxis back to the hotel.) And the day after the Seminar the British Council has arranged a public meeting with a panel of speakers, one of whom is to be me.

This morning I went into the city to buy a bush shirt and a pair of thin trousers, and had a fascinating walk through crowded narrow streets with all sorts of metal workers and leather workers etc. in niches along the way. This is a medieval city with slices of modernity thrown in at random. One little shop was that of a bone-setter. There are ancient contrivances for weighing things, and vast metal pots, people dressed in all sorts of different things from practically nothing upwards.

A few days later:

I am writing this during an unintelligible paper at the Seminar, having just come in from a most fascinating morning of playing truant. I wanted to take a number of photos of down town Madras whilst it is all new and astonishing to me. We [an interpreter provided by the British Council and I] strolled about all morning in the markets expending a roll of thirty-six pictures – ordinary street scenes, bicycle rickshaws, etc. We visited the main Hindu temple, which is very magnificent, with a huge tower carved all over with gods and goddesses and mythological scenes, inner temples, and a big lake in which people bathed at certain festivals, lots of carving and gold paint and colour.

The landscape is always with figures, and the great majority of the people walking about are men – I should think fully 90%. The women live their lives at home and the man does everything outside the house, including the shopping. The standard wear is a short-sleeved shirt and a dhoti, the latter being simply a wide length of cloth which is worn in several different ways, as an ankle-length skirt, or folded in half as something more like a Scottish kilt, or full length but draped in folds, this being I gather the Bengali style. Probably 70% of men wear the dhoti and the rest western clothes. The women, including many European women, wear saris.

The International Seminar itself is not much good. The papers are not on a high level. They are read out, followed by two ten-minutes prepared comments. Most people exceed their time, so that there is practically none left for discussion. However all this is more than compensated for by being here and by meetings with people outside the official sessions.

A few days later:

I gave my public lecture yesterday evening on 'The Problem of Reincarnation, a Western Approach', and it seemed to meet with a good deal of interest and caused quite a stir! There was a torrent of questions and discussion after it (including a twenty minutes remark by the chairman!), and ever since lots of people have been buttonholing me about it.

I later got used to the Indian method of chairing a lecture. The chairperson gives his/her own independent thoughts, usually prepared in advance, after the main speech, on the same subject but not necessarily referring to the original paper. In the Madras case the chairman was the very distinguished philosopher T.M.P. Mahadevan, who expounded the orthodox advaitic view over against my European version. (On another occasion a few years later I was chaired in Delhi by the Chief Justice of the Supreme Court of India who after my own lecture gave a long but interesting lecture of his own about his particular form of Hinduism. At that time, under the Indira Gandhi government, his position was controversial and dangerous and there were armed guards behind the curtains on either side of the stage.)

One day we were all taken by bus to visit Mahabalipuram and Kanchipuram, where we had an audience with the Shankaracharia of Kanchi.

> He is an old man with a very beautiful face and intelligent, twinkling eyes. He came into the barn-like room and sat cross-legged on a table precariously held together with string, and we were each introduced to him, after which there was some discussion, someone translating throughout. I can well believe that he is a saint; but he did not have anything particularly interesting or illuminating to say to the assembled philosophers.

The meeting was, in Hindu terms, more in the nature of darshan, simply being in the presence of a holy person.

As the Seminar drew to an end:

> Everything is inefficient. Everything that pours, spills. Lights are never bright enough or in the right place. When you buy anything, even a postcard, there is elaborate paperwork. All travel and other arrangements have to be made several times over. In a garage I saw the logically baffling notice on a door: No Entry Even With Permission ... [However] I think my dominant impression of India so far, which I find that the others from abroad share, is the pervasive atmosphere of friendliness. Not only the Indian philosophers but everyone else as well is friendly

and make one feel at home. Walking about in the streets and among the crowds in the market one has no feeling that the people – nearly all of whom are desperately poor by western standards – are looking at one resentfully or enviously or in any but a friendly way. They are securely in their own way of life and religious culture, which one is welcome to share, but from within which Western existence is not a matter of envy. And in fact a much bigger proportion of faces look carefree than in the west.

From Madras I went south to Pondicherry.

I went to Pondy on the bus – 100 miles for 5 rupees – and came back in style in a chauffeured car from the Sri Aurobindo ashram. Pondicherry is Franco-Indian, as Madras is Anglo-Indian ... I stayed in an ashram guest house kept by a multi-lingual Hungarian in a very European style. We ate to the sound of Chopin or Bach played on LPs, and our host chatted in French, English and German ...

Professor Basu (who once taught Sanscrit at Durham) showed me round the Aurobindo ashram, and I met several times with two interesting retired philosophers there, Indra Sen and H. N. Bannerjee, the latter having been on the commission which investigated the famous Shanti Devi case of a child apparently remembering a recent previous life, these memories being confirmed by investigators. However when I pressed him he told me that although he had signed the report authenticating the child's memories he was not certain that this was indeed a case of reincarnation. There are also a number of European and American student types around who are partly on holiday (apparently by dropping out for six months) and partly seeking the 'wisdom of the East'.

I went on next to Bangalore, staying in the United Theological College of which Russell Chandran, whom I had met before in the States, was the principal, and had Christmas dinner in his house.

I am invited out quite a lot to meals with different members of the staff, who all live in houses within the college compound. About half are Indian and half British or American. The foreign staff whom I have met (all sent out by missionary societies) are, apparently at least, mostly academically second-rate, though one or two of the Indians seem rather good. The head of the graduate programme is a Dr John, with a Heidelberg doctorate in OT, who seems academically strong; and a lecturer in theology called

Duraisingh has interesting ideas and is thinking hard about the distinctively Indian development of Christian theology. [Both have subsequently become deservedly well known.] And of course Russell Chandran is an intellectual as well as ecclesiastical leader.

I also visited the very interesting neighbouring Christian Institute for the Study of Religion and Society, whose director was then M.M. Thomas, and later Stanley Samartha – of the Rubicon conference at Claremont.

From Bangalore, it now being January 1971, I flew to Calcutta and from there by train to Santiniketan (Abode of Peace), the small liberal arts university, Visva-Bharati, about a hundred miles further north, founded in 1921 by Rabindranath Tagore.

Santiniketan is a somewhat idyllic place – a loosely spread-out university in the country, with trees and flowers all around. Ox carts, students on bikes, and cycle-rickshaws mingle in the lanes. The guest house is a one-storey circular building, with six double guest rooms opening onto a wide circular verandah bordered with large flowers. The beds have mosquito nets and each room has a ceiling fan and adequate lighting. Each room has a bathroom – no hot water but a shower, basin and toilet. Hot water is brought in a bucket on request. The water here, although boiled, does something to one at first, resulting in a day or two of tummy trouble. The main part of the day is like a very good English summer. At night two blankets.

The colour of Indians ranges from black to off-white, and this range seems to be connected with caste – the lighter the skin the higher the caste, and the darker the skin the lower. The other day I asked the man who cleans my room to clean the bathroom as well, and when he had not done so I reminded him. I was told that they had to send for a cleaner, who later arrived and did the job. An Indian professor staying in the guest house explained that this had been a problem of caste. The man who cleaned the room was not of the right caste to clean a bathroom.

When I went I tipped the lower caste man extra.

I was a visiting professor in the Centre for Advanced Study of Philosophy, whose new concrete building was still unbuilt at one end and already falling down at the other. The director was Santosh Sengupta, who had already visited us in Birmingham.

Yesterday I spent a pleasant evening at the Sengupta house, where I went to give a present to the youngest Master Sengupta, whose

9th birthday it was. Santosh was lolling comfortably in something like a Roman toga, and there were delicious Bengali sweets and tea. I think that Mrs S. is on the way with another baby, though it is difficult to be sure through the folds of a sari.

The teaching of philosophy of religion here is in a most deplorable state. One of the set books, the one being taught this term, is Hocking's *The Meaning of God in Human Experience*, published in 1912, and hopelessly out of date. Further, there are only two copies of it. Consequently the students themselves do not read it! The lecturer is supposed to relay its contents to them. Nothing could be more absurd.

Indeed the whole teaching ethos was, in western terms, medieval. The students were not being taught to think for themselves but to believe whatever their teachers said and then reproduce it in the exams. I was supposed to meet my class three times a week for four weeks. But in fact almost every week one or two sessions were cancelled, with the University closed either for a religious festival or because someone, such as a relative of one of the governors, had died.

I went one day to the bank, with an armed guard outside carrying a very ancient rifle, to cash a traveller's cheque, handing in my passport as identification. It gave my occupation as Minister of Religion. Presently the manager came out, bowed deeply, and said what an honour it was to welcome a member of the British government to his bank! If I had been quick witted enough I might have said something like, 'Shush, incognito, you know.' But in fact I merely explained prosaically that any clergyman was called a minister of religion in official documents, thus depriving the manager of a little reflected glory.

During my time at Santiniketan I had many useful discussions with individual philosophers. My interest throughout the India trip was to learn more about Hinduism (and later Sikhism), both philosophical and popular. As is well known, the 'ism' which makes Indian religion sound like a monolithic unity is a modern western export. The reality is a vast, infinitely varied range and mixture of religious traditions and movements which are generally mutually entirely tolerant. There are no quarrels between devotees of different gods and goddesses about which is the true deity, because they all are, and are all manifestations of the mysterious ultimate reality of Brahman. The outlook is thus quite different from that of the 'Western' monotheisms.

During my term at Santiniketan I went by train to Magadh university in Bihar to give a lecture and visit Bodh Gaya.

My host, Prof. Masih (who is an Edinburgh graduate) took me there this morning. This is Buddhism's most sacred place, with the Bodhi tree under which the Buddha received his enlightenment. There is a vast seventh century Buddhist temple with innumerable carvings, and next to it a modern Tibetan monastery and temple, very brightly painted in red and gold, with many figures of the Buddha – the Tibetan Buddha having a sardonic smile on his face. Dozens of rolls of books on shelves, prayer mats on the floor. Also a room with a huge prayer wheel, a cylindrical metal drum about twenty five feet high, and filled with written prayers; and pilgrims take turns to move it round on its axis by handles near the bottom. We also visited a brightly painted Thai Buddhist temple with a big golden Buddha; and the next day the remains of the ancient Buddhist university at Nalanda, which flourished in the seventh century with some ten thousand students. The return journey was probably a typical Indian rail journey. I got up at 5.30 in the morning to catch the train, and then had a two hour wait for it to be late. It was even later at the other end, so that I missed my connection, and arrived back here at 6 p.m.

Hazel was able to join me at Santiniketan for a couple of weeks, beginning with two days in Calcutta where we stayed at the Ramakrishna Mission Institute of Culture at Golpark, where I also gave a lecture. I noted that, 'The contrast between the poverty and simplicity of Ramakrishna himself, two generations ago, and the style of the Swami in charge today is like that between Jesus and the Pope.' This was the time of the Naxalite movement, when Calcutta was in a state of unrest and some parts blocked off because of popular demonstrations. The Indian communists, who were powerful in Bengal in the north and Kerala in the south, had split into the Communist Party of India and the Communist Party of India (Marxist), and a group of the latter had staged an armed insurrection in a village in Bengal, Naxalbari. The Naxalites were spreading and causing violence in many places, and on the increase at the time when Hazel arrived. At Santiniketan two buildings were burned down, the vice-chancellor went round with an armed bodyguard, the university registrar was stabbed to death, some trucks were burned, and for a while there was a tent full of soldiers camped outside the guest house.

According to the *Calcutta Statesman*, 'The pattern of attack is the same as in Calcutta and elsewhere. Groups of young men storm colleges, set fire to laboratories, damage property and escape almost in no time.' The paper adds that, 'A section of teachers and employees spoke bitterly of Santiniketan as having grown over the years into a pocket of affluence in the midst of an economically depressed area, which according to them is apt to create resentment among local people.' This was probably a correct analysis. Santiniketan had long since ceased to be the simple ashram-like place of Tagore and was now living off the great man's memory. The philosophers however took the disturbances 'philosophically' and carried on as normal.

We went in a bicycle rickshaw (or pram, as Hazel called it) to the nearby small town of Bolepur to buy presents – she had brought an extra suitcase in which to take them home. Whilst she was at Santiniketan the University held its annual convocation, at which the chancellor, Mrs Indira Gandhi the prime minister, herself a Santiniketan graduate, came to speak arriving by helicopter accompanied by two other armed helicopters. The convocation was out of doors in a mango grove but amidst strong security. I was struck by the fact that the University officials, who had previously been wearing western clothes in which they looked shabby and undistinguished, looked magnificent in the Bengali garb which they wore for the ceremony.

One day we were invited to the puja (worship) of the Goddess of Learning, Saraswati. This was in the house of one of the philosophy professors who has a puja room. We all sat on the floor before an image, made of painted wood, of the goddess symbolising learning, verses from the Vedas were chanted, and then we all threw our flowers to the goddess. Then to another room for a meal, served on disposable plates made of leaves tacked together, everyone sitting on the floor.

When Hazel left to go back to England and I to go on to Benares,

there were various mild alarms and excursions on the way to the airport for her plane to Bombay. The British Council met us at Howrah station in Calcutta and took us out to the Dum Dum airport. The driver said that a car had recently had a bomb thrown at it on this road and he had orders to turn back if he saw any sign of trouble. However there was none, and we arrived at the airport safely. Then we saw a notice saying that Flight 206, Hazel's flight to Bombay, was to be five hours late, which would have left very little time for her connection to London. However we next discovered that this notice referred to the previous day and had just been left up, and she was able to depart more or less on time. Then I discovered that my own flight to Benares had been cancelled and I re-booked for a flight at 6 a.m. the next day, and Indian Airlines put me up in a hotel appropriately called the Grand. I got up at 4 a.m. to be at the Indian Airline city office at 4.40, only to be told that the flight was postponed to 11 a.m. In the end it did in fact take off shortly before 11.30.

Benares, as it was then, but now restored to its original name of Varanasi, is the holiest city of Hinduism, and I stayed on the campus of the Benares Hindu University.

On arriving there was a little battle over accommodation. The guest house where I was for the first night is very nice, with the luxury of hot water on tap. But they told me that after one night I was to move into an 'apartment' that was being got ready for me, because there was a rule that no one can stay in the guest house for more than a day or two. I saw the 'apartment', consisting of two absolutely filthy basement rooms, unused for many months or years, and likely to be just as dirty and dark when they had cleaned it. The guest house is half empty. I announced to an alarmed man from the Registrar's office that I would stay as long as the University saw fit to accommodate me in the guest house and would then go on to Delhi. The next morning Dr Deveraja, head of the Centre of Advanced Study, saw the Registrar who said that I could not stay in the guest house, whereupon he went to see the vice-chancellor who said that of course I must stay in the guest house ...

and so I stayed for a very interesting couple of weeks.

The BHU campus is very fine, a semi-circle of about a mile in diameter, centering on a magnificent temple, and with half circle roads – faculty houses on the outer road, student hostels and other buildings on the middle one, and other big buildings on the inner half circle. The whole thing is spaciously laid out, and the buildings, all in a style which I associate with India during the British period, are in good order and good state of painting. The campus was planned and built as a whole about 1918, the original college on the site having been founded by Annie Besant, the Theosophist leader, who worked hard for Indian independence.

There are shops and little open air markets, a hospital attached to the Faculty of Medicine, and vast playing fields between the rings of buildings.

I have been on a conducted tour of the city, beginning with a trip on the river at 6.30 a.m. We were rowed past the centre of the city where the river is lined by huge maharajas' palaces, now hotels for pilgrims. Many people were bathing in the Ganges, the most sacred river in India. They begin about four in the morning and there are people bathing there all day, to the sound of music and chanting. We also passed a burning ghat where the dead are burned on piles of wood, each body taking about four hours to be consumed, with the ashes then scattered on the water. In the city I have seen bodies being carried on stretchers, covered with flowers, towards the river. Then we visited some of the principal temples, including the Golden Temple, with roof of beaten gold, and the monkey temple, with twenty or thirty monkeys loose in it from the forest that was previously there. This is a Durga temple, painted dark red because animal sacrifices are made there. The city itself has crowded narrow streets, but is pleasant to walk about in, without the fears and tensions of Calcutta. Transport is mainly by cycle rickshaw, though there are also pony traps. For heavy transport there are big leathery swaying camels – a very graceful animal. There are also a great many book shops, selling of course mainly Hindi books.

Someone at the University asked me when I was going to meet the party. This puzzled me until I realised that 'the party' was the correct way of pronouncing Tripathi, one of the senior BHU philosophers. Dr Tripathi, or as I think of him The Party, is a very nice chap, a devout Hindu who gets up at four every morning to bathe in the Ganges, then spends an hour or so in prayer and meditation before breakfast. Another was Dr Sharma. The Sharmas, with whom I had tea the other day, keep a buffalo. Apparently unless one keeps one's own cow or buffalo, milk is hard to get and is invariably sold diluted with water. He told me that he has two daughters, the oldest fourteen, and that in a few years he will have to arrange marriages for them, within his own caste and sub-caste, and will have to pay the bridegroom's father about Rs 20,000 in each case. He also has two sons, and will recoup when they are married! He said that so far from dying out, the institution of arranged marriages with substantial dowries is as strong as ever.

One evening Sharma and The Party took me for a row on the river to see the scene by moonlight. It was really most beautiful, with the pinnacles, towers and minarets of the old palaces catching the moonlight. The music and chanting was still going on. And to this background we discussed Brahman and karma and the jivatman! Then we landed at the biggest of the ghats, the Dasashwamadh Ghat, and walked into the town for coffee and then betal leaves – these are wrapped with various mouth staining pastes and chewed. In the town, which was a mass of flaring lights and moving crowds, we saw a wedding procession, and an elephant lumbering along with passengers on his back. In one narrow street everyone had to jump out of the way as a bull came charging through, chasing two cows!

This morning I did some work for the University by talking to a comparative religion class about Christianity and conferring with two PhD students about their theses. Then this afternoon sitting on the lawn (there are genuine lawns here) talking about Hinduism with The Party. In the evening The Party and I went to dinner at the Sharmas. Mrs S., who does not speak English, hardly appeared. We had a magnificent meal of fourteen different dishes, and a lot of uncritical religious stories (about people remembering their former lives etc) from The Party.

I learned a lot in Benares, but moved on after two weeks to Delhi, staying at the Cambridge Brotherhood, an Anglican monastic community where the brothers do all sorts of different things and where I had some interesting conversations, and caught a glimpse of the reclusive Hindu–Christian Swami Abhishiktananda who was briefly staying there. I gave some lectures and papers at Delhi University and was much more impressed by the philosophers there than at Madras, Santiniketan or BHU. Some of the younger philosophers, who had done their post-graduate work at Oxford, were fully of a calibre to hold their own there. One, whom I was to get to know well later, was Ramchandra Gandhi, a grandson of the Mahatma. I also made the standard visit to Agra and shall never forget my first sight of the Taj Mahal. 'This more than lives up to its reputation. When one first sees it, it almost takes your breath away. It is built of shining white marble, and is so perfectly proportioned that although it is immense it seems quite small and delicate, so controlled and effortless, virtually perfect.'

I must pass more quickly over later visits to India. One was in 1975–6 to give the Teape lectures in Delhi, Calcutta and Madras. In Delhi this time I got to know better Ramu (Ramchandra) Gandhi, who lectured in St Stephen's College, a brilliant young philosopher with doctorates from both Delhi and Oxford, and with something of the spirit of his grandfather in him. I kept in touch with him for many years, both in India and in the United States. When I first knew him he was embarrassed to be known as one of the Mahatma's grandsons, but later became fully reconciled to his grandfather's memory and was proud of his achievements. Ramu later became a devotee of Sri Ramana Maharshi, the Bengali saint who died in 1950, whose message Ramu encapsulated in the title of his book *I am Thou* (1984).

On that same trip Hazel and Eleanor and I went on a tour of Rajastan and spent Christmas with a former Birmingham doctoral student, Sam Joshua, who wrote his PhD thesis comparing the systems of Shankara and Paul Tillich. He was then the Church of North India priest at Ajmeer and his wife a practicing doctor. On Christmas day the church was full with vast crowds outside unable to get in. We also spent another Christmas with them later, in 1990, in Bombay where he was now bishop. If all Indian Christian leaders were as faithful and dedicated as Samuel Joshua, the church would be fortunate indeed.

Another visit was in 1984, with Hazel, when our planned trip was cut short in Delhi by turmoil caused by the assassination of Indira Gandhi. As a result of this I had to miss a meeting that had been arranged with Sai Baba, the 'living God' near Bangalore. Because the two assassins had been Sikhs in her bodyguard the Sikhs in Delhi and throughout the country were being attacked by Hindu extremists. One result, for tourists, was that since most of the taxi-drivers are Sikhs there were very few taxis in operation. But Sikh shops were being burned down and Sikhs in general unjustly vilified. Was it an example of what Jung calls synchronicity that when we got home the ceremonial Sikh sword (given to me by one of the Birmingham gurudwaras) on the wall above my study door had fallen to the floor, the only time this has happened?

Westerners who spend more than tourist time in India either love it or hate it. I love it. Despite the appalling poverty, despite all the dirt and the inefficiency – I am referring back to the 1970s – there is an indefinable something that makes the westerner, who in many ways is so fortunate, feel very respectful, even humble, in face of the patience and hospitality and friendliness that one finds there.

18

With Sikhs in the Punjab

From Delhi, after a short visit to Chandigarh University which had another relatively strong philosophy department, I moved to my last visiting professorship, at Punjabi University at Patiala in the Punjab where I hoped to learn something about Sikhism. I was attached to the Guru Gobind Singh Department of Religious Studies. Its building has five two-storied wings devoted to Sikhism, Hinduism, Buddhism, Islam and Christianity, each including a small temple, mosque, chapel or gurudwara. The head of the department, Dr Harbans Singh, was a courtly gentleman who welcomed me heartily and was a perfect host throughout. He had spent a year or so at Cantwell Smith's Center for the Study of World Religions at Harvard where he had written his life of Guru Nanak, the founder of the Sikh tradition, using western canons of historical research so far as he dared.[1] He was now editing a vast *Encyclopedia of Sikhism* on the same principle. Probably the best scholar at the Centre, however, was Lalman Joshi, reader in Buddhist studies. I had a room in the Hindu wing, where there happened to be one spare, and I lived in the large and comfortable University guest house with a balcony in the front for the morning sun and another at the back for the afternoon sun. The Christian lecturer, Christanand Pillai, a Catholic priest, took me on the back of his motor bike into Patiala a number of times including once, dressed in old clothes, to join in the Hindu Holi festival where amidst much jollity and laughter we got, like everyone else, sprayed with coloured water and covered with brightly coloured powder.

My impression of the Punjab was that it was

in some ways like one's image of the American west in the late nineteenth century – energetic, building going on everywhere, and rapidly becoming prosperous. There is also a frontier air in that one sees a sprinkling of men carrying old-fashioned rifles and quite a lot from the villages carrying a full-length sword in scabbard (in addition to the Sikh's dagger) ... The Punjab is prosperous and progressive and the Punjabis energetic and active. People have enough surplus energy to smile and laugh and play the fool – just now I saw two students on a bike, one standing on the other's shoulders and declaiming in Punjabi to an imaginary audience.

I went last night (Sunday) to a very informal mass in the sitting room of Christanand Pillai attended by one or two Punjabi RCs, a Muslim and his wife, a Hindu and his wife, and a Protestant – me. Then Christanand and I went on to dinner with a Punjabi Sikh sociologist and his French wife. He has a Yale PhD and has also studied at the Sorbonne. He was very scornful of the Guru Gobind Singh Dept., which he described as pure window dressing. It has a magnificent building but a very poor library incapable of sustaining serious research. Everything is Sikhism oriented – the Muslim researching on the Muslim background of Sikhism, the Christian on the relation between Christian and Sikh theism, the Buddhist translating Buddhist texts into Punjabi. And they engage in no organised discussion, although they are all personally on friendly terms. The director's (Harbans Singh) field is not religious studies at all, but English literature. So far as I can check, all this is true ... Cashing a traveller's cheque in the local bank this morning I was sitting in the manager's office along with another customer, who was addressed as 'Your Excellency', when a tremendous three-party discussion started about belief in God in an age of science, with bank clerks occasionally coming in to listen or join in.

On Saturday I went with Sardar Harbans Singh (Sardar being a mark of respect, and when people meet him they very often bow down and touch his foot) to the sports day of a public, i.e. private, school of which he is a governor. We sat in state under a great awning with the nobs, including His Highness Maharajadhiraj Yadavindra Singh of Patiala, who is a fine looking six-foot-three Sikh, topped by a magnificent turban, enormously wealthy and owning much land, living in a palace, and going about in a cadillac. The Maharajas of Patiala used to be leading rulers of the Punjab, and the present one's father, I was told, had some three hundred 'wives' and thousands of children. The Maharaja, who was friendly and conversational, gave away prizes, and others were given by Mrs Pandit, sister of Nehru and aunt of the Prime Minister, Indira Gandhi. Mrs Pandit has been a cabinet minister, High Commissioner in London, Ambassador to Moscow and to the UN, and has been President of the United Nations. She is pro the Maharajas, whereas her niece, who has just won a landslide victory in the general election, intends (rightly I would think) to abolish their 'privy purse'. I later visited the Maharaja's palace and noticed signed photographs of Hitler and Mussolini: the present Maharaja's father had been selected by Hitler to be king of India after Germany had won the war and taken over the British empire. A Raja, who is one of the Maharaja's brothers, showed me the palace's historical collection – masses of old manuscripts and historical records, thousands of medals and coins with diamonds and sapphires and other precious stones, lots of maps and manuscript state documents and treaties and letters, and other precious things such as Guru Gobind Singh's sword. The collection is permanently guarded by two armed soldiers.

Before leaving the Punjab I went on a three-day trip across it with Harbans Singh, visiting the Golden Temple at Amritsar and spending two days in the home of the district administrator at nearby Gurdaspur.

> Everything was very leisurely, and very lacking in privacy ... At night the head of the house slept in an inner room, opening into another room, where Harbans Singh and I slept, opening onto a verandah where the women of the house slept, opening onto a courtyard where the servants slept, and the son, who is a student who has rebelled against the Sikh hair and turban etc. and is in disgrace with the elders. There was tea at about 6.45 a.m. and then a couple of hours in which people wandered about in their pyjamas and sat on one another's beds talking. Our host Iqbal Singh even met official visitors on the porch in his pyjamas. Breakfast was about 9 a.m. To complete the communal, non-private character of life, there is a real family four-seater loo in a shed at the bottom of the garden.

I suspect that I am a good listener, and I recall an example of this in the Gurdaspur household. The teenage daughter of the family sought me out and talked to me excitedly for at least half an hour in Punjabi, assuming that I spoke the language. I did not understand a word, but she was obviously unloading her teenage grievances and I simply nodded occasionally and made sympathetic noises. She seemed to feel better when she had finished, and probably felt even better still when she realised that I had not understood any of it! (Another example occurred when I spent a month at the luxurious Rockefeller study center at Bellagio on Lake Como. A fellow guest was a French lady philosopher who several times sat next to me at dinner and talked about her philosophy in French that was much too fast for me to catch more than the very general drift of what she was saying. But I listened attentively, with an occasion 'vraiment' or 'oui', without her ever realising how inadequate my French was.) Continuing my diary,

> When we drove back to Patiala we stopped at Hoshiapur to visit a famous astrologer's place where there is a book, supposed to be thousands of years old, in which people's future is written. My name was produced, supposedly written in ancient Sanscrit, on old brown parchment paper. But I had given my name on arrival and the man had gone away for fifteen minutes to fetch the page, during which I have no doubt that he added my name with a suitable brown ink. It said that on this particular day a foreigner called John Hick would come, but would have to come again another time to receive his horoscope.

Harbans Singh was profoundly shocked when afterwards I said that in my opinion the astrologer was a fraud. The University's vice-chancellor, when I saw him to say goodbye, said that obviously I would be coming to Patiala again and would be welcome.

It was at Patiala that I met Kushdeva Singh, one of the few genuine saints or mahatmas whom I have been lucky enough to know.[2] By this I do not mean a perfect human being, for there is no such thing, but one who is manifestly much more advanced than the great majority of us in the transformation from natural self-centeredness to a new orientation centred in the Transcendent, the Divine, the Ultimate, a transformation expressed in unrestricted love and compassion for all their fellow humans – or in some cases for all life. Kushdeva Singh was a doctor and TB specialist who was responsible for the existence in Patiala of a big TB hospital; an orphanage; an ashram with a school for the destitute; a leper hospital; a refuge for women thrown out of their families; a place for indigent incurables to die in relative comfort instead of lying in the gutter; and nursery schools at four places in the old city. He took me round these one day, driving at breakneck speed in his ancient car. At the home for the dying he introduced me to the woman in charge, 'This is my sister Anita', then to the orphanage where he introduced his sister Sushila, and the sanitorium where he introduced his brother Darshan. At first I wondered if his whole family was involved, but since I was introduced as his brother John I realised that for Kushdeva we were all one family, the human family. He had met Gandhi when a young medical student, had been indelibly impressed by him, and had later been one of the vast multitude who travelled to Delhi from all over India to attend Gandhi's funeral in 1948. The great lesson that he had learned from Gandhi was that 'a mere man with high aspirations and ceaseless effort can grow into a formidable personality, and with his utter fearlessness and devotion to the cause of humanity can achieve the summit of human endeavour'.[3]

Kushdeva had the same pluralistic understanding of religion as Gandhi. He said, 'The Hindu religion is as good as the Sikh religion, which is as good as Islam – if people actually practice them.' And as we passed a temple, 'We have so many temples because people prefer to talk about their religion than practice it. Who needs to be told that we ought to be truthful and help one another?' He gave me a copy of a book of his mystical poetry, and later of other writings as we corresponded over the years until his death in 1988. When I was with him in Patiala he did not speak about himself and the remarkable things he had done in the past or the fact that the Indian government had awarded him the Order of Merit (Civil) and the title of Padam Shri. But later he wrote about his experiences (which were 'as fresh in my mind as if they occurred only yesterday'[4]) at the time of Partition in 1947 when about a million people died violently as Punjabi Hindus and Sikhs tried to cross from what was now Pakistan into India whilst Muslims in the Indian Punjab tried to cross to Pakistan. In 1947 Kushdeva was medical superintendent of the Hardinge TB sanitorium at Dharampore in the Simla hills. The people of Dharampore were mainly Hindus and Muslims, with a few Sikhs, and 'there was always quietness and peace in the atmosphere.

IF YOU WISH TO BE PLACED ON OUR MAILING LIST, PLEASE RETURN THIS CARD

NAME:

ADDRESS:

ZIP/POSTAL CODE: CCUNTRY (IF OUTSIDE UK):

EMAIL:

O N E W O R L D
O X F O R D

To ensure we send you the correct information, please could you answer the following questions:

In which book/catalogue did you find this card?

If in a book, where did you purchase it?

Which of these best describes your interest in our books? Please tick as appropriate:

You use them for personal use or as gifts

You work in book retail

You are a student and our book(s) are recommended

Other reason?

You are an academic
if so, do you have responsibility for selecting books for course adoption? Yes/No
If yes, for what course?

PLEASE INDICATE ANY AREAS OF PARTICULAR INTEREST

☐ Comparative Religion

World Religions:

☐ Hinduism ☐ Buddhism ☐ Baha'i Faith

☐ Judaism ☐ Christianity ☐ Other (specify)

☐ Islam ☐ Sufism

☐ Mysticism ☐ Inspirational

☐ Middle East

☐ Politics

☐ History

☐ Philosophy

☐ Popular Science

☐ Psychology and/or Self-help

☐ Other (please specify)

For further information, please e-mail us at info@oneworld-publications.com or visit our website at http://www.oneworld-publications.com

NE PAS AFFRANCHIR

NO STAMP REQUIRED

By air mail
Par avion

IBRS/CCRI NUMBER:
PHQ/D/1154/OX

REPONSE PAYEE
GRANDE-BRETAGNE

Oneworld Publications
185 Banbury Road
OXFORD
GREAT BRITAIN
OX2 7BR

Complete communal harmony prevailed among the people.'[5] But shortly after partition Hindus and Sikhs from what was now Pakistan began to pour into the Indian Punjab and refugee camps were set up. Kushdeva Singh was a leader in organising food, clothing and shelter for camps at nearby Ambala and then in Dharampore itself. Soon stories began to circulate of the horrendous murder of Hindus fleeing from Pakistan and the growing hatred that this evoked was turned against the local Muslims. A shopkeeper began to manufacture and sell daggers, which were eagerly bought for three or four rupees by young men of both the Hindu and Muslim communities, and guns were sold to the wealthy for seven hundred to a thousand rupees by British officers leaving India. Soon a Muslim was murdered by a Sikh or a Hindu, and the communal tension became acute, with muttered threats to murder all the Dharampore Muslims. They now knew that they must leave their homes, jobs and possessions and try to make their way to Pakistan, even though Muslims travelling west were being slaughtered on the same scale and with the same ferocity as Hindus travelling east.

Kushdeva Singh was probably the only Sikh in the region to be trusted by the Muslim community and they sought his help. He was a tall, commanding figure, holding the rank of major from his wartime service in the Indian army medical corps and able by his personal authority to get things done. He arranged trucks to take the Muslim families to a transit camp at Subathu.

> Next day two trucks arrived at about ten o'clock in the morning. The Muslims were getting ready to leave. It appeared as if all would go well. But it was not to be. I got disturbing information that some of the [Hindu] refugees and miscreants had blocked the road from Dharampore to Subathu at four different places with tree trunks and coaltar drums. Some refugees were also seen moving about near these blockades. I was further informed that the truck drivers had been bribed.[6]

So he changed the evacuation plan without telling anyone, even the Muslims themselves. When they were almost ready to leave he sent the two truck drivers to his hospital on some pretence, produced two new drivers and told them to drive immediately to Dagshai, which was in a different direction and where there was a cantonment in which the Muslims would be protected until they could move on further. The ruse succeeded, although the infuriated mob promptly looted all the now empty Muslim houses.

Kushdeva next went to nearby Kasuli where the Muslim community had decided to leave as soon as possible. They wanted to take their possessions with them but he advised them not to: this would almost certainly invite an attack on the journey. He also advised them not to use the road but to go on foot by a bridle-path through the hills. They agreed to do so, sending their possessions separately by truck. The trucks were ambushed and everything stolen but the refugees reached their destination safely. Kushdeva also personally escorted some Muslim women to Delhi and worked successfully in many ways to enable the local Muslim community to escape safely to Pakistan, in spite of constant danger to himself from people maddened by hatred.

Two years later he was returning by air from Oslo, where he had been doing postgraduate work on TB, and decided to stop at Karachi on the way. Memories of the carnage were still vivid and emotions were still running high. It was therefore astonishing that a turbaned and bearded Sikh should turn up at Karachi. He was asked on arrival if he had come on some mission. Yes, he had come on a goodwill mission. Did he then represent some society? Yes, he was a member of the largest society on earth – the society of mankind. He had come to Pakistan on his way back to India because he did not accept that the relationship between the two countries should continue to be one of enmity. At the airport he was recognised by some of the Muslim policemen who had known him in Dharampore and whose families he had rescued. Word of his presence spread rapidly among those he had helped to escape, their friends and relations, and he was greeted with delight and feasted by a growing number of his former neighbours. The superintendent of police, Abdul Waheed Khan, was among them and when Kushdeva's plane was ready next morning

> I embraced Waheed and took leave of him and proceeded towards the plane. The constables accompanied me right up to the plane, and, when I was about to enter the aircraft, all of them stood in line and presented a salute. I acknowledged with folded hands and tears dripping from my eyes.[7]

He was inevitably involved in the big political issue in the Punjab, the demand of the Sikh nationalist party for an independent Punjab,

Khalistan, the Sikh state. Kushdeva was opposed to this. He argued that a Sikh homeland

> would have been a landlocked state of five or six districts, sandwiched between India and Pakistan, and our status in India would have been that of foreigners. The only persons who would have benefited from it would have been a few power-hungry politicians for whom the glow of freedom meant ministerial chair.[8]

Because of his public opposition to the Khalistan movement a young man once came to visit him, intending to assassinate him. But after talking with Kushdeva Singh for some time he was so impressed that he confessed his purpose, which he now saw to be wrong, and departed leaving his knife behind.

Kushdeva was a Sikh in the original mould of Guru Nanak (1469-1539), the founder of the Sikh tradition, who was a profoundly ecumenical spirit. Nanak composed what became part of the Sikh morning prayers:

> There is but one God. He is all that is.
> He is the Creator of all things and He is all-pervasive.
> He is without fear and without enmity.
> He is timeless, unborn and self-existent.
> He is the Enlightener
> And can be realized by grace of Himself alone
> He was on the beginning; He was in all ages.
> The True One is, was, O Nanak, and shall for ever be.

This gives something of the flavour of the Sikhism expressed in Kushdeva Singh's own mystical poetry:

> People go to their temples
> To greet Me;
> How simple and ignorant are My children
> Who think that I live in isolation.
>
> Why don't they come and greet Me
> In the procession of life, where I always live,
> In the farms, the factories, and the markets,
> Where I encourage those
> Who earn their living by the sweat of their brow?
>
> Why don't they come and greet Me
> In the cottages of the poor

And find me blessing the poor and the needy,
And wiping the tears of widows and orphans?

Why don't they come and greet Me
Among those who are trampled upon
By those proud of wealth and power,
And see Me beholding their suffering and pouring out
    compassion?
And why don't they come and greet Me
Among women sunk in sin and shame
Where I sit by them to bless and uplift?

I am sure
They can never miss Me
If they try to meet Me
In the sweat and struggle of life
And in the tears and tragedies of the poor.[9]

This reflects Kushdeva's own experience of finding God in the service of those in special need in his own place, Patiala. 'Religion', he said, 'is based on eternal faith in and unshakable love of God, and an overflowing urge from within to serve all living beings – men, animals, birds, insects and all that is life, because of there being oneness of life pervading the whole universe.'[10] What was so impressive about him was that this was not for him just a beautiful idea but the actual stuff of his daily life.

In a letter written near the end of his life he says, 'I am still living, a physical wreck, but I am more than happy and contented.' One of his poems is on immortality:

Some people pray to become immortal.
If they think of becoming immortal
Along with this mortal frame,
They are aspiring for something that is impossible,
Because this mortal frame must perish.

But if however they want to become immortal
Through their mortal frame,
This is possible,
Because a life led in complete dedication
Becomes life-eternal, deathless.
    It lives on in the Infinite.

A life lived for one's own self is like a pond
That stagnates, stinks and dries up,
But a life lived for Him
Is an ocean, ever fresh and perennial,
That never exhausts.[11]

As to what happens after death, he believed, like other religious Sikhs, in reincarnation. He said in a letter, 'Dr Kushdeva Singh once dead will never be born as such, but the soul shall have some other covering.' This is the last I heard from him before his final illness:

The ball no questions of Ayes or Noes makes,
But right or left as strikes the player goes,
And He that tossed it down into the field
He knows about it all – He knows. (Omar Kayyam)

This applies to the story of my life. In His graciousness He not only blessed me with a human figure, but chose me as a ball to play with. The player enjoyed the play, and the ball in turn enjoyed the surprisingly beautiful, ever changing phenomenon, the world. After playing for over eighty-two years the player has closed the game, and the ball is slowing its speed to come to a halt. At least for the time being. The ball in all sincerity offers you its parting affection and regards for the close ties of friendship over the decades. Yours affectionately, Kushdeva Singh.

You can see why I count Kushdeva Singh as one of the small band of saints knowing whom has helped me to believe that there is more to our existence than any purely materialist or naturalistic account is aware of. (The others whom I count in the same band are the Christians Desmond Tutu and Patrick O'Mahoney and the Buddhist Nyanaponika Mahathera.)

After Patiala I spent a week at Simla, steeped in imperial history, before returning to Delhi for my flight home, my previous merely book knowledge of Indian religion now greatly deepened and enriched.

NOTES

1. Harbans Singh, *Guru Nanak and the Origins of the Sikh Faith*, Bombay: Asia Publishing House, 1969.
2. My account of Kushdeva Singh here is shortened from a chapter in

my *The Fifth Dimension*, Oxford: Oneworld, 1999, used with the publisher's permission.

3. Kushdeva Singh, *Mahatma Gandhi*, Patiala: Rotary Club, 1983, p. 5.
4. Kushdeva Singh, *Love is Stronger than Hate*, Patiala: Guru Nanak Mission, 1973, p. 11.
5. Ibid., p. 13.
6. Ibid., p. 26.
7. Ibid., pp. 40-1.
8. Kushdeva Singh, *Sikhs and Sikhism*, Patiala: Guru Nanak Mission, 1982, p. 18.
9. Kushdeva Singh, *In Dedication*, 2nd edn, Patiala: Guru Nanak Mission, 1974, pp. 31-2.
10. Ibid., p. 55.
11. Ibid., p. 40.

19

With Buddhists in Sri Lanka

I had a spring term sabbatical in 1974 and with the aid of a British
Academy Overseas Visiting Fellowship spent it in Sri Lanka
attached to the philosophy department of the University of Sri Lanka
at Peradeniya. On arriving in Colombo, the capital, I spent a few
days with Lynn de Silva at his Ecumenical Institute, which is
concerned with Buddhist–Christian dialogue, and then went by train
up to Kandy in the central highlands, the Peradeniya campus being
just outside the town. I stayed in the university guest house on a hill
overlooking the campus, looked after by the slightly villainous –
though not so to me – Lionel and his family. He spoke no English
and I no Sinhala but we managed to communicate sufficiently. I see
from my letters home that I paid eighteen rupees a day for
accommodation and meals which with the special tourist rate of
exchange was less than £1 a day. I also gave Lionel an extra ten
rupees a week for doing things like bringing buckets of hot water up
to fill my bath each evening. The only other long-term guests were
two Indian post-graduate students from Bihar researching on new
strains of rice, whilst other occasional visitors came and went. The
other house on the hill was occupied by the professor of English,
Ashley Halpé, and his family, whom I got to know well. Ashley and
Bridget are highly cultured, he widely read in English literature and
she very musical – there were both an upright and a grand piano in
their spacious sitting room. I often had rides into Kandy with them,
and years later Ashley stayed with us in Birmingham a couple of
times after Shakespeare conferences at Stratford, he being probably

the leading Sri Lankan authority on Shakespeare. He had also been dean of the University at the time, then very recent, when troops occupied the campus and arrested and beat up many students for suspected opposition to the government, and had done all he could to protect them.

My daily routine was to get up and go for a half-hour or so walk in the cool of the early morning, then a substantial English-style breakfast of fried eggs, toast, coffee, the other meals being Singalese but not as spicy as the Singalese themselves like them. The sky was blue and the sun hot during the day and I sat out in the garden a lot of the time, reading the scriptures in the Pali Text Society translations and numerous books about Buddhism from the university library. I also often walked down to the Peradeniya Botanical Garden, the finest I have seen anywhere. This is huge, containing more kinds of palm trees than I knew existed, big spreading banyan trees, tall trees inhabited by large hanging bats who darkened the sky when a swarm of them took to the air, an amazing variety of bushes and shrubs and flowers, lots of monkeys and parrots and other exotic birds, plenty of places to sit to read or write, and plenty of long walks. There were also snakes, and one day I was sitting under a banyan tree writing a Preface for the new Fontana paperback edition of *Faith and Knowledge* when I heard a rustling behind me and looking round saw a four or so foot-long snake gliding towards me out of the spreading roots of the tree – whereupon I decamped.

The Mahavale river runs through the Garden and at the right time of day one could watch elephants rolling in the water, and could also look down from a bridge on crocodiles moving about below. Elephants were used as tractors and I often saw them at work dragging logs, etc. – the first time I met an elephant outside a zoo was on the path down from the guest house to the campus. Once when I was walking through the Botanical Garden I came upon Mrs Bandaranaika, the Prime Minister, and her party picnicking (with a few armed guards standing around) under a tree that was famous for its wide spread of branches. This was some years before the bitter fighting which has now tragically continued so long and so destructively between the Tamil Tigers and the Singalese government. It was in the Botanical Garden, incidentally, that much of *The Bridge on the River Kwai* was filmed, with its wooden bridge built over the Mahavale.

Kandy itself was once the capital of what the west then called Ceylon, and includes a large artificial lake on whose shore is the Temple of the Tooth holding what is reputed to be a tooth of the Buddha which is carried through the streets once a year in a colourful procession of many brightly painted elephants, watched and enjoyed by vast crowds. The Buddhist Publications Society also had its office by the lake and I bought the *Dhammapada*, a collection of sayings of the Buddha which constitutes the Theravadins' Bible, as well as a good deal of contemporary Theravada writings.

The University seemed to me to be in a better state, academically, than most of the Indian universities I had visited. All of the teaching staff had to spend a year abroad, in the USA or Britain, before becoming full lecturers and were thus in touch with the wider world of scholarship. The head of the philosophy department, Padmasiri de Silva, was extremely helpful and we have kept in touch. His successful *Introduction to Buddhist Psychology* has gone through three editions in my Macmillan Library of Philosophy and Religion.

The guest house was half-way up a hill which had a Hindu temple on top, a mosque further down, then a Catholic church, a Protestant church, and finally a Buddhist stupa. The Anglican priest, the Rev. J.R. Ratnanayagam, who was also a university chaplain, was very hospitable. I preached in his church and spoke at a meeting afterwards on interfaith matters. I also had some good discussions with Bishop Lacksman Wickramasinge, who had read my *Evil and the God of Love* and felt, probably rightly, that it would have benefited from some input from Buddhism – about which I knew very little when I wrote the book.

From Peradeniya of course I visited the tourist sites of Sri Lanka, once with Hazel, who came out for a fortnight, and once with Shirley and Norman, who also came for a visit. We went to the mountain fortress of Sigiri; the remains of the ancient cities of Anaradapura and Polonnaruwa, where there are the huge standing and reclining statues of the Buddha; the two vast wild game parks where we saw mongooses, crocodiles, parrots, an eagle, a large leopard, innumerable monkeys, iguanas, buffaloes, tortoises and elephants; and the naval port of Trincomalee. I also spent a weekend at Nuwara Eliya in the middle of the tea-growing highlands, and visited a tea plantation run by a relative of Padmasiri de Silva.

My purpose in going to Sri Lanka was to learn something at first hand about Theravada Buddhism. The Theravada, the Way of the Elders, is the southern Buddhist tradition (mainly in Burma, Thailand, Sri Lanka), representing the Buddhist tradition in India before it spread northwards into China, Tibet, Korea and Japan to form the Mahayana or Great Vehicle, which then produced a wealth of new scriptures notionally ascribed to the Buddha. I was later to learn more about Mahayana Buddhism, and particularly Zen, at Claremont and on visits to Japan. However the Theravada claims to continue the earliest tradition embodied in the Pali scriptures.

I was greatly helped by the Saturday morning discussion group which was formed for my benefit. It included several bikkhus (monks), several Buddhist scholars from the University, and an intellectually and spiritually outstanding Englishman, Bryan Cooke, with a Singalese wife, who had lived at Peredeniya for many years. The group discussed every aspect of Buddhist thought and practice. One topic was nirvana, a central Buddhist term, particularly in the Theravada. It is often taken by westerners to refer to a blissfully tranquil state of mind which is the fruit of prolonged meditation. But it was made clear to me that it is this but also much more than this. The word means literally 'blowing out', as in the blowing out of a flame, and thus might suggest that the solution to the problem of *dukkha* (suffering, more generally unsatisfactoriness) is the ultimate extinction of the self. But this is a misunderstanding. The attainment of nirvana does involve blowing out or destruction, but what the Buddha taught is that, 'The destruction of lust, the destruction of hatred, the destruction of illusion, friend, is called Nibbana'[1] – Nibbana being the Pali equivalent of the Sanscrit Nirvana. Nor is nirvana only a subjective state of consciousness but one that is continuous with the eternal transcendent reality that is Nirvana, also called in the Mahayana the universal Buddha nature. In his authoritative exposition of Theravada Buddhism Walpola Rahula equates nirvana with Ultimate Reality,[2] and Nerada Thera describes it as 'the permanent, immortal, supramundane state which cannot be expressed in mundane terms'.[3] Other topics discussed included the Buddhist teachings of *anatta* (no substantial self), *anicca* (impermanence, flow), and the ideas of karma and rebirth, and much else. My first use of all this, together with other reading and discussions, comes in *Death and Eternal Life*, chapter 21.

But my most important Buddhist source was Nyanaponika Mahathera, a mahathera being a monk who has been ordained for twenty years or more. He lived in a forest heritage in the Udawattakle Forest Reserve just outside Kandy.[4] This was not a hut but a well-built bungalow with an extensive library within it. At first I saw Nyanaponika as simply a learned and interesting scholar. But I became aware that he also embodied the transcendence of the self-centred ego that Buddhism seeks. He incarnated to a significant extent the dharma that he taught.

He was originally a German Jew. Apparently he was always religiously inclined, and learned Hebrew to study the scriptures at first hand. As he grew, however, and read voraciously in many fields, he began to have disturbing doubts about some of the traditional teachings. This led to a search for new insights, and he found these when he began to read about Buddhism. Although he had never met a Buddhist, by the age of twenty he identified himself as one. When the family moved to Berlin in 1922 he was able to join a Buddhist group and gain access to a much wider range of Buddhist literature. He also came to hear of some German Buddhists who had settled in Buddhist countries, particularly Burma and Ceylon, and decided that one day he would, like them, become a monk in that part of the world. This did not happen however until some years later. In 1933 Hitler came to power in Germany and the persecution of the Jews began. Now in his early thirties Sigmund Feniger, as he was then, joined the Central Committee of German Jews for Help and Self-Protection. But he wanted to get his widowed mother out of Germany and in 1935 they moved to Vienna where they had relatives. He was now in touch with a German Jew who a generation earlier had become a Buddhist monk in Ceylon and in 1936 he set out to join him. He lived as an upsaka or lay disciple, preparing for ordination, and a year later became a bikkhu or monk, being given the name of Nyanaponika meaning inclined to learning. He studied Pali, the ancient language of the Buddhist scriptures, and later translated and commented on parts of the Pali canon in both German and English.

When the Nazis invaded Austria in 1938 he arranged for his elderly mother to come to Colombo where he was able to visit her regularly. However when war broke out the next year Nyanaponika was interned as a German, in spite of being a German Jew. He spent most of the war in an internment camp at Dehra Dun in India, where he came to know another German Buddhist, this time in the Tibetan tradition, Lama Govinda, with whom he had many friendly discussions about the differences between their two branches of Buddhism and from whom he learned Sanscrit. In 1946 he was released and returned to what was about to become the independent republic of Sri Lanka, of which he became a citizen.

In 1951 Nyanaponika moved to the forest hermitage where he spent his time in meditation, in talking with people who came to consult him, in writing and translating for the Buddhist Publication Society, and travelling to Switzerland once a year as spiritual adviser to Theravadins living in Europe. I was one of those who visited him several times in the hermitage, discussing various aspects of Buddhist thought and meditation. He also came to Kandy to hear me lecture at the British Council and then to discuss this with me. He said that he liked the spirit in which I spoke, although he disagreed with my criticisms of some aspects of Theravada philosophy. One point of disagreement that I remember concerned his explanation of the *anatta*, no substantial self, doctrine. He used the analogy of a ceiling fan, of which there are many in hot countries such as Sri Lanka. Because its shafts move round so quickly they seem, illusorily, to form a solid and static circle. Likewise, because the stream of successive discrete moments of consciousness succeed one another so quickly they create the illusory appearance of a substantial enduring self. I argued that the same analysis could not apply to the consciousness observing the fan, which had itself to be continuous if it was to see the moving states of the blade as forming a continuous whole. But of course if this illustration was faulty that does not affect the truth or falsity of the doctrine itself.

The method of meditation which Nyanaponika practiced and which he describes in detail in *The Heart of Buddhist Meditation*[5] is known as satipatthana or mindfulness meditation. The basic idea is that by concentrating on something, namely one's own breathing, that has no intrinsic meaning, one empties the consciousness of its ordinary ever-changing contents and thereby opens it to a greater reality of which we are not normally aware. However this can become not just a special moment achieved in meditation but a state of mind that pervades much of life. The procedure is very simple. You sit down comfortably with straight back, make a deliberate mental intention to open yourself to the reality beyond our ordinary experience, take a few deep breaths, and then with eyes closed simply attend to your breathing, its coming in and going out, preferably (according to Nyanaponika) at the diaphragm. The mind wanders again and again and again and you return to the breathing, continuing as long as you feel like it. Sometimes after a while you reach a second stage at which the mind remains effortlessly focused on the breathing and you feel as though you could continue indefinitely. I have once, but so far only once, experienced what was to me a startling breakthrough into a new form or level of consciousness. I was in that second stage and when eventually I opened my eyes the world was quite different in two ways. Whereas normally I am here and the environment is there, separate from me, there was now no such distinction; and more importantly, the total universe of which I was part was friendly, benign, good, so that there could not possibly be anything to fear or worry about. It was a state of profound delight in being. This only lasted a short time, probably not more than two minutes. But I can see that to anyone living, or being for long periods, in such a state of mind there would be a profound serenity, and that the unselfcentred compassion, feeling with and for others, which is so central to Buddhist teaching would be entirely natural. Even to have tasted this fleetingly has been to me very significant. And short of that nirvanic state there are other times when meditation leaves me in some indescribable way uplifted, made deeply happy.

I note that the Dalai Lama, also teaching mindfulness meditation, recommends, as one method, keeping the eyes open and fixed upon some object,' and I sometimes also try this

One thing that one realises in meditation is how extraordinarily complex and multi-dimensional our mental life is, like a vast ocean in which fishes of many shapes and sizes swim in all directions in and out of the small spotlight of consciousness. And surrounding that well-lit area is a penumbra of half conscious thoughts which continually intrude or retreat. So whilst being directly aware of your breathing other thoughts, including a second order awareness of your first order awareness, flit in and out of consciousness. All this in what I have called the first stage, beyond which I myself only rarely proceed.

The psychologist Eric Fromm, who met Nyanaponika in Switzerland, was struck by his emphasis that 'peace and joy, not destruction and nihilism, are essential for the "feeling-world" ', and concluded, 'I am convinced that Nyanaponika Thera's work may become one of the most important contributions to spiritual renewal in the West, if it can reach the knowledge of a sufficient number of people.' Fromm's assessment is included in a volume of Nyanaponika's writings edited by his successor in the forest heritage.[7] To give just a flavour of his teaching:

> Among those calling themselves 'believers' or 'religious people' or, in our case, Buddhists, there are still too few who have that kind of genuine faith in the actual power of the Good to transform and elevate the life of the individual and of society, to secure them against the resistance of the evil in themselves and in the world outside. Too few dare to entrust themselves to the powerful current of the Good, too many secretly believe, in spite of a vague sort of 'faith', that the power of the evil in themselves and the world is stronger − too strong to be contended with. Many politicians everywhere in the world seem to believe the same, particularly those who call themselves 'realists', obviously implying that only the evil is 'real'. They think that of necessity they have to submit to its greater power. If they are not willing to put it to the test, it is no wonder that they cannot achieve much good.

Again, 'Let us teach real joy to others! Many have unlearned it. Life, though full of woe, holds also sources of happiness and joy, unknown to most. Let us teach people to seek and to find real joy within themselves and to rejoice with the joy of others.'[8] His understanding and practice of Buddhism were always positive and always informed by the inner liberation taught by the Buddha.

In 1994, just after Nyanaponika's ninety-third birthday and his fifty-eighth rains retreat, in the words of the head of his order 'his body succumbed to the universal law of impermanence which holds sway over all conditioned things'. Buddhists believe that the great compassion of buddhahood flowed through him and many monks did a 'loving-kindness meditation' for him, wishing him a smooth transition to his next life. For my part, I have been greatly enriched by knowing him.

It was after these visits to India and Sri Lanka, and partly as a result of them, that I wrote my longest book, *Death and Eternal Life* (1976). Amongst a wide range of topics I treated the mainly Hindu and Buddhist belief in reincarnation more seriously than any but a very few other western philosophers. In approaching this I criticised the standard Christian doctrine of an eternal heaven or hell on the ground that, in almost all cases, at death we are not yet ready for either an eternal heaven (or heaven via purgatory) nor have we deserved an eternal hell, or obliteration. We need further moral and spiritual growth or development – for which the traditional purgatory doctrine does not allow. And such development happens in this life, to the extent to which it does happen, because of the shape of life, bounded as it is by birth and death. It is the pressure of these boundaries, as distinguished from an endless vista of the same life, that gives urgent meaning to our time here. We have to get on with whatever we are going to do. And so continued progress may well be in further finite lives.

My eventual conclusion is that something like the Buddhist conception of rebirth is quite likely to be true. This depends upon a distinction between the present conscious self, which is not immortal but is a temporary and changing expression of a deeper reality, an underlying psychic structure, a dispositional or karmic continuant, which affects and is affected by the activities of the present self, and which will be expressed again many times in new conscious personalities, reflecting a gradual development towards unity with the eternal ultimate reality. These rebirths may not be in this world; there may be many worlds in many universes or sub-universes. But the many lives are linked by a latent continuity of memory of which we are not normally conscious but which constitutes the identity of the series. To repeat the way that I have put it in *The Fifth Dimension*, so long as we cling to our fragmentary and very imperfect ego its approaching demise is the worst possible news and we will go to great lengths to shut it out of our minds. But if we can each come to see ourself as the present moment within a long creative process and can trust in the value of that process, we can accept our mortality without fear or resentment and can try to live to the full within our present life span. For everything that we do is contributing, positively or negatively, to the future selves who will continue the project that is presently embodied in us. We are like the runners in a relay race: the torch has been handed to us and for a short time the whole project depends upon us. Our life thus has an urgent meaning. We are contributing something unique, not only to the world that will continue after our death but also to our own future selves who will, one after another, embody the basic dispositional character-structure – the soul, or jiva, or karmic nexus – which we have inherited and are now all the time modifying in small ways for good or for ill.

I should add that I am not greatly impressed by the stories of regression under hypnosis to previous lives, or of reported waking memories of previous lives, although I assume that a memory of the entire series of lives exists within the karmic continuant, and it is presumably possible that sometimes flashes of this leak into the present consciousness. But a simpler and more popular version of reincarnation belief seems to be surprisingly widespread in contemporary western society, surveys reporting that about seventy per cent of people, including church members, profess some kind of reincarnation belief. In most cases they probably have in mind the popular conception of the present self living again, rather than the more complex Buddhist/Hindu idea. I imagine that they have seen the implausibility of the traditional Christian belief, but share the basic cosmic optimism of all the great world religions and find some kind of reincarnation to be the most plausible possibility.

NOTES

1. Samyutta-Nikaya, IV, 250. (*The Book of the Kindred Sayings*, Part IV, p. 170, in the Pali Text Society translation.)
2. Walpola Rahula, *What the Buddha Taught*, Oxford, Oneworld, 1997.
3. Narada Thera, trans., *The Dhammapada*, Colombo: Vajrarama, 1972, pp. 24–5.
4. My account of him here is based on *The Fifth Dimension*, chap. 23, used with the publisher's permission.
5. Nyanaponika Mahathera, *The Heart of Buddhist Meditation*, 2nd edn, London: Rider, 1969.
6. The Dalai Lama, *A Policy of Kindness*, Ithaca, N.Y.: Snow Lion Publications, 1990, chap. 8.
7. *The Vision of Dhamma: Buddhist Writings of Nyanaponika Thera*, ed. Bhikkhu Bodi, 2nd edn, Kandy: Buddhist Publication Society, 1994.
8. Ibid., pp. 304 and 255.

20

The Myth of God Incarnate

In my inaugural lecture at Birmingham in 1967 on 'Theology's Central Problem', namely the realist/non-realist debate, I ended by listing other major problems coming up over the horizon, including the relation between Christianity and the other world religions. I had now moved a long way from my evangelical/fundamentalist beginning, and through orthodoxy to heterodoxy, and although I did not see any solution to this problem posed by the reality of the other world religions – at that time only beginning to emerge in the consciousness of most western theologians – I did see the problem very clearly, and this was later accentuated by becoming involved in community and race relations affairs in the city and by my visits to India and Sri Lanka. I came fairly soon to see that for Christianity the problem of religious plurality hinged on the central doctrine of the incarnation. If Jesus was God incarnate, Christianity alone among the world religions was founded by God in person and must therefore be uniquely superior to all others. This made me look again at the traditional doctrine and its history. As several critics have correctly suggested – though I do not see this as in any way a damaging fact – it was the multi-faith issue that led me to this; and as I proceeded I developed grave doubts about the accepted formulations. I was a long way behind-hand in this, for many other theologians had long had similar doubts. I conceived the idea of a book of essays bringing the issues to the fore. For while the incarnation doctrine was generally regarded as the central Christian truth, and in Britain was especially treasured in Anglican circles,

227

theologically educated clergy and ministers were aware that it is enormously improbable that Jesus himself taught that he was God (or God the Son) incarnate. His deification was a gradual development. It was not the Jesus of history but the Christ of the faith as officially defined at Nicea (325 CE) and Chalcedon (451 CE) who proclaimed himself as sole saviour of the world; and the Chalcedonian definition was in error when it claimed that the theory of Jesus' two natures, one divine and the other human, is as 'our Lord Jesus Christ himself taught us'. That he did not in fact teach it raised issues that were familiar to theologians and biblical scholars but that could still come as startling news to the general public. I knew that my former colleagues at Cambridge, Maurice Wiles, then Regius professor at Oxford and recent chairman of the Church of England's Doctrinal Commission, and Dennis Nineham, then warden of Keble College, Oxford, and Frances Young and Michael Goulder in Birmingham, might well be interested. They were, and we were joined by Leslie Houlden, principal of Cuddesdon College, the leading Anglican theological college at Oxford, later lecturer and professor in NT at King's College, London. Later again Don Cupitt at Cambridge came in. We met and decided to draft essays, circulate them, and then have several more meetings to discuss them. Oxford was the most convenient place for access from both Birmingham and Cambridge, as well as having three of the contributors already there, and we usually met in the Warden's Lodge at Keble for discussion and a cheese, fruit and wine lunch, though we also met once in my house in Birmingham. The central and programmatic piece was Maurice's on 'Christianity without Incarnation?'. My own essay was on 'Jesus and the World Religions'.

What was the book to be called? We could have chosen an academic title, such as *Studies in Christian Origins*, in which case the book would have been reviewed a year later in the learned journals but would have had no more effect on the churches or the general public than all the other academic volumes over the years saying many of the same things. But we wanted to break the taboo. And so we chose *The Myth of God Incarnate*, a title first suggested – paradoxically in view of her later move back in the direction of traditional orthodoxy – by Frances Young. The title was much criticised as deliberately provocative and sensationalist. And so it was

– we wanted its message to be heard. But the critics failed to take in Maurice's careful explanation, in his chapter on 'Myth in theology', that scholars today do not mean by myth that which is simply false, but that which expresses truth in stories or descriptions which are not literally true but which nevertheless point to some important reality, in this case Jesus' exceptional openness to God and the embodiment in his own life of God's love for humanity.

The book was finally ready in 1976 and John Bowden of the SCM Press enthusiastically took it up. I have known John ever since he became editor of the Press and for years until he retired we enjoyed an annual lunch together in London, sharing thoughts on the theological scene. In a letter after his retirement he said that 'the Myth press conference was the most exciting theological event in my life'. The launch was in the summer of 1977. I wrote a couple of pages of diary on The Week of the Book:

The week began on Tuesday 29 June, when Peter and I – Pete there 'just for the beer' – and Frances Young and Michael Goulder caught the 9.48 to Euston and then a taxi to St Paul's Cathedral where we walked around looking for the Chapter House. It is in fact a large house separate from the cathedral, and going into the spacious hall we heard a loud buzz of conversation upstairs. Here was a big room full of people of the kind who, I imagine, go to literary cocktail parties. Wine and various kinds of nibbles were being served and everyone was talking (and presumably no one listening). I spotted John Bowden who turned out to be talking with Clifford Longley, Times religious affairs correspondent, who was very cross about the Observer's leak last Sunday. [I presume in retrospect that John had done the leaking himself as a good publicity move.] Presently John took me into the next room – with a long table covered with microphones, facing three rows of chairs – to explain the procedure of the press conference and to tell me that The Myth had already sold out to the book shops and was now reprinting, and that the Observer article had brought a much larger number of press people than he had expected. Going back into the cocktail room I recognised a few people and chatted to them and then we were all summoned into the conference room. I reckoned that there were seventy or so people, though one of the newspapers said over a hundred.

John Bowden talked about the embargo until Friday and was

challenged on this by several people, who wanted to be able to report the present occasion, and before the meeting ended he changed his mind and lifted the embargo. Then I read a short prepared statement. According to the *Church Times*,

> Dr Hick opened the proceedings in come-let-us-reason-together tones that extracted the sting of sensation from his words. People could take comfort, he said, from the fact that other books which had seemed shocking and heretical had later been accepted as valuable instruments of the Church's mission. There was nothing new about the central themes of *The Myth of God Incarnate*, he added, still conversationally: it was now agreed by virtually all scholars that Jesus had not presented himself as divine, 'although many church members are not aware of this'. They are not indeed. Anyway, the point of the book, he said, was to bring this 'gently and responsibly' into the consciousness and understanding of the Church.

Then David Edwards, advertised as *advocatus dei*, spoke saying nothing very critical about the book except that its title is provocative. Next Maurice Wiles spoke briefly though I can't now remember what he said. Then there were questions. These came thick and fast, often with two or three trying to speak at once; and the meeting went on for half an hour longer than planned. Most of the questions were more or less hostile: Is Jesus the Son of God or not; is the wooden cross in my pocket being devalued; aren't you Unitarians; what about the cross and resurrection? etc. Generally the answer, whether from Maurice, Dennis or myself, consisted in saying it depends on what you mean by ____, which was frustrating to journalists who have never wondered what 'Son of God', for example, means. There were also others who asked questions, or spoke to me afterwards, who were sympathetic to the book.

After the press conference we were each nabbed by journalists for further interviews, and then went outside for photographs on the steps of St Paul's and further words into a microphone for the BBC. Eventually – nearly three o'clock – we got away for a magnificent lunch in the Mermaid Theatre restaurant. After a long and jolly lunch, with German white wine, I felt like nothing more energetic than sitting on the embankment and watching the barges go by on the Thames.

Wednesday's papers had quite a lot about the news conference. During the day I was rung up from Oslo by a journalist wanting to know how to get hold of the book, and from New York asking what the book had to say about miracles. *The Birmingham Mail* rang up to read me a statement by the Moderator of the Church of Scotland, Dr John Gray, saying that the *Myth* authors 'would, if they were honourable men, resign their professorships and divest themselves of their status as Christian ministers', and asking for a comment. I asked them to ring back in an hour and then said that I presumed that the Moderator had not yet read the book, but that when he did he would find that it makes accessible work done by theologians in recent years which, in the opinion of many, will help to make the gospel more relevant to the modern world. When the reporter asked what I had to say about the Moderator's resignation demand, I said that I didn't want to add anything. The next day the *Mail*'s headline was "'I won't quit," says Jesus-row man'. There was also a call from the *Observer* saying that the Archbishop of Canterbury is likely to condemn the book at the Synod on Tuesday, that a counter-book called *The Fact of God Incarnate* is to be published in August, and that someone had preached against our book in St Paul's at a service on Wednesday.

As I kept telling people who asked, the central theme of the book is that the language of divine incarnation, in which we speak of Jesus as God incarnate, God the Son, Son of God, Second Person of the Trinity living a human life, is symbolic, mythological, or poetic language. Nearly all the letters I have received so far (today being Tuesday 5 July) have, curiously enough, been congratulatory. Today someone in California sent me $10 to send him a copy by airmail. Just now a press man has rung up from London asking if I could meet with a group of international press in London – which I could only do on Sunday, when I spend a night in London before catching a plane to Accra on Monday.

Yesterday evening Michael Goulder and I did an hour and a half phone-in for BRMB [a local Birmingham radio station] which seemed to go quite well. None of those who phoned in had read the book, and most were conservative Christians, but charitable and friendly. Radio Birmingham want a phone-in in September and it may be interesting to see what difference it makes that people have had time to read the book.

In my opening statement at the press conference I had presented the book

as the latest in a series of volumes of essays in which groups of theologians have suggested new theological moves or emphases. These include *Essays and Reviews* (1860), *Lux Mundi* (1889), *Foundations* (1912), *Essays Catholic and Critical* (1926), and *Soundings* (1962). It has been the standard pattern for such books to be regarded when they first appeared as controversial and even sometimes as heretical and shocking, and then later to be accepted as vehicles of theological progress. *Essays and Reviews*, for example, was ferociously attacked as a wicked undermining of the Christian faith and its seven authors were branded as 'Seven Against Christ'; and there were actions in the courts against those of them who were Anglican clergymen. But within a generation their argument and point of view had become accepted by nearly all educated Christians in this country, and one of them [Frederick Temple, father of another archbishop, William Temple] had become Archbishop of Canterbury! So if anyone is tempted to react with alarm to the present volume, let him take comfort from history ...

(I see that I had scribbled on the back of my statement a note to John Bowden, 'I would have thought that you could allow this Conf. to be reported as an event in itself – but it's up to you. John.') David Edwards in his remarks said that he thought I should be the one to become Archbishop of Canterbury!

The immediate hubbub was intense. At the Anglican Synod a few days later we were likened (in a prayer!) to the 'German Christians' who had supported Hitler. However Archbishops Donald Coggan of Canterbury and Stuart Blanch of York, as joint chairmen, resisted the call for an emergency debate about the book, saying that 'it would be irresponsible to engage in discussion of a book published only last Friday, which few of us can have read'; and Dr Coggan also tried to avoid discussion by saying that the book was unimportant and had caused 'more hubbub than it was worth'. He was perhaps wary of attacking some of the Church's leading theologians and perhaps also remembered how his predecessor, Michael Ramsey, had attacked John Robinson's *Honest to God* the moment it appeared and then regretted having done so. The archbishop's prudent caution was also shown in my being invited, as the only non-Anglican, to join the unpublicised group called Caps and Mitres, an annual informal meeting in London of theologians and bishops, and that Dr Coggan came to the first meeting at which I was present and was friendly to me. But the *Church Times* carried photos of us under the headline 'Seven Against Christ?' and concluded its leading article, 'All in all, *The Myth of God Incarnate* furthers only one discernible objective. It constitutes a notably unconvincing contribution to the cause of unbelief.' Athenagoras, Orthodox Archbishop of Great Britain, declared that the writers of *The Myth* had 'fallen prey to an opposition of a demonic character'. John Stott, the evangelical vicar of All Souls, Langham Place, London declared us to be heretics, and the moderator of the Church of Scotland called upon us to resign from our positions, as also did the Church of England Evangelical Council. The *Sunday Telegraph* had a cartoon of Christ on the cross with the book nailed to it above his head. Another headline was 'Anti-Christ in St Paul's'. There was a spate of mostly hostile articles and letters to the newspapers for several weeks – I have four large volumes of press cuttings. And only seven weeks later *The Truth of God Incarnate* was published by Hodder & Stoughton, edited by a leading evangelical, Michael Green, the other contributors being Bishop Christopher Butler, the Rev. Brian Hebblethwaite of Cambridge [later a good friend], Bishop Stephen Neill, and Professor John Macquarrie. I reviewed the book in *Reform*, the journal of the United Reformed Church. Also in 1997 a pamphlet, *God Incarnate*, appeared by the future Archbishop of Canterbury, George Carey, published by the Inter-Varsity Press.

It will be evident from all this that my Anglican colleagues, Maurice, Dennis, Michael, Don and Leslie came in for far more 'stick' than Frances, as a Methodist lay person, or myself as a URC minister. Probably from an Anglican point of view we Nonconformists did not count. If there was ever a move within the URC to dismiss me, I never knew of it and it cannot have got very far. But there were strong calls for the Anglican authors to resign their orders, though these never finally came to anything. In the spring of the following year the Birmingham diocesan *Lookout* carried an article by Michael, then an Anglican priest in good standing, explaining 'why neither the Bishop nor I thought I should leave the Church'.

More positively, professor Geoffrey Lampe of Cambridge, a distinguished Anglican theologian, put out a statement welcoming the book, and Peter Baelz another leading Anglican defended it. On the noticeboard of the theology department at Birmingham:

> Said a wise and articulate don,
> 'Incarnation is simply not on!
> Two natures in one,
> It just can't be done -
> It's a most mysterious con!'

The book sold thirty thousand copies in the first six months. A German translation (*Wurde Gott Mencsh?*) appeared in 1979, and a partial Arabic translation with commentary was published by Abdus-Samad Sharafuddin in Jeddah. The book was simultaneously published in the States but made smaller waves in this much larger pond. *Time* magazine devoted a page to it with a fairly balanced account of both sides of the debate, as also did the *San Francisco Chronicle* and the *Los Angeles Times*, and there were some positive book reviews. But an article in the *Christian Century* correctly remarked that

> There are few surprises in it for anyone who is at all familiar with the work of Karl Rahner, Hans Küng and other European theologians, and it is a measure of the continuing insularity of British theology that the present controversy has been delayed until 1977.

But there was of course plenty of condemnation from within the American fundamentalist world. The book and the resulting controversy were also covered by the press in Canada, Italy and South Africa

I was reminded of a small after-shock of this controversy when re-reading my files about AFFOR (see chapter 16). Kenneth Leech, a very fine Anglican priest in London, author of valuable writings both on spirituality and on social justice, wrote a paper urging the church to mobilise itself against the contemporary fascism of such movements as the National Front, and invited AFFOR to publish it, our then director David Jennings being a friend of his. In the course of it Ken presented the traditional incarnation doctrine as the basis for Christian resistance to fascism and referred to the non-incarnational theology of 'the Wiles/Nineham school' as undermining this. I objected to AFFOR associating itself with this charge, writing to David that

> Most of [Ken's paper] seems to me excellent. There is however one aspect of it which seems to me better omitted. There is, as you know, a considerable debate going on about the viability of a non-incarnational Christian faith, which its proponents claim to represent the religion of Jesus. The issue concerns, not the principle that God is concerned for love and justice between men – a principle which is not peculiar to Christianity – but the principle of the uniqueness and universal authority of Christ and hence of Christianity. Leech gets into this debate when he uncritically accepts the thesis that the rejection of Chalcedonian Christology, associated with Wiles, Nineham, Lampe and others [including myself], promotes or is sympathetic to fascism ...

Ken Leech replied to David that 'I am not prepared to omit those crucial passages simply because he [Hick] disagrees with them', and suggesting that the pamphlet could be published with a note saying that the publisher does not necessarily agree with everything in it, or with some other such disclaimer. I wrote again to David reminding him that it was our custom for anything we published to be read and approved by the committee; and that in some previous cases a number of changes had been made in the text.

> It is true that Ken Leech does not say that non-incarnational theologians are paving the way to fascism. But in the context of a pamphlet about Fascism, to attack this school of thought, along with the other groups discussed, can only have the effect of suggesting this ... There is at the very least an implied suggestion of a connection of some kind between this school of theology and the subject-matter of the pamphlet. Otherwise why bring it in? Again, in the passage about the German Christians [who supported Hitler] there is an implied connection between their position and that of The Myth of God Incarnate authors.

After some further discussion we did not publish Ken's pamphlet but it was I believe published elsewhere.

My prediction that the central information disclosed in The Myth would become generally acknowledged has proved correct. When the book was reissued sixteen years later there was a meeting in Birmingham Cathedral hosted by the provost, Peter Berry (who was far in advance of the Church of England as a whole on race relations and relations with people of other faiths), and I began my remarks by reading this passage, 'To speak of Jesus as "Son of God" is to use a metaphor ... it does not imply deification ... I would argue that the potentiality for becoming a Son of God belongs to humanity as such ...', and asked which of *The Myth* authors had written this? I then revealed that it was in fact written in 1990 by one of the authors of the anti-book, *The Truth of God Incarnate*, John Macquarrie.[1] The significance of *The Myth* was not that it contained startling new thinking but that it made public by people who could not be ignored much current thinking that had long been unpublicised because it might disturb the faithful. And of course the longer one delays telling what is bad news to the hearer the harder it becomes to do so. But this 'letting of the cat out of the bag' was inevitable sooner or later and could only in the long run be salutary. For it is not really bad news at all. It only seems so because the churches had failed for so long to share with their members the findings of modern biblical scholarship and the resulting rethinking of some of the traditional formulations. I received letters from clergy thanking me for the book, saying that they had long thought along these lines but of course could not tell their people; and from lay people thanking me for it, and saying that they had long thought along these lines but of course could not tell their pastor!

But whilst it is generally accepted, outside fundamentalist and extreme evangelical circles, that Jesus himself did not teach the doctrine of the Incarnation, controversy continues in full spate about the significance of this fact. For there are many fall-back positions which conservatives can take: although Jesus himself did not teach his own deity, it is implied in his words and actions, or it only became evident to his followers as a result of his resurrection, or in developing the official doctrine the church was divinely guided. The year after *The Myth* was published we organised a conference in Birmingham (with a grant from one of the Cadbury Trusts) bringing together *The Myth* authors and some of our most prominent critics, Charles Moule, Brian Hebblethwaite, Nicholas Lash, John Rodwell, Stephen Sykes, Graham Stanton, and Lesslie Newbigin. This resulted in some genuinely illuminating discussion and produced an excellent book, *Incarnation and Myth: The Debate Continued*, edited by Michael

Goulder, who also discomforted Moule in a public debate. As well as Michael Green's rapid response book and George Carey's pamphlet there followed *The Myth/Truth of God Incarnate* (McDonald 1979), *The Art of God Incarnate* (Nichols 1980), *God Incarnate Story and Belief* (Harvey 1981), *The Logic of God Incarnate* (Morris 1986), and *The Saga of God Incarnate* (Crawford 1988). I made my own contribution to the continuing discussion in *The Metaphor of God Incarnate*, 1993. This is, in my humble opinion, actually a better book than the original *Myth*, because it is by a single author and so is able to present a sustained argument. But of course it has not had anything like the same impact, although unlike the original *Myth* book it has been widely read in the Far East through translations in Japanese, Chinese, Korean, and also in Portuguese for readers in Brazil.

Since *The Myth* we have moved in three different directions. Maurice Wiles, Leslie Houlden and myself have proceeded, I would say, in the same direction as the book. Frances Young, who has been ordained into the Methodist ministry – though remaining an academic and a university administrator – has moved in the direction of, but not quite back to, Chalcedonian orthodoxy. Michael Goulder has become an atheist, as described in chapter 13. Don Cupitt has become a total anti-realist but remains an Anglican priest. Denis Nineham maintains his position on the incarnation doctrine but with (I think) a certain degree of sympathy for Don's non realist form of religion. All remain good friends both with myself and with one another. The whole *Myth* group, except Maurice who was unable to come, together with the publisher and spouses were at my pseudo eightieth birthday party and it was good to catch up with them there and in subsequent phone conversations.

NOTES

1. John Macquarrie, *Jesus Christ in Modern Thought*, London: SCM Press, 1990, pp. 42–3.

21

Botswana and apartheid South Africa

I, and Hazel most of the time, spent three months in the summer of 1980 in South Africa, preceded by a visit to Botswana with which she had a family connection. The (Congregationalist) London Missionary Society had been working there since 1813 and Hazel's mother Frances Bowers, as a secretary of the Society, had appointed many of its present staff in Africa and sometimes visited them. And Seretse Kama, the first President of Botswana when it became independent in 1966 – though he had previously been banned by the British Government whilst the country was the Protectorate of Bechuanaland – had been a fellow student at Oxford with Hazel's brother Michael. The family were always hospitable to foreign students and Seretse was often in their house in London. They also knew Miss Chiepe, who had been Botswana's High Commissioner in London and was now Minister of Mineral Development and Water Affairs. We flew to Johannesburg and were there for a few days, being conscious immediately of the master race mentality of the white society, before flying on to Gaborone, the capital of Botswana.

This was then a comparatively new 'frontier town', centring on the Mall surrounded by shops and offices and the President Hotel where we stayed at first. In marked contrast to Johannesburg, Gaborone had a relaxed and friendly atmosphere. Whereas in Jo'burg in the late afternoon the blacks were hurrying to buses to take them back to Soweto and the other black townships, in Gaborone they were at home and strolling about at leisure and did not look, or avoid looking, at whites in the same way as in South Africa. The few police visible were unarmed, there was no atmosphere of fear or tension, and when we visited Miss (Dr) Chiepe in her office in the Mineral Development ministry the only guard was an old man sitting outside in a chair and armed with a wooden stick. Miss Chiepe was extremely friendly and spent some time with us, with occasional telephone interruptions. She told us that Botswana had immense mineral resources but that the main problem was a lack of the water needed to mine them. We would have visited Seretse Kama himself but alas he had died only a few days earlier of a sudden cancer of the spleen.

We attended the meeting of the National Assembly at which his successor Dr Masire was elected. We did not know whether we would be able to get in but were in fact seated with the foreign diplomats – probably because we were foreign and suitably dressed! There was no visible security and the public in the gallery joined in the Amen after the chaplain's opening prayer, and joined in the clapping after the new President had spoken. He was then sworn in before a huge crowd outside, and we later went to a big open-air service in memory of Seretse.

A student friend of Pete's at Manchester had been Jerry Mosala, then teaching at the university in Gabarone. We then all called him Jerry, but later under his proper name of Itumeleng he has become a prominent and controversial figure in the new South Africa. He introduced me to his colleagues in the theology department and Hazel visited schools and a teacher training college. About seventy per cent of the population of the country were literate. Itumeleng and his wife Louisa invited us to stay with them in their house, and we moved there after a day or two. She had lived in Sharpeville and was about ten at the time of the Sharpeville massacre in 1960 when sixty-seven Africans were killed and one-hundred and eighty-six wounded. She remembered her shirt being covered with blood from someone who was shot next to her in the crowd. Itumeleng's younger brother was recently arrested and given a severe blow on the head, charged with being part of a rioting group although he was in fact walking on his own. The police tried without success to make him sign a confession and he was now out on bail awaiting trial. One of the people we met at the Mosalas' was the local Methodist superintendent minister, a black South African who had recently been in prison for five months awaiting trial on a charge of possessing World Council of Churches literature! But Itumeleng said that the big difference in South Africa since he returned from two years in England was that the people were no longer afraid of prison or the police. A spirit of change was in the air.

One of Frances Bowers' LMS friends, the principal of Moeding College out in the country, came to collect us and we spent a few days there, being taken to numerous interesting sights (such as the ruins of Livingstone's house, and Molepolole with its caves and the execution rock). I preached on Sunday in the college chapel. Among the interesting people whom we visited were Dr Alfred Merryweather and his wife. He was in charge of the local hospital, had at one time been speaker of the National Assembly, and had been Seretse's personal physician. He had recently been with Seretse for medical treatment in London and had accompanied him back. At the request of the Foreign Secretary the RAF had adapted a DC10 into a one-bed hospital so that the President could come home to die in his own country. Dr Merryweather was to preach, in Setswana, the main Botswanan language, at the President's funeral in his own village of Serowe. The majority of the population of Botswana were nominal Christians, with 20–30 % being church attenders, which is much more than the proportion in Britain. Dr Merryweather seemed to us the ideal missionary type, having identified himself with the country, playing an active and constructive part in its life, and being highly respected.

Returning to Johannesburg, one of the first things I did was to go to see Bishop Desmond Tutu who was then the General Secretary of the South Africa Council of Churches. (He later became bishop of Johannesburg and then archbishop of Cape Town, and was awarded the Nobel Peace Prize in 1984.) I found that he already knew me as the author of *Evil and the God of Love*. Until the release of Nelson Mandela in 1990 Desmond was the most prominent public opponent of apartheid in the country who was not in prison. As he said in a sermon,

> Many people think Christians should be neutral or that the Church should be neutral. But in an oppressive and unjust situation, such as we have in South Africa, not to choose to oppose is, in fact, already to have chosen to side with the powerful, with the exploiter, with the oppressor.

The Council's offices were behind heavily barred doors to prevent a sudden police raid. Desmond had recently been arrested at a demonstration, along with a number of other church leaders, and then released the next day. He said that it was great fun and had done a lot to raise their spirits. The authorities had bungled the event, gaining a lot of bad publicity abroad, and were 'silly asses'. The time for passing resolutions, as a substitute for action, was over. He thought, however, that a universal disinvestment from South Africa was not at that time practical politics and the best policy was to insist on certain conditions: the workers to be able to live with their families near their place of work; trades unions to be allowed; and a proportion of each company's profits to go into black educational projects. (Later, as the situation developed, he called for international disinvestment and an economic boycott.) He was vital, buoyant and humorous and confident that the apartheid regime would end within the next ten years. He was not far out, for in 1990 Nelson Mandela was freed and then the election of an African National Congress government. He said that he would send someone with me to visit Soweto when I was in Johannesburg again at the end of August, which he did, and told me when in Natal to visit some of the camps for workers. I saw him again before leaving South Africa and after that have met him on various occasions in the USA.

In South Africa he lived dangerously every day. Whilst we were there, there was a death threat from the Wit Kommando, a violent underground organisation dedicated to eliminating advocates of racial integration, who told Desmond to leave the country within a month or be killed. He had of course no intention of leaving, even if his passport had not been confiscated by the government the previous March! But he was always lively and humorous and optimistic, and with a much wider religious outlook – in relation for example to people of other faiths – than most Anglican bishops. He must have an enormous number of friends around the world, and I am very happy to be one of them. We have continued to correspond and I have a number of letters in his spidery handwriting, but the one I treasure most is a card in reply to my own card of congratulations to him and his country when in 1994 the African National Congress won South Africa's first genuinely democratic election, 'My dear John, Thanks for your beautiful card & its splendid message. We have all won, & especially such as yourself who supported us in the struggle. Much love and God's blessings, Desmond.'

From Johannesburg we flew to Durban, where we were collected by Vic Bredenkamp and Martin Prozesky (who I was to get to know well through his writings and his visits to us in Claremont) of the department of religion at the University of Natal at Pietermaritzburg where I was to be a visiting professor for the term. South Africa's winter weather, mirroring the northern hemisphere's summer, was marvellous, with blue skies and warm sun. We were given a flat constituting half a large bungalow near the university – 165B King Edward Road – with a white family living in the other half. Separate from the house was a garage with two small rooms built onto the back in each of which there lived a middle-aged black maid, one working next door and the other elsewhere. Unlike our own flat these two small rooms had no electricity and were lit by candles and oil lamps. They had no running water and used a tap in the yard. There was one outside toilet, of the hole in the ground variety, for the pair. A black maid came in once a week to clean our flat, having an hour-and-a-half journey each way. The exchange rate then was roughly R2 to £1. The average wage for live-in (i.e. live in a hut in the back yard) black maids was R35 a month, and for live-out maids R50 a month, which had to include the bus fares which could amount to as much as R20 a month. (Hazel of course paid our own cleaner at a proper rate.) Although legally the maid cannot have her husband living with her in the servants' quarters we heard of a number of cases in which the husband did in fact live there, the white employer turning a blind eye. It was not however possible for their children to live with them – these had to be left with a granny or with another family in the 'homeland' or a black township.

The other group of blacks living in the white cities were the men in the vast workers' hostels. I visited one of these in Johannesburg, like a prison except without bars, housing 4000 men, with hundreds of rooms in tiers round several courtyards, four or six men in a room in which the beds almost filled the floor space. The hostels were for men only, their families whom they supported with payments from their wages being hundreds of miles away in one of the 'homelands', the vast black ghettoes recognised as states by no other country than

South Africa. There was no privacy in the hostel, and there were no recreations except for the numerous 'bottlestores' in the street outside and no doubt brothels somewhere in the neighbourhood. Nothing could be less conducive to family life than a labour system based on these hostels for separated men. It was one of the most inhuman aspects of apartheid that it destroyed for so many the traditional close African family life.

We also visited several 'black spots' in Natal, places long inhabited by black communities which the government had now decided to evict for white development. About two million people had already been moved under the various resettlement schemes and another million were scheduled to be moved – initially into identical small lots containing a metal hut with a small metal toilet. Here they would work in a nearby factory.

At the University, among the English as distinguished from the Afrikaans academics, one could almost take a theoretical rejection of apartheid for granted. But whilst they and the English language press were mostly opposed to the National Party government and its policies, the great majority of English-speaking South Africans were living happily enough on the proceeds of apartheid – the deprived social status, low wages, education for servitude and appalling living conditions of the black workers, including their own servants. The dirty work of imposing apartheid had been done by the Afrikaners, who therefore bore the blame, but the English South Africans seemed ready enough to share its benefits as members of the white master race. When we went to a service at the nearby Presbyterian church the worship was clearly directed to the God of the white tribe of Africa, with prayers for our rulers in Pretoria and for our boys on the frontiers, but with no reference at all to the black majority among whom the congregation lived, and their problems, or to the drought and famine then afflicting nearby Kwa Zulu.

There were however several in the theology department who were deeply opposed to apartheid and were acting as best they could, necessarily in inconspicuous ways, against it. But they were a small minority among a white population who looked down on blacks as a lower species, at the same time fearing their presence and the growing signs of future change. For example, Professor Bredenkamp (who was always very hospitable to us) was interested in research into forms of birth control that would reduce the, to him, overwhelming size of the black population. People whom we met casually in Johannesburg had all spoken of the blacks as lesser creatures who constituted a threat. To most white people whom we met the black majority were individually invisible but collectively constituted a dark menace. When I went to Kimberley in Afrikaans (Boer) country I was told repeatedly that the blacks needed to be kept under control. On an internal flight I sat next to an elderly white man just back from a holiday in Europe. He said he was glad to be back and would not want to live anywhere except in South Africa. Meat was incredibly expensive in England and it was impossible to afford servants there. Here you can have one living in a hut in the backyard for very little. I said that perhaps this system is more costly than it seems but that the cost is borne by the black servants and their families. 'Yes,' he replied, 'but they're still just savages, you know.'

On the other hand I met some atypical Afrikaners who, at great cost to themselves, opposed apartheid. We went out once with the Wittenburgs, at the University, on their Tuesday round, first buying vegetables wholesale, then delivering half of them to an old peoples' home in a black township, and the rest elsewhere. (The Wittenburgs knew that their mail was intercepted because her father wrote regularly to the family, using carbon copies, and their own copy always arrived three days later than the others.) I also, incidentally, met Alan Paton, author of the famous anti-apartheid novel, *Cry, the Beloved Country* (1948) which brought international attention to apartheid, although latterly he had become much less radical.

From Pietermaritzburg we were taken by anti-apartheid workers to black townships, many of which were not on the official maps, to visit schools and other institutions. The townships varied greatly in the quality of housing – from rows of identical small brick bunga-lows to a sprawl of mud shanties; and such amenities as water varying from water laid on to a tap outside each house to a communal tap for many houses. It was reported in the local paper that in Sweetwater, one of the black townships that was on the map, no one had to walk more than two kilometres for water!

The annual per capita expenditure on education in South Africa was then R640 for a white, R297 for an Indian, R197 for a coloured (mixed race), and R68 (£34 a year) for a black. The blacks were being educated only to the level at which they could supply manual labour for the whites. We visited several black schools. One for example was a primary school for fifteen hundred pupils with an all black staff and presided over by an able and dedicated black head. He had no secretarial help and the school had no janitor, the children themselves doing all the cleaning and maintenance. Each teacher had a class of one hundred children in an overcrowded hut, fifty coming for the first third of the day, joined by the other fifty for the second part so that she was then teaching a hundred children, and finally in the third part just the second group of fifty. The children sat two or three at a desk or stood or sat on the floor. Many could not afford the textbooks and shared or did without and others could not afford exercise books. All equipment, such as chalk, had to be bought from a fund created by the parents' contributions. The parents also contributed to a building fund which the government matched rand for rand, so that one day there would be a proper school building. Because the parents generally have to leave home by 5 a.m. or so they give their children breakfast before they leave and the next meal when they get back at night. In this school a white charity was providing milk and a slice of bread for each child at midday. The whole system constituted a deliberate policy of restricting the vast majority of the black population to a minimal education. As prime minister Verword had said, 'The Bantu must be educated for a certain status in life.'

But mainly English-speaking Natal was in fact nevertheless in general more 'liberal' than the much larger Afrikaans-speaking South Africa. We met some very brave people who were working to end apartheid, particularly Peter Kerchoff who ran the Pietermaritzburg Agency for Christian Social Awareness (PACSA). *The Natal Witness* was opposed to apartheid, seeing it as an Afrikaans project. Being unable to do more than express a sense of solidarity with such people I felt a bit ashamed when a *Natal Witness* reporter who interviewed me said that a lot of young people regarded me as a kind of guru. I was later told of other people who had been praying that I would not come to South Africa! Possibly this explains why, when we first arrived at Johannesburg airport, the immigration officer looked at a list and then went away for ten minutes before coming back to admit us. The South African government certainly did not like my report,

Apartheid Observed, based on a detailed diary and published in Birmingham by AFFOR, and it was promptly put on the banned list when copies arrived in South Africa.

To return to Natal, I was made welcome at the black Federal Theological Seminary at Edendale where I was invited to speak and where every one of the students individually came to shake hands. The Seminary's president, Dr Sigqibo Dwane, was an outstanding leader – people of such high calibre were obviously important for the future free South Africa. I also had a great reception at the St Joseph's Scholastica, a black Catholic seminary, where again one could recognise some likely leaders for the future, for example Dr Jabulani Nxumalo. Hazel and I visited the Durban–Westville University in Durban as guests of 'Pipin' Oosthuizen, head of the Department for the Study of Religion, an Afrikaner who was opposed to apartheid. The students were almost entirely Indian in origin, the largest number being Hindus and the next largest Muslims. I had an hour-and-a-half session with about seventy students, talking about the relationship between different religions; my viewpoint did not shock them at all and evoked good questions. Another day Pipin took us to visit the Phoenix Settlement fourteen miles from Durban where Gandhi had lived and edited *Indian Opinion* and where one can see the wooden bungalow where he lived and the desk at which he wrote. Then on to the African township of Kwa Mashu consisting of small houses without electricity or running water or flush toilets and with water having to be carried in buckets from a communal tap. The buses ran from here into Durban from 4.30 a.m., the workers leaving before dawn to begin work at 7 a.m., and returning after dark – presumably seeing virtually nothing of their children during five days each week.

We also visited the University of Zululand, with good modern buildings but a very weak staff of academically mediocre Afrikaners and a few ill-equipped blacks. The Zulu students were of course also academically ill-equipped after the kind of school education that we had seen. Our hosts saw them, not as young people with unfulfilled potential but as inherently capable only of very limited and inferior education.

It was only three years earlier that Steve Biko had been beaten to death by the police when in custody, becoming an internationally known martyr of the Black Consciousness movement. He had been a medical student at the University of Natal's black Medical School at Durban which I visited on what turned out to be the anniversary of the death of Brother Stephen Bantu Biko. There was a lunch-hour meeting at which we all stood for a minute in silence. We were then addressed by a friend of Biko's, and then by the white dean of the medical school, who described in detail how the police doctors had flouted all the rules of medical ethics in leaving him battered, chained and untreated for many hours; and supporting the call for an inquiry into his death. Then another speech from another black student, and finally we all (except for the white professors, who were sympathetic to the students but could not associate themselves with them politically) stood with raised clenched fist to sing the national anthem of the future democratic South Africa, *N'kosi sekelel i'Afrika*. Although I did not know the Bantu words the whole occasion was deeply moving. I was then invited to the students' council office to meet with a number of their leaders, active in the Black Consciousness movement. They saw no chance of radical change without revolution. Buthelezi and Inkatha (the Zulu organisation in Natal) were dismissed as having sold out to the government. The attitude of the churches was ambiguous, and associated in the past with the repression of Africa. But Tutu and the South Africa Council of Churches were respected. These students seemed to me to be young men of high calibre, likely to be leaders in the future free South Africa. One of them said, 'We're grateful for all the help we can get from abroad, but we know that in the end we have got to do it ourselves.' I could only wish them well. In the end, they and innumerable other blacks did do it for themselves.

But the police state, of which Steve Biko was a victim, was pervasive. Opponents of apartheid had to be careful about what they said on the phone. We met a number of people who knew that their letters had been opened before being delivered. Well-known dissidents were placed under a banning order, not allowed to meet more than one person at a time and nothing that they said could be reported. There were then about a hundred and fifty banned individuals. I visited two of them, one being Beyers Naude, a prominent Afrikaner and former member of the Bruderbond, who openly opposed apartheid and was reviled by Afrikanerdom. There was an unmarked police car parked outside his house, and we went out to have tea in the garden at the back where, he thought, our conversation could not be picked up by their electronic equipment. (Others however told me later that he was deluded in this and that they could probably hear most of it.) His estimate was that black violence was very likely. He thought the black population would like the rest of the world to disinvest from South Africa in spite of the economic hardship that this would cause, but because this is not realistically possible we should advocate the same basic conditions that Desmond had stated. Naude was clear, level headed, dedicated, but did not strike me as the great charismatic leader depicted by some. His wife, who sat with us much of the time (contrary to the provisions of the banning order), gave me a packet to deliver to a Christian group.

After Durban we flew to Cape Town, where we were met by John de Gruchy, a notable critic of apartheid, and John Cumsty, an English professor at Cape Town University, who seemed to tolerate apartheid without too much difficulty. John de Gruchy, as an ordained minister, was about to marry (illegally) a black man and white woman. I lectured at Cape Town University, and was also invited to preach in the cathedral, my sermon including a statement about apartheid at which a women in the congregation got up and walked out. At University of the Western Cape for Coloureds I met some fine Afrikaners who rejected apartheid and were regarded as traitors by the powerful Broederbond. I also later visited Stellenbosch, the heart of Afrikaanadom. Some cousins of Hazel's took us out for the day to the Cape Peninsula and Cape Point, stopping for coffee on the way at Scarborough beach. Hazel's maternal grandfather had been minister of the Observatory Congregational church in Cape Town, which we visited. He also wrote a life of Seretse's father.[1] We went up Table Mountain, with its magnificent view, including the Robben Island prison whose most famous inhabitant, Nelson Mandela, I silently saluted.

I felt privileged to have visited South Africa at this point in its history. On the one hand, the white treatment of the blacks was wicked, sinful, inhuman, and their general blindness to this fact, even among very decent people, made it all the more so. On the other hand, I saw the human spirit asserting itself in many young blacks and a few whites. The younger generation, particularly school children and students, were beginning boldly to assert their existence as human beings. One could see this in the faces and in the bearing of many young men in Pietermaritzburg. The end of apartheid was, if not in sight, at least just over the horizon. Sach de Beer, the industrialist and opposition member of parliament whom I met in Johannesburg, told me that he expected a black government within ten years, but more as a result of black trades union pressure than direct violence. The development of the country's industries would require a more educated work force than the present policy allowed and the ending of apartheid was an economic as well as a moral necessity. John Rees, Director of the Institute for Race Relations, likewise predicted a black government within ten years. (I noticed a small tape recorder on his desk as we talked – I presume he had to protect himself against being misquoted.)

A final visit was to Desmond again, surveying the church situation. The largest white church, the Dutch Reformed, supported apartheid and defended it on biblical grounds; most of the English-speaking church leaders opposed apartheid but did not have the support of their laity; the black churches were generally too frightened to take part in the liberation struggle, so that their young people were becoming increasingly alienated from them. I had already learned that the strong evangelical/charismatic movement within the Anglican church enabled people to shut the whole racial situation out of their minds. Desmond said that the situation was immensely complicated in some ways but very simple essentially. Treat the blacks as fellow citizens of South Africa and the implications of this could be worked out over several years. What would be the position of the churches in the post-apartheid South Africa? The acid test would be: what was your contribution to the struggle?

NOTES

1. John Charles Harris, *Kama*, London: Livingstone Press, 1922.

22

Graduate teaching in California

I had not expected to have a second US incarnation. But in 1978 I was at a conference in San Francisco and was invited, whilst in California, to give a lecture at the Claremont Graduate School, later Claremont Graduate University, just outside Los Angeles. I did not know at the time that their Danforth professor of the philosophy of religion, John A. Hutchison, was due to retire and that they were looking for a successor. In due course they invited me to take the Danforth chair, and in due course I accepted. For my first three years there, with Hazel also after the first year, I taught in the spring semester only, January to May, and was back in Birmingham in time for the end of year examining and the autumn term. But from 1982 and for the next ten years Hazel and I moved fully to Claremont. In the summer the region became much too hot, drawing in the frightful LA smog; but we missed this by returning to England for the three summer months, when we were able to keep directly in touch with the rest of the family. We kept our house in Birmingham (21 Greening Drive, Edgbaston), renting it out whilst we were away, and renting out our Claremont house whilst we were in England. Sometimes the renting arrangement worked well, sometimes not.

The San Francisco conference which I was at when I was first contacted by Claremont was one of those hosted by the 'Moonies', the Unification Church (changing its name several times since) founded by the Korean evangelist, Sun Myung Moon. I attended three of these, all big international events, the other two to which Hazel also came being in Hawaii and Istanbul. The latter conference was on the theme of inter-faith relations. From Istanbul we visited several other places including the church where the Council of Nicea had met. Someone there suggested that we should all, standing on the ruined wall, recite the Nicene creed. Some did this is Greek, some in Latin, some in English, and some (including me) in inverted commas! The great majority of us, academics from a number of countries, who accepted invitations to these conferences (of which there were many more than these three) did so because, although we were not attracted at all by the Unification movement the conferences themselves were not only in nice places and lavishly funded (travel and hotel paid for both participant and spouse or partner) but were also intrinsically very interesting and not in any way interfered with by their sponsor. At the Hawaii and Washington conferences a good deal of attention was given to science/religion issues, often led by Nobel prize winners and other top experts in physics and other fields.

The Moonies had a bad press in many quarters and were accused of brainwashing vulnerable young people. Colleagues who knew far more about them than I did discounted most of this. In the late 1970s the Unification Church made the experiment of sending a number of its potential future leaders to do graduate work in major American universities and there were several of them in the religion department at Claremont. They were all bright, highly motivated, morally 'upstanding', as well as being deeply dedicated disciples of Sun Myung Moon. However the experiment was later terminated because too many of them, exposed to wider ideas and more critical thinking, sooner or later defected! At about the same time the Unification Church was drawing serious criticism for its business enterprises in Korea, which included arms manufacture, and was later charged with tax fraud (Moon himself being convicted of this in 1984) and it was denied charitable status on the grounds that its strongly anti-communist stance made it a political organisation. Learning more about its wider policies and activities than I knew at the time, I might well not have accepted those conference invitations.

To return to Claremont, this is outside Los Angeles city but inside LA county and lies at the foot of Mount Baldy, the nearest part of the massive San Gabriel mountains – in twenty minutes one could drive to above 6000 feet. Claremont town (but called a city) is formed round the cluster of Claremont Colleges.

CGU (Claremont Graduate University) is one of the USA's numerous private universities but the only free-standing purely graduate one, i.e., not part of a university based mainly on undergraduate teaching. It is one of a consortium of five institutions in Claremont, the others being undergraduate colleges: Pomona, one of the top liberal arts colleges on the west coast, Harvey Mudd, one of the top undergraduate colleges in the country for engineers, McKenna, a liberal arts college for men and Scripps for women. They share certain common facilities, above all an excellent library (larger than Birmingham's), and a faculty club. CGU had departments of history, literature, psychology, art, business administration, sociology, philosophy and religion. The Southern California School of Theology, basically Methodist but widely ecumenical in character, is also in Claremont. This gives its own degrees, but those of its graduate students wanting a PhD (rather than a ThD or the – academically bogus – DMin) did so at CGU, and a number of its faculty also taught at CGU, as did some of the Pomona, McKenna and Scripps faculties who were interested in doing some graduate teaching. The CGU faculty in Religion of which I was a member numbered twenty, plus fifteen others from the colleges.

Some of my colleagues were very distinguished in their fields. In PRT (Philosophy of Religion and Theology) they included John Cobb, the well known process theologian and founder of the Center for Process Studies in the School of Theology, his disciple David Griffin, the analytical philosopher of religion Stephen Davis (whom I had taught at the Princeton Seminary), Marjorie Suchocki, John Roth, and Frederick Sontag, and in the rapidly growing field of feminist studies, Karen Torjesen; and my predecessor Jack Hutcheson continued to do some occasional teaching. There was also a strong team in NT studies: James Robinson (famous for his work on the Nag Hammadi Coptic Gnostic manuscripts and on the International Q Project, as well as *The New Quest of the Historical Jesus* and other books), and James Sanders and Burton Mack. And there were many others in various fields. In general, a strong academic environment.

The attraction to me of CGU was two-fold. One was that it was a delight to move from mostly undergraduate to purely graduate teaching. And the other was the academic climate in the States, which was much more open and enquiring than in Britain. Whereas at Birmingham the philosophy of religion had a marginal place, it had a central place in the Religion programme at CGU. And the topics that had become high on my own agenda, broadening philosophy of religion from the philosophy of the Christian religion to the philosophy of religion globally, were already high on the agenda at Claremont, thanks to Jack Hutcheson and to the general academic climate. Alongside the religion department there was the Blaisdell Programs in World Religions and Cultures, which at first had a full-time director, although later when its funding ran low it became a smaller operation, with myself as director, sponsoring annual lectures – whilst I was there, Wilfred Cantwell Smith from Harvard, Muhammed Arkoun from the Sorbonne, Takeuchi Yoshinori from Kyoto, and Zwi Werblowsky from the Hebrew University, Jerusalem. Before its funds ran out I also used them to hold some excellent international conferences, the first on Gandhi with contributions from several leading authorities – Raghavan Iyer, Margaret Chatterjee, Sugata Dasgupta, Kees Bolle, Geoffrey Ostergaard, Ashis Nandy, Sushila Gudwani, and an excellent paper from Rex Ambler from Birmingham. Dr Dasgupta was son of the author of the standard multi-volume *History of Indian Philosophy*, and had been part of the Dasgupta household in Calcutta when Mircea Eliade, as a young man, lived with them whilst studying Hinduism. The present Dasgupta rang up Eliade in Chicago to charge him with having in his autobiography falsified his relationship with his, Dasgupta's, sister – according to him Eliade had behaved disgracefully. But it was a long time ago and who now knows the truth of the matter? The book coming out of the conference, *Gandhi's Significance for Today* (1989), was edited by the public policy expert Lamont Hempel and myself and published by Macmillan and has done quite well. We also had at this conference Rodrigo Carazo, rector of the UN Peace University and former President of Costa Rica, who had been influenced by Gandhi's thought, and Jerry Brown, the former Governor of California.

Another Blaisdell conference was a Jewish–Christian–Muslim encounter, with papers on all aspects of these faiths by their own scholars with comments from each of the other two faiths. This produced *Three Faiths, One God* (1989), edited by Edmund Meltzer and myself, and published by Macmillan and the SUNY, Press which has also done well.

In addition to the Blaisdell conferences I organised a series of philosophy of religion conferences which helped to raise Claremont's profile considerably in this field. To organise an international conference, bringing people from abroad, arranging accommodation, setting up the programme and carrying it through, involves a great deal of work, and each time I paid a competent student to do all this after I had myself made the basic plan and chosen the people to be invited. It also required a substantial budget which, thanks to the President of CGU, John Maguire, was made available. I invited others to edit the resulting books, which were *Death and Afterlife* (1989) edited by Stephen Davis; *Concepts of the Ultimate* (1989) edited by one of our best students, Linda Tessier; *Ethics, Religion and the Good Society* (1992) edited by Joseph Runzo, professor of philosophy at Chapman University; *Inter-religious Models and Criteria* (1993) edited by James Kellenberger, professor of philosophy at California State University at Northridge; and *Is God Real?* (1993) again edited by Joseph Runzo. And the year before I retired from Claremont Steve Davis organised a conference on my own work, with critical papers on a series of topics, with responses by myself. We had a particularly lively and useful session on the problem of evil, with William Rowe, one of the leading American philosophers of religion, arguing powerfully against Linda Zagzebski and myself. Amongst the other conference participants there were a former student, Gavin D'Costa, and Gerard Loughlin and Chester Gillis, all of whom had written critical doctoral dissertations about my work[1] (though Chester later came to agree with me[2]), and critics Brian Hebblethwaite and Julius Lipner – all of them friends as well as critics. The resulting book, *Problems in the Philosophy of Religion: Critical Studies of the Work of John Hick* (1991) was edited by one of our students, Harold Hewitt. All of these were published by Macmillan. My successor in the Danforth chair, Dewi Phillips, has continued the programme of annual conferences, in one of which I have participated, and has had the brilliant idea which I ought to have thought of myself of the *Claremont Studies in the Philosophy of Religion*, published by Macmillan and St Martin's Press (now jointly the Palgrave Press).

Various friends also came to give guest lectures from time to time. For example, Michael Goulder. 'Saturday until today Michael has been staying in our guest room. His two lectures were triumphs – complete command of biblical material, complete lucidity of argument, very impressive intellectual presence.' Although I differ from Michael totally about the validity of religious experience, and am often agnostic – due to ignorance – about his theories in biblical interpretation, I nevertheless have a lot in common with him in that we both value clear thought, accurate reasoning, and the lucid expression thereof, and can spot feeble and lazy thinking a mile off!

At CGU the requirements for the PhD in religion were those of all the major US universities: first, master's level exams across the field of religious studies, and reading exams in French and German (plus further ancient languages for biblical subjects), then two years of graduate seminars chosen by the student out of the range of departmental offerings, then a qualifying exam related to the student's chosen dissertation topic, and finally the writing of the dissertation. For the dissertation the student had a committee of three faculty supervisors. This has both advantages and disadvantages in comparison with the British system in which there is normally only one supervisor. The advantage is that the student cannot be dominated by a single professor with his or her sometimes dictatorial directions. The disadvantage is that the three may sometimes disagree amongst themselves and give confusing or contradictory advice. But normally both systems have in practice worked satisfactorily.

I was responsible for two seminars in each of the two semesters, and these took place on Mondays and Tuesdays from three to six in the afternoon. My teaching method was as follows. Each of the fifteen three-hour sessions divided naturally, by a coffee break, into two. In each of these slightly less than one-and-a-half-hour periods there was a short paper written by one of the students on a chapter or an article prescribed for that week and read by everyone. These student papers, which were not intended to be summaries but critical responses, were handed or faxed in the previous day – or Saturday in the case of a Monday seminar – and photocopied and distributed at the seminar, so that everyone had a copy in front of them. The writer began to read the paper aloud, but anyone could interrupt for discussion at any point – and sometimes, when the paper was successfully provocative we never reached the end of it. In addition when anyone felt that some issue had not been sufficiently worked through, he or she was encouraged to write a one-page discussion note which was likewise photocopied and distributed and taken as the first item of business next time. Sometimes these themselves provoked responses, with discussion continuing for two or three weeks. I sometimes contributed discussion notes myself, and also occasionally longer pieces to introduce a new topic or to summarise a concluded part of the course. The students' discussion notes were deliberately restricted to one side of a sheet of paper to encourage the concentration of thought that brevity demands. They should be the result of a repeated filtering out of the irrelevant and the redundant in aid of a sharp focusing on the central issue. And they should aim at maximum clarity, eschewing would-be impressive vagueness and rhetoric.

This format worked best with the really good students. Two or three or four such could make a seminar go well. In the course of twelve years I learned a lot, particularly from this minority of first-rate students. But I hope that all the seminar members also learned something through their participation in what was intended to be an intellectually demanding experience. The more a student put into a seminar discussion the more he or she gained from it.

But as well as the teaching I had to do some administrative chores. Throughout my career I have avoided administration like the plague and have usually got away with membership of a committee or two which hardly ever met. But about halfway through my time at Claremont I was asked to become chair of the religion department on the grounds that for publicity purposes there ought to be a 'high profile' chair, but with someone else, Edmund Meltzer, as associate chair. He was supposed to do all the work downwards, in relation to the students, which was the major because almost daily work, and I all the work upwards, in relation to the dean and president. I thought that my own part would be minimal – fixing the salaries once a year, and dealing with new appointments, but not much more. But as time went on I became involved in unwelcome committees, emergency breakfast meetings, crisis talks and other ephemeral but time-consuming events. And yet even so Claremont was a much better place for me to be than anywhere else I knew of.

From Claremont I travelled all over the States to give lectures and take part in conferences. A few trips were into the deep south, where the American Civil War was still called by some the War of Northern Aggression. One such was to a College in Mobile, Alabama. Whilst there I went on Sunday to the large Southern Baptist church which had been famously photographed in the 1960s with the deacons standing in a row at the door to keep blacks out. There was a white congregation of perhaps a thousand, and a large choir with orchestra. The sermon centred on Sin, in narrow legalistic language, the preacher mostly shouting, and then people were called to the front to be saved, one or two who did so making obviously rehearsed speeches. When I got home it was reported in the *LA Times* that a Southern Baptist minister had been expelled for holding that Jews go to heaven!

When I retired from the Danforth chair in 1992 the department office prepared for me a sixty-three page document called 'Leftover Thoughts' consisting of a number of the short discussion papers and longer introductory and summarising papers that I had produced for different courses over the years, together with my 'exaugural' lecture.

Here is an example of my own brief discussion notes:

Plantinga's ontological argument

Can one 'do a Gaunilo' on Plantinga with the following argument [which mirrors Plantinga's own argument for a maximally good God]?

1. There is a possible world W in which maximal evil is instantiated.
2. Necessarily, a being is maximally evil if it has the property of being maximally evil in every (possible) world.
3. Necessarily, a being has the property of being maximally evil in every (possible) world only if it has omnipotence, omniscience, and absolute moral depravity in every (possible) world.
4. If W were actual, (5) 'There is no omnipotent, omniscient, and absolutely morally depraved being', would be impossible.
6. But since (5) is impossible in one possible world, it is impossible in all possible worlds.
7. Therefore there is an omnipotent, omniscient, and absolutely morally depraved being!

Each student also had to write a major term paper on a topic of their own choice, agreed by me. I gave them:

A Little Essay on Essays

I hope that you have started or are about to start writing your term paper. The following advice is offered for use in so far as it is apposite and for oblivion in so far as it is superfluous.

Choose a topic which genuinely interests you and in which you are eager to invest your time and effort. There is nothing worse than writing a major paper merely as a course requirement – except perhaps reading such a paper. There is no reason why a really good term paper, on a suitable topic, should not be developed into an article for publication. I have occasionally in the past received such papers. But if you aim for this, the topic has to be one on which an article is needed. But whether or not the topic is one that might justify publication, make publishability your aim so far as quality is concerned.

If you are going to expound and criticise some writer, take great care with your exposition. Make it so fair and balanced that the author would be able to accept it as an accurate account of his/her thought. And quote with 100 % accuracy. Do not be tempted to set up a caricature in order to have something easy to demolish. And try to see the value of a point of view from which you differ. No thinker who is worth criticising is likely to be wholly wrong. Make the effort to discriminate.

If possible, a paper should be built around a central thesis. Be very clear in your own mind what your central thesis is, and then exclude material which is not relevant to it. Second only to a pen (or typewriter or PC), a wastepaper basket is probably the writer's most important item of equipment. Be prepared to discard – sometimes an agonising thing to do. (If you want to digress, do so visibly – saying what you are doing, and perhaps even putting the digresssion in brackets.) Don't leave the reader puzzled about the connection between what you are now saying and what you said in the previous paragraph. If the link is not self-evident, spell it out.

Words work best when used economically. They lose their value in inflation. So if you can cut any words out of a sentence whilst leaving the meaning intact, the slimmer sentence will communicate more effectively. And don't overload a sentence. If you find yourself having to add more and more qualifying clauses, so that the sentence gets ever longer and more complex, consider breaking it into two.

Use words precisely. Ask yourself whether what you have written says exactly what you want to say.

Finally, criticise your own work ruthlessly. If, when you read a paragraph through, you feel that there is something wrong with it, don't rest until you have seen what is wrong and put it right. The difference between good and poor writing is often roughly proportionate to the number of times it or parts of it have been rewritten. So produce a first draft, and then let it grow and develop, and perhaps change shape, with repeated reworkings. Every time you see reason to cross something out you are probably on the way to a better paper. One can see a paper as a piece of sculpture to which one returns day after day, adding bits on, having an eye to its proportions, and working away at it until it comes out right – or as nearly right as you can get it.

During my time at Claremont I offered seminars on the epistemology of religion; the problem of evil; death and eternal life; contemporary philosophies of religion; Locke, Berkeley and Hume; Christianity and other religions; Buddhism and Christianity (with Masao Abe); and the entire draft of what became my book *An Interpretation of Religion*.

I am not sure that I would have been able to write this if I had not gone to Claremont with its pervasive spirit of openness to the global reality of religion. At any rate it was here that I developed my 'pluralistic hypothesis' about the relation between the religions – although that only occupies about half the book. I had long had the 'pluralistic insight' expressed in Rumi's saying about the religions that, 'The lamps are different but the Light is the same – it comes from beyond', and had written about it a number of times. But in *Interpretation* it is developed much more fully.

A major influence here had been Wilfred Cantwell Smith, who became a good friend and admired mentor.[3] He was enormously learned – able to use Arabic and Sanscrit and Chinese as well as Hebrew and Greek and six modern European languages – and could back up the pluralistic insight with the authority of a major historian of religion. He was famous for the fact that his scholarly endnotes often occupied almost as many pages as the main text of his books. Wilfred's critical scholarly conscience also shows itself in his writing style, with all the careful qualifications and qualifications of qualifications by which he seeks to do justice to the endless complexities of his subject. His sense of the complexity of meanings, and his instinctive avoidance of over-simplification – which sometimes makes him less easy to read than he might otherwise be – came out when I asked him once whether he had now finished his last book, a comparative study of world scriptures.[4] He said, 'Yes, in six of the seventeen senses of "finished".' His scholarly scrupulousness may reflect the Calvinist conscience that is symbolized for me by the time when we had a meal together at some conference, each paying for ourselves but with Wilfred ending up owing me ten cents. Of course I told him to forget it. But a few days later a ten cent coin arrived, taped to a card in an envelope. As a fellow Calvinist, though only in the same very loose sense as himself, I appreciated this; but as a lay economist I noted that the stamp on the envelope had cost twenty-five cents! I said that Wilfred is a Calvinist in a very loose sense. If, per impossibile, he had published his thoughts in Calvin's Geneva he would very probably have met the same fate as Servetus, who was burned alive as a heretic. (So would I.)

Wilfred, then, was a major comparative religion scholar, with a specialisation in Islam. But what made him unique is that he used his prodigious range of knowledge to further the cause of mutual human understanding and the awareness of our common humanity. Whilst he delved deeply into the particular traditions in their unique particularity, his vast knowledge made him aware of fascinating parallels and historical interconnections between the different religious traditions.[5] Further, he was not an armchair scholar. He had worked for six years in what is now Pakistan, and throughout his life he interacted with people of many faiths, insisting at McGill, Dalhousie and Harvard that the study of other faiths required not only book knowledge but also personal knowledge of people who embodied those faiths. He was interested, in other words, in religion as the living and lived faith of his fellow human beings, not merely as illustrating types or as material for sociological analysis.

Wilfred's contributions to thought within and beyond the academic history of religions were immensely important and influential. He deconstructed the familiar western concept of a religion as a bounded socio-religious entity over against other such entities, tracing the modern origins and showing the inadequacy of this way of thinking.[6] It is largely due to him that today we are accustomed to speak of religious traditions, as internally diverse and changing movements, rather than of religions as vast static entities. And he steered us away from asking the typically western question about another religious community, What do they believe? to an interest in their lives as a whole, in which propositional beliefs sometimes play a major but often only a peripheral part.

Another major contribution was Wilfred's distinction between, on the one hand, what he called faith and, on the other hand, the cumulative traditions. The latter are historical phenomena interacting with all the other forces which together make up human history. By faith he means the individual's inner spiritual response to the Divine. This distinction is enormously important, for the inner life of faith is regularly ignored in the media's focus upon the religious organisations; and whereas these divide, faith (in his sense of the word) unites.

Through his intellectually liberating work on the world-wide religious dimension of human life Wilfred has been the father of contemporary religious pluralism, rightly so regarded by critics as well as by friends and colleagues.[7] His rejection of the idea that Christianity is the one and only true faith and context of salvation has been a major influence for the growing acceptance of a wider vision.

As my own contribution I applied to the epistemology of religion Kant's distinction between the world as it is in itself and as perceived by us in terms of the system of concepts that structures our own consciousness. I distinguished between, on the one hand, the ultimate transcategorial (or ineffable) Real which is universally present around and within us, and on the other hand the range of different forms of human awareness of that reality as the various personae (Jahweh, Heavenly Father, Allah, Vishnu, Shiva, etc.) and impersonae (Brahman, Tao, Dharmakaya, etc.) formed by our different conceptual systems and – very importantly – spiritual practices. But there is a lot more to it than this miniature summary can convey. *An Interpretation of Religion* has been widely discussed, and indeed almost every treatment of the problem of religious diversity since has had something to say about it. It has helped to stir up a number – at the moment nearly thirty – books about my work, mostly by conservative Christian theologians and philosophers, a few of them making useful critical points.

From my diary in February 1982:

Life has continued too busily for the diary to get a fair deal. But one event should be recorded. Yesterday Mark told me on the phone of a letter from the V.C. at Edinburgh U., inviting me to give the Gifford Lectures there in 1986-7. This is both an unexpected delight and a half-expected relief! What if I had never been invited to do the Giffords, when some who have less to say have given them? Indeed ever since student days in Edinburgh I think I have nursed some kind of assumption that I would one day deliver the Gifford lectures! So it is a relief that my presumption is not rebuffed.

The lectures were endowed at the end of the nineteenth century by a Scottish judge, Lord Gifford, and I was shocked to find that his great, great grandson, the present Lord Gifford, who is a barrister with some very good ideas about law reform, pronounces Gifford as though it were Jifford – who is he to presume to know, better than generations of philosophers of religion, how to pronounce his own name? Many Gifford series have been given during the last hundred years, some notable (by such as A.N. Whitehead, Reinhold Niebuhr, Karl Barth, Paul Tillich, Emil Brunner, William Temple, and the best of all by William James, and many others also, including such contemporaries as Alvin Plantinga, Richard Swinburne, Keith Ward, etc.) with yet others long since forgotten. There are some important thinkers, however, who ought to have been asked to present their thoughts in this forum but who were not – such as John Oman, F.R. Tennant, Charles Hartshorne, William Alston. As I see it, it is not so much that it is a great honour to be invited to give the Giffords as a bit of a slight not to be! In reality the lectures themselves were no great event, with an audience of around fifty, although it was wonderful to be in Edinburgh again, meeting old friends and seeing familiar places. Ron Murray (by then Lord Murray, a senior appeal judge) came to some of the lectures and I had a very nice lunch with Ron and Sheila in their house, and also attended a court hearing. Peter McEwan, living at Ballater in Aberdeenshire, came to lunch with me at the Faculty Club and reminded me that he and Alec Stewart and I had agreed to meet again at the Devil's Pass in the year 2000 – which we have failed to do. Ele came up to Edinburgh for one of the lectures and the weekend, and on leaving Edinburgh I was able to visit mother in Leeds. Altogether a very good trip.

These years at Claremont ended happily with one of my best graduate seminars, the best of the series of philosophy of religion conferences, and my best student during the Claremont years – Tim Musgrove – receiving his PhD. Hazel and I were both sad to leave, and yet ready to leave.

NOTES

1. Gavin's, at Cambridge, was published as *John Hick's Theology of Religions*, University Press of America, 1987; Chester's, at the University of Chicago, as *A Question of Final Belief*, Macmillan, 1988; and Gerard's dissertation at Cambridge was called 'Mirroring God's World: A Critique of John Hick's Speculative Theology', 1986.

2. Chester Gillis, *Pluralism: A New Paradigm for Theology*, Peeters Press: Louvain, and Eerdmans, 1993.

3. What follows draws on a lecture that I gave at a conference in Montreal in 1992 on the occasion of Wilfred's retirement, published in *Method and Theory in the Study of Religion*, Vol. 4, 1992, and in my Preface to a Cantwell Smith Reader.

4. Wilfred Cantwell Smith, *What is Scripture?*, Minneapolis: Fortress Press, and London: SCM Press, 1993.

5. See, e.g., his *Towards a World Theology*, London: Macmillan, 1981, containing his Cadbury Lectures at Birmingham.

6. See his *The Meaning and End of Religion*, first published in 1962 and many times reprinted, e.g. by Fortress Press of Minneapolis in 1991.

7. A Claremont graduate, Edward Hughes, wrote his PhD dissertation on Wilfred's work, published as *Wilfred Cantwell Smith: A Theology for the World*, London: SCM, 1986.

23

Life at Claremont

But of course there was much more to life in Claremont than teaching. These were, I would say, the happiest ten years for Hazel and me in our married life, spoiled only by the tragic death of Mike – about which more later. She loved America and we made many friends and, as always, she found absorbing teaching to do. She learned Spanish, the second language of California, becoming quite fluent in it. We had wonderful visits from the children. Pete and Ele delight in remembering (every year) how one Christmas we all visited San Diego and had dinner in a Mexican restaurant, where a large female singer came round the tables as she sang. I happened to be sitting on the outside so I was the one on whose lap she sat and sang. We had all seen this coming, I in increasing embarrassment and the others in increasing anticipation.

Our Claremont house, 516 West Ninth Street, an easy walk or bike ride from the campus, was a wooden bungalow with a large sitting room, two bedrooms, two bathrooms, dining room as an extension of the sitting room, kitchen, study leading out onto the sundeck, a double garage (with a mountain and lake mural painted on it by an artist friend) and added onto the garage a guest room with bathroom. There was a small lawn at the front and a bigger one at the back, kept green by pipes below the ground feeding sprinklers. We were fortunate in having very friendly neighbours on both sides, with one of whom I am still in touch.

Between them the Colleges had five open air swimming pools, one of Olympic size, and although CGU did not have one of its own we could use all of them. Swimming in the open air, surrounded in most cases by palm trees, bushes and flowers, was a tremendous pleasure. Beside one of the pools ingenious students were accustomed to use a large blackboard to write up palindromes (reversible phrases and sentences), each trying to produce a longer one than the last. The shortest was 'Pull up'. A later one was 'Madam, I'm Adam' with the answering 'Even am I, man, Eve'. But the two longest were: 'Able was I ere I saw Elba' and 'A man, a plan, a canal – Panama'. I had never swum regularly before but began a habit at Claremont which I have continued ever since, though now only three times a week instead of virtually every day. One day I listed in my diary some of life's smaller pleasures, which were: 'swimming in clear blue water of Scripps pool at an uncrowded time of day; breakfast in bed; a few minutes listening to Mozart on earphones at the end of a long session of writing; bird songs in the early morning; going out to pick up the paper before breakfast – fresh air, sun, birds'. The paper was the excellent *Los Angeles Times* delivered early in the morning by someone going along the street in a car and throwing it onto the path in front of each house – in a plastic bag on rainy days.

The climate was a delight, sunbathing weather almost every day, though with a rainy season in the spring when there could be tremendous tropical downpours. The daytime temperature was usually in the mid or upper 70s, although one Christmas it was 80 degrees. We had a south-facing sundeck at the back of the house with two comfortable sunbeds and I spent a lot of each day out there in the sun, reading and writing. I was still living BC (Before Computers) – although the department office was full of them – and wrote by hand, the result being put on a computer later. One April,

> In the high 80s yesterday. Warm enough to sit outside after dark smoking a cigar. The moon, behind the Munters' tree [next door], very bright and large, almost bursting through the foliage. Stars at rest and occasional lights of planes, too far away to be heard, crossing the night sky. Hot again today – we have just had breakfast on the sundeck. Blue sky. Bird songs.

The region had earlier been a citrus growing area and in our yard (garden) we grew oranges, lemons, grapefruits, peaches, and there were humming birds hovering among the branches. There were also some local large green parrots, powerful squawkers, who sometimes patronised our trees and phone lines.

Southern California is an earthquake area and at Claremont we were not very far from the San Andreas fault. There are apparently some eleven thousand, mostly imperceptible, earthquakes each year. We had earthquake insurance, and most of the houses were wooden and single storey so that they could stand up to a certain degree of shaking. There were several sizeable quakes during our ten years there. One was in October 1987. At 7.40 in the morning there was a quake of 6.1 on the Richter scale, centred at Whittier. I was standing on the grass in the yard and was suddenly conscious of a mighty wind which violently shook the trees, with their branches swaying frantically. A couple of thousand years ago people would probably have said that an angel passed by. But it was over in a few seconds, with no real damage in Claremont. Hazel had been driving to work at the time, and the tyres absorbed the shock, with the car only rocking a little. Another was a 5.5 quake centred at nearer Upland. I was away at a conference in New Orleans but Hazel was at home when books fell out of their shelves and a picture fell off the wall. But again no one was hurt in Claremont. However a 6.9 earthquake further north in October 1989 killed 150 people in San Francisco. And in our last year at Claremont there was a 6.1 quake centred at nearby Desert Springs, making the house sway and rock for sixty seconds. But the expected Big One is still to come.

As a URC minister I wondered whether to apply to join the local Presbytery of San Gabriel and, remembering my 'affair with the Virgin Mary' twenty years earlier, and having no desire to spend my time in ecclesiastical controversy, I consulted some Presbytery members whom I knew who made soundings and then assured me that my application would go through on the nod. However in fact some of the evangelical/fundamentalist brethren spotted it and did object. In September 1983,

> The Presbytery meeting was held last Tuesday, and I had to cancel the second half of my seminar to attend. My name was proposed by the committee chairman for membership. There was then about an hour of debate, speakers quoting from *The Myth of God Incarnate* and *God Has Many Names* and my 'Christian Century' article of 2 years ago. The tone was mostly courteous. Speakers for

the motion included Steve Davis, Jim Angell [minister of the Claremont Presbyterian church of which we were members], and Jane Douglas. After an agreed cut-off time 88 voted for and 82 against! Very close. I was then enrolled after answering the constitutional questions. Jim Sanders (whom we met at the swimming pool this afternoon) said that later in the meeting a Protest was lodged, signed by 100 names, and that the Moderator had rejected it as out of order because it dealt with substance and not order.

The situation was complicated by the recent union of the northern and southern Presbyterian churches to form the Presbyterian Church USA, with a provision that during the first three years any congregation was free to opt out. It was put about by the antis that if I was received into the Presbytery a number of the former southern congregations would secede. It was also a factor that generally the super-evangelical congregations were the largest and richest and that the Presbytery was campaigning to increase its capital funds! The very conservative Fuller Seminary in Pasadena was also a strong anti influence. Hazel and I went to dinner there with Ian Pitt-Watson (who had graduated in philosophy the year before me at Edinburgh) who was now professor of homiletics at Fuller. He had an additional angle on the Presbytery dispute. He said that there was a seepage from the Presbyterian church into the extreme right-wing sects, and if my Presbytery membership was sustained this would increase, for people on the fringe would see the Presbytery as dangerously liberal!

The thing had now escalated with an appeal against the Presbytery's action to the Synod of Southern California. In February next year, 1984,

At a lunch at STC with the Moderator of the Pres. Church, U.S.A., Randy Thompson. Then about an hour with him and the Presbytery executive. He seems to be an ecclesiastical statesman rather than a theologian, though friendly. It seems that the Synod's Judicial Commission is stuck and seeking a compromise. Suggests that Presbytery start again and examine me in open Presbytery, with the five complainants agreeing that if the vote is against them they will regard it as final. At present three agree and two not. I agreed to my proposed part – though it will not be pleasant, and could well go against me. The Moderator said he did not know how it would go.

The thing simmered in the background in complicated ecclesiastical manoeuvres, other people busy with it and I most of the time forgetting about it, until in due course when I was invited to meet with the Presbytery's Committee on Ministry. I made a short statement focusing on my attitude to other faiths – Los Angeles having the third largest Jewish community in the world; a large Buddhist community and the biggest Buddhist temple in North America; and large Muslim and Hindu communities – and my view that Christianity was not the one and only true faith. There was a good deal of discussion, after which I left them for a while, and when I returned they had decided to ask me to withdraw my application in order to avoid a split in the church. I had no wish to cause this and agreed to withdraw my application – to the jubilation, I was later told, of the fundamentalist brethren throughout the church. They had now avenged their failure to exclude me from the Presbytery of New Brunswick a quarter of a century ago. It had evidently rankled all these years.

John Dart, the well-known religion writer for the *Los Angeles Times*, reported in a way sympathetic to me and quoted Jim Angell, the minister of our church in Claremont, 'The Presbyterian church needs great creative minds like John Hick', and the campus rabbi embraced me! I was not myself bothered by the outcome. My job was not at stake, CGU not being a church related institution; and I was happy not to need to attend Presbytery meetings. But it was disturbing to see how strong the fundamentalist and extreme evangelical element was – and still is – within the Presbyterian church.

A very satisfying activity was the creation of a local – Los Angeles area – Jewish–Christian–Muslim dialogue group. Thanks largely to the work of a then student, Maura O'Neill, a good network of personal relations was developed as we met in different houses. Muzammil Siddiqui, Imam of the flourishing Orange County Islamic Center (and with a Birmingham PhD), and Rabbi Ben Beliak, campus Jewish chaplain, supported this. We generally discussed concrete matters, like family life, the rearing and education of children, food, the rituals and holy days, etc. With theology left in the background, ordinary and lasting human friendships were formed.

On a more academic level, I was also a founding member of both the international Jewish–Christian–Muslim 'Trialogue', and the international Buddhist–Christian Theological Encounter, about which more later. The Trialogue was initiated by Len Swidler, Khalid Duran and Rabbi David Blumenthal. In addition to these, John Cobb among the Christians, Rabbi Irving 'Yitz' Greenberg, and Pinches Lapide among the Jews, and Muhammed Arkoun, Rifat Hassan, and Fathi Osman among the Muslims, were among the leading members. We usually met in the USA, but once in Jerusalem. We would have liked to meet in Egypt but were not in the end able to. As we all got to know one another our discussions were extremely productive of mutual understanding. Although only articulated by a minority of us, including myself, the implicit assumption was that it is okay from God's point of view for Jews to be Jews, Christians to be Christians, and Muslims to be Muslims.

An Interpretation of Religion was published in 1989 by Macmillan and Yale University Press and had a good reception. Yale UP had entered it for the Grawemeyer Award in Religion (then an award of $150,000, now of $200,000), and early in 1991 I had a phone call from Louisville, Kentucky, to say that I was to receive the award for that year, and could I come to Louisville in ten days' time for a press conference at which the four awards would be announced? There is one in religion, this being only its second year, the first having gone to the New Testament scholar E.P. Sanders; one in international relations, which went that year to the prime minister of Norway for her leadership in the United Nations on environmental issues; one in music, which went to John Corigliano for his symphony composed in memory the world's AIDS victims; and one in education which went to Professor Kieran Egan for his book on the use of the imagination in primary education. For each field there is a small international committee changing in membership every year which makes a shortlist, and then a local committee from Louisville University together, in the case of the religion award, with the Louisville Theological Seminary, makes the final choice.

A few months later Hazel and I went to Louisville for the award-giving ceremony, where I almost disgraced myself. In southern California most men only wear a tie on special occasions. I had been told that the big dinner at which the awards would be presented would be a formal occasion, and as a Californian I thought of wearing a suit and tie as the height of formality. But when our hosts came to collect us at the hotel they were aghast. I was supposed to be in a dinner jacket and black bow tie. So they took us on a frantic chase through Louisville at eight o'clock at night looking for a shop where I could hire the correct gear – and happily we found one and turned up just as the cocktail period was ending. I made a short speech and a medal was hung round my neck on a red ribbon. John Dart in the *LA Times* had great fun reporting that I had received this prestigious award by a body including the Louisville Presbyterian Seminary for saying what I had been excluded from the San Gabriel Presbytery for saying!

From Claremont we made various expeditions, including several visits to Grand Canyon: In June 1983

> we made a second expedition to Grand Canyon, and I went down by Bright Angel Trail on the mule train, staying the night at Phantom Ranch and coming up the shorter and steeper Kaibab Trail next day. Strenuous, leaving one saddle sore but otherwise ok. The immense natural rock structures in the Canyon – like giant thrones, gothic cathedral, castles, pyramids, ziggurats etc. – are profoundly impressive. Millions of years old, with human beings as insects crawling round their feet during the last few seconds!

It was on the balcony of a restaurant overlooking the Canyon that I had my first memorable taste of pina colada, no subsequent pina coladas made anywhere else having yet measured up to it!

We also visited San Francisco and Yosemite National Park; Lake Tahoe; walks on Mount Baldy; whale watching on boats going a mile or two off shore; a weekend in Las Vegas, and several in San Diego with its marvellous zoo and much else. We also had a Christmas at Cuernavaca in Mexico where Hazel attended a Spanish language course while I sat in the sun at the hotel, and then a few days in Mexico City.

I made numerous visits to other universities and conference centres all over the States and Canada. For example, in March 1984,

> Back yesterday from an annual gathering of the Pacific Division of the American Philosophical Association, meeting on the old *Queen Mary* moored at Long Beach. A very pleasant couple of days. Drove down with Chuck Young [professor of ancient philosophy at CGU] and his partner Nancy. First class 'state

room', much larger than the 3rd class cabin in which we came across the Atlantic in January 1956. Visited the Spruce Goose – built by the reclusive multi-millionaire Howard Hughes as the biggest airplane in the world, which made only a single flight, of one mile. Dinner Thursday with Charles Crittenden, who is a commentator on my paper on Friday. Friday spent a.m. on deck writing replies to the two comment papers – Charles, and Dallas Willard of the University of Southern California. 1 p.m. chaired a session on Ethics & Theology, paper by Bob Adams – careful and interesting as always. Walked round deck several times with him afterwards talking about a possible book of his essays for Macmillan's Library of Philosophy and Religion [of which I am the General Editor], and about the Presbytery and also Princeton Seminary. At 5 p.m. gave my paper to the Phil. of Rel. Society. A full room and an excellent session. Good paper by me (!) and two good responses, then persistent questions. A number of leading people there – Adams, Mavrodes, Kellenberger, King-Farlow, Puccetti, Davis, etc., then dinner with chairman, Joe Runzo – who is applying for a job at Fuller! The Q.M. itself pleasantly nostalgic. Met a number of new people. The Prentice-Hall girl told me that the last ed. of *Philosophy of Religion* sold 110,000 copies. Tried to interest me in writing another text – but my text writing days are over.

Again,

Last week at 25th anniversary meeting of American Society for the Study of Religion at Chicago. Met the great Mircea Eliade, a somewhat shrunken old man. Stayed at McCormick Inn, room on 18th floor looking out over the cleared railway yards and curving concrete roads sweeping above and below each other, carrying ceaseless flows of traffic in every direction. Had lunch with Chester Gillis and dinner with Hiromasa Mase and family. Chicago airport lavatories ['rest rooms'/ 'comfort stations'] have wash basins with automatic taps that come on spasmodically for a few seconds, but mostly fail to work at all.

There was an amusing, but at the time embarrassing, incident once when I went to give a lecture in the University of Chicago's Divinity School. I stayed the night in the faculty Quadrangle Club, and coming down the next morning looking for breakfast I saw a large room with a big oval table obviously set for breakfast, though I was surprised that there were so many guests staying there, having only seen a few. There was a rather impressive man standing at the door and I said 'Breakfast's in here?' He said, 'Yes, go on in.' So I sat down at table and others came in until it was full. It felt slightly odd that they were all in suits or smart dresses whereas I was wearing a sports jacket and no tie. I chatted with my neighbours about nothing in particular whilst a splendid breakfast was served. Presently the impressive looking man, who was now sitting at the head of the table, got up and said, 'Ladies and gentlemen, we all know what the problem is. I'd like to hear your views', and he turned to the man on his right and said, 'Joe, what do you think we should do?' He then went on round the table, and it quickly dawned on me that this was the University's President Levy holding an emergency meeting of his deans and other senior officials to discuss a student revolt, with a big demonstration expected later that morning! What was I to do? I thought it would be unacceptably rude just to get up and walk out at this point, and equally rude to interrupt the proceeding to apologise and then go. And in the meantime as Levy called on people one after the other round the table he was getting nearer and nearer to me! Horrors! All I could do, when he came to me, was to explain that I was a visitor from Britain who had been lecturing at the Divinity School yesterday, staying the night, and apologising for being there, my mistake. Levy coped with the situation very graciously, saying that he would welcome any thoughts from a colleague from Britain. I of course disclaimed any right to an opinion, and the discussion moved on round the table, to my great relief. There was curious codicil to this incident many years later when, back in Birmingham, the department hosted a visit from a group of theology professors from another university in Chicago. I was invited to talk to them, and as an opening gambit told them my awkward experience in the Quadrangle Club. One of them immediately told us all that he had been the student leader organising the demonstration, and that the secret emergency meeting had become known and was part of university folklore. Small world!

On one occasion I visited the University of Virginia at Charlottesville to give a paper to the philosophy department, staying a few days with Peter Heath, who had been a friend from Edinburgh and Belford days and was now a professor of philosophy here. He was a brilliant teacher and an acute philosopher who has however written very little, although his article on 'Nothing' in Paul Edwards' *Encyclopedia of Philosophy* is a classic of comic seriousness. He has also made a major contribution to contemporary philosophy by his translations of many difficult German works, including much of Kant in the new comprehensive Cambridge translation. He is also an authority on *Alice in Wonderland* and the interesting logical puzzles which it contains – Peter has a room lined with hundreds of books on Lewis Carroll and Alice. In this pleasant house amid a sea of trees on the outskirts of Charlottesville the front door once became stuck and ever since, with characteristic disregard for such trivialities, he has used the back door through the garage!

It is also somehow characteristic that his letters indicate the day of the month but not the year when they were written. But when I wrote to him about my 'breakthrough' in meditation, in which I experienced a unity with the world around me and a strong awareness of the ultimately benign character of the universe of which I am a part, so that there was no room for any kind of fear or anxiety (see chapter 19), he replied:

The account of your Nirvana-type experience was intriguing, though one cannot help wondering, on reading it, what universe it is that you are talking about. It cannot very well be the physical universe, since that seems, nowadays, to be nothing more than a vast, frigid emptiness, thinly contaminated with chemicals. I wish I knew why it is there at all, and what (if anything) it is up to, and whether such questions make sense; but however that may be, it hardly seems capable, on any terms, of being well or ill disposed to anyone. We may be pleasantly surprised to be scratching a living on its doorstep; but it is only human self-importance that sees 'Welcome' written on the mat. The cozy old cosmologies invented or borrowed by the world religions made it possible to believe in a providential scheme of things, managed (perhaps) by a benevolent God; but their (pre-Copernican) notions of its scale and history are so wide (and short) of the mark that they carry no conviction in any but a local and 'spiritual' sense, of no apparent relevance to the shambolic scenery observable, e.g., via the Hubble Telescope. To put it crudely, one just cannot see Jehovah, Allah or the rest of the world's roster of individual deities having charge over some trillions of galaxies, on top of the merely local responsibility for which they were originally invoked, and in which capacity they remain believable to many, though not unfortunately to me. The only thinkable God for the material, actual, astronomical universe would seem to be Spinoza's, who just is the universe (which is no doubt why Einstein endorsed him). But then he is notorious for loving only himself (whatever that may mean), and is such an unsatisfactory God from the prayer-and-providential point of view that it's no wonder the orthodox have never had a good word to say for him.

And then in a later letter continuing on the same theme:

From your paper on the ineffable [in *Religious Studies*, March 2000], and the interesting remarks in your letter, it seems that you are indeed pretty close to the Spinozistic position of unrequited esteem for a deity whose attributes transcend both human comprehension and the rules of ordinary logic, and of which, therefore, nothing significant can be thought or said. The doctrine – as you show – has a respectable pedigree, though I can't imagine it has ever been popular with the orthodox in any of the world religions. For where does it leave those religions, if not sunk in fundamental error, and their practitioners mired in all manner of observances which (as Spinoza pointed out) are absurdly unsuited to the situation supposed?

Needless to say I have written back with my own responses to Peter's thoughts. But I quote him, not in order to continue the argument here, but to show what a valuably challenging friend he is and why I wish that he would publish more. He is also, I may add, the best conversationalist I know.

Returning to CGS (as it then was), when we began to think about honorary degrees for 1984 I proposed Desmond Tutu and this was accepted. We gave him the LLD degree and he said jokingly that he would now be able to talk to the Minister for Justice on equal terms. (He now has too many honorary degrees to list in his *Who's Who* entry). Since I already knew him I was his host whilst in Claremont. He arrived from Australia where he had been a guest of the government. After he had had time to sleep off the jet lag I took him for drinks with the President of CGU, John Maguire, and then to our house for dinner with a few other guests, others coming in later for coffee and to meet him.

Another day I took him for a long walk in the Botanical Gardens. I asked (as is my wont) about his daily routine. He gets up at 4 a.m., has some 'quiet time', conducts the eucharist at 6 a.m. in a small

Soweto church of which he is rector, then drives to the new Council of Churches office in Johannesburg – not the one in which I had earlier visited him. There are staff prayers, an exchange of news among the various organisations which share the building – Black Sash, etc. – then much time spent on the phone, visitors, reading the papers, correspondence, etc. The phone is tapped, mail tampered with, perhaps electronic listening in – he tells visitors that they may be being listened to. But he also said that Christians in South Africa are not to be pitied because of their difficulties but envied because their duty was so clear – to oppose apartheid.

I had recently received an invitation to visit Witwatersrand University. I did not need to visit South Africa again to see for myself what apartheid was like and would only want to go if I could be of some definite service to the black community, and I asked Desmond's advice. He said that if I went anywhere, the best place would not be Wits but the black Federal Seminary. Wits thinks it is liberal and progressive, but in reality is not, and it would do them good to have an invitation refused. But the anti-apartheid movement was moving towards recommending suspending all cultural links with South Africa. And so I did not go.

Another meeting was when I was at a conference at Emory university in Atlanta, Georgia, and he was on sabbatical there and took me out for a meal. I thought that if I was to appear in public with an Archbishop – he had now become Archbishop of Cape Town – I had better wear a tie. But he turned up to collect me at the hotel, with a welcoming embrace, dressed in a sweater, sweat-pants, and cloth cap, and with a huge car which the University had provided for him. He was optimistic about the future of South Africa and thought the movement towards democracy was now unstoppable. He had a great admiration for Nelson Mandela. Desmond intended to retire in four years' time so that a new Archbishop could be in place for the next Lambeth conference. He will then go back to live in Soweto. He still had to be security conscious, going in a car with darkened windows, never going out alone, never sitting by an open window. But, as he said, in a pulpit you are always a sitting duck. He is lucky to have survived, and the world is lucky that he has.

Returning to Claremont, whilst our life there was for the most part idyllic it was during this period that the greatest sorrow of our lives occurred, the sudden death of our youngest son Mike at the age of twenty-four. Mike was bright, thoughtful, with a social conscience, creative, good looking, a very promising artist and in particular sculptor, and in love with a lovely girl. One of his pieces done at College, a large wooden walking Font, was exhibited at the Yorkshire Sculpture Park until, after a few years, the wood decayed. He was fairly fluent in French and on 12 October 1985, he went to visit a friend, Marc, whom he had known for several years who, with his family, kept goats in the Alps in the French speaking part of Switzerland. When Mike arrived Marc was about to round up his seventy-eight goats to take them down to the village the next day, and Mike went with him to help. Having rounded them up, when they counted three were missing. The light was now beginning to fail but they went back to find them. It seems from Marc's statement to the police that he was on one hill top and Mike on another when they saw the goats, and moving towards them Mike slipped on the dry grass and was unable to stop himself and fell over the edge into a ravine which he did not know was there, falling about seventy meters onto the rocks below. Marc shouted and there was no reply. It was now almost dark, but knowing the area he climbed down to the bottom but could not find Mike. So he climbed back and phoned for help. Mike must have died instantly on impact. The local police were satisfied that his death was a pure accident, as was the coroner in Birmingham. Hazel and I flew over for the funeral and cremation and for a few days with the rest of the family. We all loved him and were all utterly devastated, perhaps Hazel most of all, who vividly remembered him as the mother who had nursed and fed him as a baby.

Some weeks later, back in Claremont, I had a brief vivid waking vision of Mike standing beside me and then going away through an open door, this having a positive rather than a negative feeling. But none of us have ever forgotten Mike, and we continue to miss him. To think of him sometimes still brings tears.

24

Encounters with eastern Buddhism

Whereas in Europe the Buddhist world is far away, on the American west coast it is directly across the water. It is however a long way across, and on each of my two visits to Japan I stopped off about half-way in Hawaii for a few days both going and returning. Roshi (Zen Master) Keido Fukushima, abbot of Tofoku-ji, one of the ancient Kyoto monasteries, who spoke English was an annual visitor to Claremont and I visited him in his monastery. He is also a fine calligraphist, and the piece which he gave me says, in Japanese, 'The old pine talks Satori' – satori being the state of enlightenment. This is perhaps a koan. At any rate, for several years I did not understand it, unless it is simply saying that everything points to satori. Then one morning in Birmingham when I was meditating whilst sitting up in bed after breakfast, at this point with my eyes open and looking at the old oak tree about fifty yards away on the other side of the hedge, I remembered the saying and suddenly saw its meaning. Banally expressed, it is saying that everything points to, or can trigger, satori – except that when you see it for yourself it is no longer banal but a powerfully living truth. (Another piece of calligraphy which someone else gave me, at the Doshisha Buddhist University, and which is easier to understand, says in Japanese, 'Truths bloom like a plum blossom even in snowy and windy winter.') I asked Keido, in his room in the monastery, with a large open window looking out on trees and greenery, if there was anything he could say about his own attainment of satori. He said (as I expected) that it is inexpressible but as a beginning he gestured through the window and said, 'I became part of all this.' Having met three Zen masters and a number of lay practitioners I can see that the faithful practice of zazen (Zen meditation) for a number of years undoubtedly has a marked effect on people, going beyond our ordinary self-centred awareness to a sense of unity with all life and a heightened sensitivity towards others, in a key Buddhist term compassion (*karuna*), feeling for and with others. One scientific researcher, James Austin, in his lengthy book on *Zen and the Brain*, claims that the plasticity of the brain is such that through zazen it actually develops the capacity for a new mode of experience[1], and I can believe this. I have however found this new capacity more attractive in some of the lay Buddhists that I have known than in some of the roshis themselves, I think because a roshi in the Japanese tradition has to administer a very tough regime of highly organised training, so that however compassionate he may be in reality he is an extremely formidable figure in the life of the monks in his charge. It was at Tofoku-ji that I came to think of Zen as macho-Buddhism! The life of the monastery – and it would be the same in the other Kyoto monasteries – is extremely rigorous and highly disciplined. The monks do zazen for six hours in the course of each day. The Master's authority is absolute. When a monk comes into his presence he prostrates himself to the floor with his forehead touching the ground. It normally takes at least ten years of zazen to attain satori and Keido told me that a roshi's most important task is to identify a suitable successor. For the Zen tradition has continued in its purity for so many centuries entirely on the basis of the transmission of the authentic satori experience. He was highly critical of many American self-styled roshis who, he said, had often been practicing for only two or three years.

It was made clear to me by the roshis with whom I have had discussions that satori is not to be thought of as a once-only event like, say, a conversion experience but something that happens again and again, sometimes more powerfully and sometimes less. For example, I met Roshi Akizuki, who is not a monastic, for two long discussions in Tokyo, with Seiichi Yagi – a very interesting and original Japanese Christian deeply involved in dialogue with Buddhists – very kindly translating. On one occasion I was taken by one of Akizuki's students to a restaurant, where Yagi and Akizuki were already installed in a private room where we sat on cushions with our legs in a trench under the low table. Akizuki showed me an easy way for a westerner to use chopsticks: separate them with a wad of paper and hold them together with an elastic band – it works well. I asked him – as is my wont – how he spends a typical day. He does a good deal of teaching. He meditates for about an hour a day, usually taking some forty minutes to attain satori. This is not a one-off experience but progressively repeated. He insisted on the importance of the Transcendent in Zen experience. But he said that the question, which I raised, whether the Dharmakaya (the ultimate reality) exists before and after the material universe, does not arise because serial time is an aspect of the material universe.

I am struck by the fact that all the authoritative Buddhists with whom I have held discussions in the Buddhist heartlands, both Theravada and Mahayana, insist upon an eternal ultimate reality transcending the physical universe, but do not see the ultimate reality as a personal creator God – although there are multitudes of *devas*, or in western terms angels. This is in contrast to many westerners who practice some form of Buddhist meditation but who see it as simply a valuable therapeutic exercise, or theologians (for example, Don Cupitt) who seek to conscript Buddhism in support of a non-realist form of religion.

In Kyoto I also visited Keiji Nishitani, one of the leaders of the Kyoto school of philosophy, author of a classic book, *Religion and Nothingness*, and then in his eighties, a little frail but fully alert. He spoke English and was very friendly. I gave him a copy of my *God Has Many Names*, and he murmured, 'The devil also has many names.' I asked him at one point if he had ever considered becoming a monk and then a roshi and he said that this had never appealed to him.

The Kyoto school is well known for its engagement with Western thought but unfortunately, in my opinion, it has fastened upon continental thinkers, particularly Heidegger, whose lack of rigorous precision mirrors their own. When, for example, in discussions with Masao Abe at Claremont I protested against his use of the idea of a circle with a centre but no circumference, pointing out that a figure without a circumference is not a circle, the point passed him by as irrelevant.

It is evident that the Zen roshis whom I have encountered, not only Keido Fukushima but also Soko Morinage of Ryoan-Ji monastery (with its famous Zen garden) in Kyoto, and Roshi Akizuki, are all extremely powerful personalities. If they have attained 'the death of the ego' and moved beyond self-centredness, this does not weaken but on the contrary empowers the individual as he engages in the world. The same is true of Kushdeva Singh within Sikhism and, in a different way, Nyanaponika Mahathera within Theravada Buddhism, and Desmond Tutu within the Anglican church and Patrick O'Mahoney within the Catholic church. To be unselfcentered makes people more not less powerful in their dealings with others and with the problems of the world.

Masao Abe from Kyoto joined our department at Claremont for five years. Durwood Foster correctly describes him as 'a master teacher of Zen who was probably also the world's leading figure, from within Buddhism, of the dialogue with Christianity'.[2] Masao (actually Abe is the first name, but we all treated Masao as that) and I conducted joint seminars and I learned a great deal about Zen from him, much of it very much in line with my own thinking. I kept a record of some of our discussions. For example on 9 May 1980:

> Starting from John's treatment of 'the death of the human ego' as the death of selfishness, leaving the cognitive machinery intact, Masao raised the question whether one can think of one aspect of the self as having died whilst other aspects continue unaffected. He emphasised that the death of the ego, resulting in conversion from the old self to the new self, is a transformation at the deepest level of our being. It is a fundamental turning from the space-time world to the transcendent Ultimate Reality. He also stressed that this occurs in all the great religious traditions, including the theistic traditions. John then suggested relating this to the differences between the various experiences of Ultimate Reality in different religions, theistic and non-theistic, and suggested that in each case there is, through the death of the ego, an experience of the same Ultimate Reality, but that this experience takes different forms, as the experience of a personal God or of nonpersonal Brahman or Sunyata, etc., because of the different cultural and religious conditioning of the experiencers – including their religious training as a Zen Buddhist, or as a Christian, or a Muslim, etc., including their religious practices, the scriptures which feed their spirits, the communities which

support them, etc., etc. Masao agreed that this conditioning is important, and mentioned that there are even differences between the Japanese and the Chinese forms of the Zen experience, due to the different cultural contexts. He believed that the differences in ways of experiencing Ultimate Reality all hinge upon the different ways of experiencing and understanding the death of the human ego. In the theistic religions this death is experienced in relation to a personal God, as submission to him, acceptance of his forgiveness, etc., whereas in Buddhism it is experienced in relation to the non-personal process of karma. Thus the experience of Ultimate Reality takes different forms according to the form taken by the death of the ego.

A couple of weeks later:

John asked Masao to say something about Sunyatta [Emptyness]. Masao said that it is a state that lies beyond nirvana. Having attained to nirvana one enjoys a private, personal state, divorced from samsara and from the human suffering of which it is full. One must then return to samsara, the process of the world, and to solidarity with suffering humanity. Then 'samsara and nirvana are one', but one in a dynamic sense, each negating the other. This dynamic double negation is sunyatta. We then returned to the question of religious pluralism. Masao said that culture provides the conditions for a Christian, as distinguished from a Zen (or vice versa) experience of Ultimate Reality, but that the Reality itself is the cause or ground of the experience. John agreed, and offered the analogy of differently coloured spectacles. The Pure Light of Reality shines upon us all, but among those who are conscious of it some wear theistic spectacles, and experience Reality as a personal God, whilst others wear Zen spectacles, and experience reality as Sunyatta. Masao was not quite happy with this. He raised the question – to be pursued next time – whether one pair of spectacles may give a more adequate view of Reality than another, and of the interaction between different experiences of Reality.

Unfortunately I do not have a record of that next time.

I do however have a piece of paper written during a long discussion that we had on a plane flying back together to Ontario airport – not the one in Canada but the one a few miles from Claremont – from a conference at Forth Worth:

Sunyatta – metaphorically a limitlessly large sphere. The word has both negative and positive connotations. Negatively, as Emptiness, Absolute Nothingness, Void, it rejects all conceptualisation and the dualistic distinction between self and Sunyata. Positively, this negation points to the limitless ground or reality, the source of creativity, the unity of opposites, the dynamic matrix.

And Masao added in Japanese, 'True Emptiness is Wondrous Being.' I also have my 'Attempt to understand':

We ordinarily experience the world from the standpoint of the self, and with the aid of the intellect, which imposes its categories, concepts and distinctions upon the world in the act of perceiving it. The satori experience (which is also the experience of sunyatta) consists in experiencing the world, and one's life in the world, from a selfless standpoint and without the intervention of the intellect. In experiencing self-centredly one values everything in its relation to oneself, as being good or bad for one. But in emptiness of self one experiences things as they are, not from a particular ego-perspective. Again, the intellect is always distinguishing. Thus one experiences the bird as a bird in distinction from a non-bird, and as black in distinction from white, and as here in distinction from elsewhere. But in an experience that is empty of intellectual activity, one is conscious of things as they are, and not in distinction from or in comparison with other things. Accordingly, if we express in language this distinctionless mode of experiencing (language having been developed to express distinctions), we utter paradoxes and contradiction – for what is experienced in satori is not experienced as black-as-distinguished-from-white etc., but simply as itself. It is just what it is, in its unique suchness, and is enjoyed as such. Thus the emptiness of sunyata is emptiness of self and of the distinguishing intellect; and it is at the same time fullness of undistorted being. The world as it is, is reality, and reality is 'the greatest mystery as it is daily and hourly performed ... it makes us live in the world as if walking in the Garden of Eden ... ' (D.T. Suzuki). It is 'Wondrous Being' (Abe).

It occurs to me that the Buddhist attempt to achieve a non-ego, impartial or universal, point of view is analogous to the Kantian ethic. For Kant's 'universalisability' criterion – in effect, would your action be right for anyone and everyone in those circumstances, not just for you? – seeks to replace the ego's point of view with a universal standpoint.

It was clear to me from my first contacts with the Theravada tradition of Buddhism in Sri Lanka, and again with the Mahayana in its Zen form to which I was introduced at Claremont, that my own thinking had a good deal in common with Buddhist teaching; and as my ideas have developed they have undoubtedly been influenced by it. This comes out in *An Interpretation of Religion*, which is the nearest that I shall ever get to a magnum opus. This is a fairly comprehensive book, arguing for the rationality of basing beliefs on religious as well as sense experience; noting the subjective contribution to all conscious experience, so that religious experience takes different forms within different religio-cultural traditions; and suggesting that in order to make sense of this variety we have to postulate an ultimate ineffable (or transcategorial) Real whose universal presence is humanly experienced in these different ways. This is my 'pluralistic hypothesis'. In the course of the book I make use of several Buddhist themes: the Buddha's teaching about the 'unanswered questions' (*avykata*), some of which have answers, although we do not at present know what they are, and others of which have no answer because they are posed in terms of human categories of thought which do not apply, so that it is a mistake to make theorising about them central in religion, and his teaching that religious doctrines are not literal truths but 'skilful means' (*upaya*) to lead us forward from one stage to another on our spiritual journey and are to be left behind when they have done their work; and I treat the idea of Sunyatta (Emptiness) as the Buddhist way of saying that the Ultimate Reality, the Real, is ineffable, transcategorial, i.e. empty of everything that the human mind projects in the activity of cognition.

Another important forum in which I learned more and more about Buddhism was as a member of the international Buddhist–Christian dialogue which was initiated by John Cobb and Masao Abe at Claremont and met annually at different places in the USA. The Buddhist participants were from Japan and were in both the Zen and the Jodo, or Amida or Pure Land, traditions. The Christian participants included many of the then leading American theologians: David Tracy and Langdon Gilkey (Chicago), Schubert Ogden (Southern Methodist University), Rosemary Ruether (a

Claremont graduate, then teaching at Northwestern University) John Cobb (Claremont), Gordon Kaufman (Harvard), Paul Knitter (Xavier University), and also Hans Küng from Germany. The discussions and personal interactions were very illuminating, and it is noteworthy that the subsequent work of all the Christians involved has shown evidence of this in their subsequent writings. I would say that on the whole we were more influenced by the Buddhists than they were by us.

During my two visits to Japan I also encountered one of its many new religions, Tenrikyo, which began in the early nineteenth century and now has some three million followers in Japan and elsewhere. (It is not to be confused with the sect, with a slightly similar name, which put sarin gas into the Tokyo underground system.) I was invited to spend several days at its holy city, Tenri, where I visited its central temple and took part in various discussions. Tenrikyo families come to Tenri for varying periods of time for refreshment, healing and service to the community. I was very impressed by the dedication and altruism expressed in their way of life, combined paradoxically with some beliefs which no one not brought up within their community could possibly (or so I would think) come to accept. One could see, for example, the exact place, within the main temple, where the world was created! But which is more important, the admirable way of life or the superstructure of beliefs? Surely the former.

I mentioned that one of the participants in the dialogue was Paul Knitter, the leading Catholic exponent of religious pluralism. Paul is a laicised priest, happily married and now retired from teaching at the Catholic Xavier University in Cincinnati. Already knowing his book *No Other Name?* I first met him in person at a Buddhist–Christian meeting in Hawaii. It was there that we planned the book *The Myth of Christian Uniqueness* (1995) which we jointly edited on the basis of a Blaisdell conference at Claremont. Paul has now long been a good friend as well as ally. His special angle on religious pluralism is as a basis for human liberation in an unjust world. Here I fully agree with him, though we differ at another point. He is trying hard to make the pluralist position acceptable within the Catholic church (and other churches). To this end he tends, as it seems to me, to try to make it seem less radical in its implications than it ultimately is. I on the other hand do not see its acceptance, or even tolerance, by the Vatican[3] or the Catholic church generally as a present possibility, but only as a long-term project, and in order eventually to get there I want to present pluralism now in its full undiluted challenge to traditional orthodoxy. So we see ourselves as having different but complementary missions: he is an apostle to the church and I to the unchurched! I wish him well in his mission, but we argue about, for example, whether he has trimmed his Christology too much in the attempt to make it acceptable.[4]

This is perhaps the point at which to refer to the reciprocal influence of my writings in the far east through the translation of several of them into Japanese, Chinese and Korean. *Philosophy of Religion* and *The Metaphor of God Incarnate* are in Japanese, Chinese and Korean. *The Rainbow of Faiths* and *Problems of Religious Pluralism* are in Japanese and Chinese, *The Fifth Dimension* is in Indonesian as well, and *God Has Many Names* is in Japanese. *An Interpretation of Religion* is in Chinese, and Dr Wang Zhicheng of Zhejiang University who translated it has published a book of his own whose title in English would be *Interpretation and Salvation* (1997), which is an introduction to my thought, and another which would be in English *Religion, Interpretation, and Peace: A Study of Religious Pluralism in John Hick's Writings* (1998). I have a note of a number of articles on my work in Chinese academic journals – none of which of course I can read. There is a considerable interest in China today in attempts to find a true meaning in life and my hope is that I may be able to contribute something to this quest. In Japan *Explorations in Religious Pluralism: John Hick Studies* (in Japanese), edited by Hiromasa Mase and Hisakazu Inagaki, was published in 1995. Hiromasa was until recently professor of philosophy at Keio University in Tokyo and is one of the two leading exponents of religious pluralism in Japan, the other being Seiichi Yagi. I first met Hiromasa when he and his family spent a sabbatical in Birmingham, and again when they spent another sabbatical at Claremont. They were often in our house in each place, and I stayed with them in Shin Yokahama after giving a lecture at Keio University. The family have now long been good friends. Sono, Hiromasa's wife, came to my pre-eightieth birthday party in Birmingham to represent her husband, who was unable to come, and their daughter Emi, then doing doctoral research on religious pluralism in Sweden, and her little son Gen, were also able to come.

I learned fairly recently of the Japanese novelist Shusaku Endo (1923–96) who won many major literary awards and of whom Graham Greene said, 'Endo to my mind is one of the finest living novelists.' His books have been translated into twenty-eight languages. Endo's last novel was *Deep River*, and since his death his writing journal has been published in Mitya-Bungaku (1997). This tells how before starting to write *Deep River* he came in a book shop upon

> Hick's *Problems of Religious Pluralism* [in Japanese]. It was as if my unconsciousness had summoned it, rather than mere accident ... This shocking book has been overwhelming me since. And I am now absorbed in reading the same author's *God Has Many Names* that the editor of Iwanami Publishing Company gave me when he came ... I went to my study and read and worked; yet, after Hick's shocking book, any book seemed boring, so I went to Taiseido [bookstore] in this heat of the late summer. Yet there was no book that I wanted to buy ... Hick is a Christian. Yet he says world religions are seeking the same God through different paths, cultures, and symbols, and criticises Christianity for maintaining a tendency towards Christian inclusivism despite its assertion, after the Second Vatican Council, of holding dialogue with other religions. He dares to claim that religious pluralism should give up such a theology as to see Jesus as Messiah, and so should reconsider the problem of Jesus's incarnation and of the Holy Trinity.

Hiromasa Mase tells how he was asked by Endo to give a lecture at Getsuyo-kai, the 'Monday Meeting Society', to which Endo listened intently. In his diary Endo wrote, 'Lecture on Hick's theology. On Christology, there was a heated discussion, or rather quarrel, between the panellist, Prof. Mase, and Father Kadowski. Heavy rain outside. As the chairman, I was embarrassed between Hick's view and orthodox Christology.'[5]

In *Deep River* the pluralist theme is expressed by Otsu, a young man who is studying for the Catholic priesthood but is rejected because of his unorthodox views. In a letter Otsu writes,

> I now somewhat regret having spoken so foolishly in front of the brethren of the Church. But it seems perfectly natural to me that

people select the God in whom they place their faith on the basis of the culture and traditions and climate of the land of their birth. I think that Europeans chose Christianity because it was the faith of their forefathers, and because Christian culture dominated their native land. You can't say that the people of the Middle East chose to become Muslims and many Indians become Hindus after conducting rigorous comparisons of their religions with those of other people ... God has many different faces. I don't think God exists exclusively in the churches and chapels of Europe. I think he is also among the Jews and the Buddhists and the Hindus.[6]

In my two visits to Japan I was, on the one hand, overwhelmed by the wonderful hospitality of my hosts, and at the same time baffled by what was to me the inscrutability of Japanese culture. I am sorry that although I have had invitations to visit China and Korea I have not been able, for various practical reasons each time, to accept them. But I am very happy that some of my ideas seem to be known and considered in these far eastern countries whose traditions I recognise as extremely profound and very important for us in the west.

NOTES

1. James H. Austin, *Zen and the Brain*, Massachusetts Institute of Technology, 1999.
2. Donald W. Mitchell, ed., *Masao Abe, a Life of Dialogue*, Boston: Charles E. Tuttle Co., 1998, p. 115.
3. This was brought home to me, as a non-Catholic, by an attack on me by Cardinal Joseph Ratzinger, Prefect of the Congregation for the Doctrine of the Faith (formerly known as the Holy Inquisition), in an address to numerous bishops in 1996. Speaking of 'the so-called pluralist theology of religion', which he declared constitutes today the main threat to the Faith, he said that, 'The situation can clearly be seen in one of its founders and eminent representatives, the American (*sic*) John Hick ' I was his public enemy number one, and my friend Paul Knitter (who is a Catholic) number two. He proceeded to give an account of my pluralist hypothesis which was very misleading, suggesting that it denies any transcendent reality, a picture that was clearly based on a biased secondary source, although Ratzinger is himself competent in English. But he had obviously not read any of my books himself. For example, he cited as a source for his criticism *Evil and the God of Love*, which is on a different subject altogether and does not mention the theology of religions, and for which he gave an incorrect date and place of publication. Again, he cited a block of

pages in *An Interpretation of Religion* which have no bearing on the particular topic he was discussing. And so on. I wrote a 'Response' which was published in *New Blackfriars* (November 1997) and reprinted, together with the relevant section of the Cardinal's original publicly reported address, in my *Dialogues in the Philosophy of Religion* (Basingstoke and New York: Palgrave, 2001, pp. 149–60). He was equally reliant on the same unreliable secondary source for his treatment of Paul Knitter's work. Ratzinger was himself earlier a highly respected professor of theology, and he would not then have accepted his present official level of scholarship in a graduate, or even an undergraduate, student!

4. See Leonard Swidler & Paul Mojzes, eds., *The Uniqueness of Christ: A Dialogue with Paul F. Knitter*, Maryknoll: Orbis Books, 1997.

5. Hiromasa Mase, 'Shusaku Endo and Religious Pluralism – in relation to his Journal of Deep River', *The Hiyoshi Review of the Humanities*, Keio University, Tokyo, No. 14, 1999.

6. Sushaku Endo, *Deep River*, trans. Van C. Gessel, New York: New Directions, 1994, p. 121.

25

Interlude – return trips to the States

Each year since I left Claremont in 1992, until 1999, I have visited the States at least once and some years several times. I was at a philosophy of religion conference at Claremont organised by my good (personal, not philosophical!) friend and successor in the Danforth chair, Dewi Phillips, as well as on other occasions. Two other conferences were at Chapman University in Los Angeles, and other conferences and lectures in Wisconsin, Boston, Indianopolis, Notre Dame, etc. There were several visits to the annual meetings of the American Academy of Religion in different places, one to give a plenary address, one to have a Festschrift presented, one for a reception to launch *The Fifth Dimension*. On one visit, to give a lecture at the Boston University Institute for Philosophy and Religion and to receive one of its volumes dedicated to me, Pete also came and we stayed in the venerable but in parts decayed Harvard Club, meeting many interesting people and Pete seeing Boston as well as coming to some of my meetings. I used some of the Grawemeyer money to upgrade to business class, which made long flights much more tolerable. I must have crossed the Atlantic some fifty times since 1953, but latterly each time I have thought that surely this must be the last time. So on what has in fact been the last (so far), in November 1999, I kept a diary:

> On Wednesday November 3 from Birmingham at 8.20 a.m. to Amsterdam by KLM, and then from Amsterdam, this time in business class, to LAX [Los Angeles]. Business class is so much more comfortable than cabin/coach class – a wider seat, more leg

room, fewer people around you, a foot rest at the front of the seat as you recline it backwards, champagne etc. offered as soon as you board, a tablecloth for meals and proper tableware, linen napkin, wine glasses, as much food and drink as you want, an individual TV screen with a variety of films. Landing at LAX in the afternoon, a taxi to the Marriott hotel on Century Boulevard near the airport. The black porter who takes my luggage to my room asks, How're you doing? and before we get there has told me all about the house he owns in Oregon. I like this American social, if not (because so many poorer people are not yet registered to vote) political, democracy.

I hardly ever manage to sleep on a plane so sleep a bit now, then have an excellent meal, and watch TV. When you go through the many channels you seem to land in ads all the time – they occupy much more screen time than on commercial TV in Britain.

The next morning I pick up my pre-booked car from the Hertz depot in the hotel and drive to Palm Springs. Like most American cars it has automatic gears, power steering, etc. Driving through Los Angeles itself I find that drivers are more ruthlessly selfish than when I was last here, with cars shooting through red lights, hooting angrily at one another and generally behaving dangerously. I do not remember it having been so bad in the past, and Bob and Marilyn Adams whom I have met since confirm that the situation has got worse during recent years. But out on the freeway – the No. 10 – the traffic is more orderly.

At a rest area on the way I put my walking stick on top of the car whilst rearranging things inside, forget it and drive off with it on the roof from which it soon falls off and is crunched by the next car. I would be completely stuck without a stick when out of doors. However I remember that on the main street through Palm Springs there are numerous antique shops and stopping at the first am able to buy an antique cane, which may have been as much as fifteen or twenty years old! Whereas in England you walk with a stick and cane people with a cane, in the US you walk with a cane and hit people with a stick.

What was the Erewhon Hotel when Hazel and I stayed there some four or five years ago is now the Miramonte Resort. The two storied buildings are the same, and I have a large ground floor room, half bedroom with TV and bathroom, plus safe in which you enter your own code number, and half sitting room with another TV plus minibar. Saw new *Star Wars* film on pay TV – not as good as the earlier ones. The main swimming pool is bigger and better – and now has oriental tents along one side, for parties, each with its own fridge. I swim once or twice a day. But the hotel now has only one dining room, with a not very large menu which does not include much that I like. Some of the waiters, from Mexico, know enough English to say a few things but not enough to understand what is said to them. However when I dine here I do so out of doors, with a clear sky and the stars. But I more often drive out to eat elsewhere in the evening. Breakfast of course is always at the Resort, again usually out of doors. During the day the temperature is in the 80s, very nice, and with a view of the mountains in the background. I generally have just a banana or apple for lunch, bought at a nearby Vons – where in a newspaper rack I saw the headline 'Ancient Photo of Jesus Discovered'!

Here for nine days (at over £100 a day not including meals), spending the time reading round the pool, swimming, eating, watching TV, sleeping. Very enjoyable, although with moments of great sadness also because Hazel is not here this time.

On Friday, Nov. 12, drive back, past row after row of thin steel windmills up and down the hills, looking like invading creatures from Wells' *War of the Worlds*, along the number 10 and down the 57, to Orange County and the Doubletree hotel where the participants in Chapman University's 'Images of Jesus' conference are housed, I being the first to arrive.[1] A very comfortable hotel, where a single room costs $219 a night (but paid by the conference). Steve Davis from Claremont McKenna College was to have come down for dinner with me today, but calls to say that he has a detached retina, recently operated on but leaving his eye bandaged so that he does not yet know how successful the operation has been. Obviously he cannot drive, but we have a long chat on the phone. He is just back from a trip to China, but is advised that the detached retina is not caused by the long flight, but that detachments are unpredictable but more frequent in short-sighted people because of the direction in which this slightly stretches the retina. He thinks that CGU is doing well under its new President and Provost, and PRT (philosophy of religion & theology) doing particularly well. Dewi a popular teacher. But I get a less optimistic picture of the finances later from Jim Robinson who is at the conference.

At the hotel next evening and prior to the conference Maura O'Neill (who did her PhD at Claremont with me) and her husband Michael Harnett come to dinner – she a former nun and he a former priest. Both are going to the World Parliament of

Religions in Cape Town next month. She and a colleague, Ben Hubbard, come next morning for coffee to discuss a book which they are jointly writing about religious pluralism. On Sunday, with the conference starting on Monday, I am taken to a splendid lunch by Joseph Runzo and Nancy in their very posh home, together with others on the international committee of their new Center for the Study of Global Ethics and Religion, including Jim Kellenberger, Fr Raphael Luevano (for whom I must get some literature about multi-faith services), and others.

The 'Images of Jesus' conference is extremely interesting and I have learned a lot. The lecture I enjoyed most was John Dominic Crossan's – he is a brilliant and scintillating speaker – and he is the person there I took to most. He told me that he has almost retired from university teaching in order to communicate more widely through public lectures and books. His latest, *The Birth of Christianity* which I have been reading is fascinating. I was also glad to meet the English evangelical Tom Wright, about to go to Westminster Abbey as canon theologian. He is a powerful upholder of what I regard as out-of-date positions, defending the bodily resurrection of Jesus in his paper; but like many British evangelicals he is a highly civilized person with whom one can talk freely, unlike many of the US 'born agains' who can sometimes be vicious and thoroughly unpleasant. I asked him in the mini-bus going back to the hotel whether his Christian faith would be destroyed if it was proved that no physical resurrection took place, and he said Yes. Richard Swinburne gave an extraordinary paper using Bayes' theorem to try to demonstrate that the Incarnation is highly probable. One of the key premises which made the Jesus-phenomenon as anything other than a divine incarnation highly improbable, according to him, is that Jesus claimed to be God incarnate, and he was quite unmoved by the NT scholars who told him that this could not be sustained. I have known Richard for quite a long time and feel that under layers of shyness there is a very nice and kindly person. So I regard him as, like Dewi, a personal friend who is also a philosophical and theological foe.

Jim Robinson gave us his not yet published complete English translation of Q.[2] I asked all the NT scholars whom I met both at Chapman and at the AAR/SBL about the status of Q today within the profession. The situation seems to be that the large majority of American scholars accept Q, whether written or oral, although many are not convinced by Jim's theory of three different stages of its formation, whereas most British scholars (including of course

Michael Goulder) reject or are doubtful about the Q hypothesis. Tom Wright told me that he is agnostic about it.

Managing to return to the hotel each day for '10 minutes'. I enjoy evening drinks with Ninian Smart, Julius Lipner, Brian Hebblethwaite, and many more; and win – when the election comes – a bet with Julius that Labour will have a majority of more than 50 at the coming general election. Incidentally, the hotel is in sight of both Disneyland and the Crystal Cathedral – symbols of the two great fantasies of contemporary America, glitzy Hollywood and glitzy Christianity. I have much enjoyed Disneyland, but when I visited the Crystal Cathedral a few years ago I found it spiritually revolting.

At the end of the conference I drive back to the Marriott at LAX and return the car. That evening Tim Musgrove to dinner. He had a good academic post in the offing, but before it was finalised the budget dropped the position and he was left without a job. So he has used his computer skills and is now the part owner and chief technical officer of an internet company in Silicon Valley. Married with two inherited children, and now two more of his own. Still very interested in the philosophy of religion. In the hotel I notice a report of problems in the health service like those in the NHS. USA Today says 'The next time you're in hospital, the registered nurse taking care of you might have five other patients. Or seven. Or even ten. You might think it's a nurse checking your vital signs, but it could be an aide with just a few weeks' training ... A decade of turmoil in health care has ushered in a new era of nursing – one where cost-cutting has reduced the proportion of RNs on wards even as patients are sicker ... ' Another article reports on US divorce rates, which are highest in the Bible Belt – it would be interesting to know why. Yet another, about the Bible Belt, reports that 'Oklahoma has joined a list of states questioning the teaching of evolution by requiring a disclaimer in school science textbooks that evolution is a "controversial theory".' The LA Times carries stories just as it was doing ten years ago about police brutality: out of 320 police shootings in the city since 1994, 37 were of mentally ill people who clearly should have been dealt with differently, one an old lady who simply turned her back on the officer. Also in the paper a report that one in ten Americans are overweight and one in five obese. On the other hand many of the younger folk keep very fit.

Thursday November 18 take the hotel shuttle to LAX and fly early, 8.15 a.m., to Boston by United, first class (there being no business class), and settle in at the Boston Sheraton, the main

AAR/SBL conference hotel, with an indoor connection to the Hynes Conference Center. The next morning breakfast with Harold Netland at the hotel, former Claremont evangelical student who worked as missionary in Japan (where I met him once in Tokyo), but who takes the multi-faith issue seriously, having published a book, *Dissonant Voices: Religious Pluralism and the Question of Truth* (1991),[3] which he says in the preface 'can be regarded as a response to the pluralism that John Hick has so vigorously championed in recent years'. We have always got on well personally. He is one of the really civilized and agreeable US evangelicals! He tells me that there is a small but significant minority in the evangelical community who are actively pursuing these issues.

Later I bump into John and Jean Cobb, now living in Pilgrim Place. John sits with me to chat whilst Jean goes shopping. Later again, I chat with Archie Spencer, whom I meet by chance whilst we are queuing for our conference badges and who has a copy of my *Fifth Dimension* with him which I sign. He tells me about a recent PhD thesis on my work by a friend of his. I also briefly meet Krister Stendahl, the eminent NT scholar, whom I have not seen since his Harvard days.

During the three day convention, attended by some nine thousand people, I have only gone to one of the innumerable sessions, and only to the first hour of that, on Tillich's view of other religions. I tried to go to a session on Radical Orthodoxy, but the room was so packed that I couldn't get a seat. I spent all my time chatting with individuals and groups, and had all my meals including breakfasts with other people. One was Paul Eddy (a civilised evangelical), who wrote his dissertation at the University of Wisconsin about my thought and later published a critical article which has been reprinted in a recent collection edited by Phil Quinn of Notre Dame. A dinner with Marjorie Suchocki from Claremont but currently visiting at Vanderbilt. Another dinner with Sumner Twiss of Brown, who also has an article reprinted in the Quinn volume, and some of his colleagues plus one of his former students, Jung Lee, who is going to send me a copy of a critical article that he has published in *Philosophy East and West*. Chatted with Kenneth Cracknell, now married and teaching in Texas, and his successor at Wesley House, Cambridge, Martin Forward; Ursula King of Bristol; Thandeka (an African name given to her by Desmond Tutu when he was at Claremont); Jim Sanders of Claremont; Farid Esack, now a Commissioner for Gender Equality in South Africa, who brings me up to date with affairs there. His position within the Muslim community in South Africa is ambiguous. He is the most publicly prominent Muslim in the country serving, as he says, the State not the Government (although he strongly supports President Thabo Mbecki) and the Muslims are proud of him for this; but they suspect him as too liberal, particularly when they see him acting impartially instead of automatically supporting the Muslim party to a dispute. A meal with Paul Waldau, now teaching at Tufts. I also meet a number of people whom I do not know but who say that they have been influenced by one or other of my books. I spend some time at the Oneworld stall in the huge book fair, chatting with Novin Doostdar and others and autograph some copies of *The Fifth Dimension*. David Blumenthal of Emory, who was the Jewish convenor of the 'Trialogue', sits down for a long chat. He tells me about a libel case to be heard in London in January in which the writer David Irving is suing a Jewish colleague of David's who accused Irving of being a Holocaust denier – which he is. (When the trial came up Irving lost the case and was confirmed as a Holocaust denier and a falsifier of history). I greet Chuck Grench of the Yale UP, who tells me that both *Interpretation* and *Disputed Questions* continue to sell well. *Interpretation* is above six thousand in the States, and must be well above ten thousand altogether, with the Macmillan edition and German and Chinese versions.[4] I have a good dinner with Huston Smith and Philip Novak, talking about Huston's curious objection to the teaching of evolution in schools. Eventually it seems that what he objects to is the naturalistic assumption behind the way in which, he thinks, it is often taught, but it could sound to some as though he is criticising Darwinianism itself. We try to talk him out of it, without success. The argument ends with he and I smiling at one another in a unity which transcends differences. Huston has grown older and is a bit deaf, but he remains a truly wonderful and impressive person who has been a major influence for good in the States. We agree over 90% of the field. Our only disagreement is about the transcategoriality of the Real, which he rejects. He maintains that It is good and loving in itself, whereas I maintain that even these are human concepts which apply, not to the transcategorial Real in itself but to its humanly experienced impact upon us.

I learn from Catholics whom I meet that the National Conference of Catholic Bishops, responding to a demand from the Vatican, have decided to extend their authority over Catholic universities and colleges. When this has been ratified in a couple of years' time theology professors in Catholic institutions will have to obtain a mandatum from the local bishop certifying that they teach in accordance with the Church's teaching. The long repressive arm of Ratzinger. Serious for people like Paul [Knitter] at Xavier. But it will also produce a general fear, particularly on the part of younger Catholic scholars, of any theological experimenting or speculation.

The Oneworld reception went okay. Joseph Runzo and Nancy Martin made long speeches. I made a short speech, and met a number of friends, including Arvind Sharma, and John Strugnell whom I have not seen for many years. He is now retired, having worked for years on the Dead Sea Scrolls in Jerusalem but leaving amidst heated controversy. Has deplorably reactionary attitudes in general. Before that, a dinner hosted by Joseph for people connected with his Center, where I sat next to Bill Wainwright with whom I have recently had a long email discussion about ineffability, etc. He is more pessimistic than I am about the extent to which US 'analytical' philosophers are taking up the issues of religious diversity – he thinks only myself, Bill Alston, Bill Rowe, and himself. But among other senior figures there are also Phil Quinn of Notre Dame and George Mavrodes of Michigan, as well as many more among the 'lower ranks'. Every new students' text now has a chapter on the topic, so I think one can say that it is now irrevocably on the map as an important issue.

On Wednesday, 24th, I return by KLM via Amsterdam, after what has been a very satisfying and satisfactory visit to the States. But on the whole I do not pine to live there, although I certainly miss the glorious sunshine of southern California. And it is curious that whilst I tremendously enjoyed my graduate seminars at Claremont I do not now miss them. But all in all America has been very, very good to Hazel and me and we would not have missed our time there for anything.

NOTES

1. The book coming out of it is *Jesus Then and Now*, edited by Marvin Meyer and Charles Hughes, Harrisburg: Trinity Press International, 2001.
2. A supposed collection of sayings of Jesus, earlier than any of the Gospels and used by the writers of Matthew and Luke.
3. Since then he has published another, *Encountering Religious Pluralism: The Challenge to Christian Faith and Mission*, Downers Grove, Illinois: InterVarsity Press, and Leicester: Apollos, 2001, with chapters on my journey to pluralism and a critique of the result.
4. And now Persian (Farsi).

26

Birmingham again

I retired from CGU in 1992 at the age of seventy. Even the sunny climate of southern California and our friends there, including those who were already in the congenial retirement community of Pilgrim Place, were outweighed by close family ties and friendships in England to which we now returned. We had already, three years earlier, bought the house in which we intended to live in the inner suburb of Selly Oak. This is a dormer bungalow with everything that we require on the ground floor, but with two more bedrooms and another bathroom upstairs, much used for family visits. We had been in the house once before many years ago when visiting the Fenns, Eric Fenn then being a big figure in the Selly Oak Colleges and the United Reformed Church who had also been assistant head of religious broadcasting in the BBC. Earlier still it was lived in by the well-known Quaker, Horace Alexander, a close friend of Gandhi,[1] and immediately before us it was owned by Harold Turner who headed the Centre for the Study of New Religious Movements in the Selly Oak Colleges. We had a number of alterations and additions made, mostly whilst we were still in Claremont, with different families living in the house at a nominal rent.

The house was built in the 1920s, when its first owners had a live-in maid and (following other owners since) we have preserved as a museum piece the box of bell signals on the wall of what was then the maid's room and is now the dining room, to which we added a bay window to make it both a little larger and a lot lighter. But the main addition is a conservatory built out from an already existing

297

south facing open loggia entered through the sitting room. This has been one of the most useful rooms in the house. There is so much of the year when the English climate does not allow you to sit out in the garden but when you can be 'virtually' in it in what we call the glass house. We also enlarged the entrance from the road, and the garage, and the front garden, and added a second garage.

When we bought the house we called it the Tip because it had been empty for over a year and had a derelict air, with the garden a jungle. Over several years a gardener coming once a week uncovered the lawns and flower beds and restored the area to a garden, presided over by a century-old oak; and we grew the hedge on the south side to twice its original height so that when this and the surrounding trees are covered with leaves one sees nothing on two sides but greenery and sky.

I began as a teenager to collect antique books.[2] In those days, before the 1939–45 war, one could sometimes pick up eighteenth century books in second-hand bookshops for a shilling or two. I continued to collect from time to time, moving up from shillings to pounds, until they became too expensive for the ordinary amateur collector. But I had by then three incunabulas, i.e. books printed in the earliest period of typography from the invention of printing in Europe in the 1450s to the end of the fifteenth century,[3] mine being dated 1483, 1486 and 1493. Incunabulas have no title page because they are printed versions of medieval manuscripts, and the information now on a title page comes in a colophon at the end. Mine are Venetian printings of Latin classics, Pliny, Ovid and Salust. It seems that by 1500 Venice had a hundred and fifty printing presses. Thus my Ovid (the most expensive of my purchases, bought in the 1970s for £120) has the colophon, '*Impreffum Veneciis per Bernadinum de Nouaria die xxvii. nouembris M.cccc.Lxxxvi. Feliciter*' (Printed in Venice by Bernard of Nouaria on 27 November 1486. Cheers!), though the present binding is nineteenth century. The paper – which was made from rag fibres until early in the nineteenth century and only since then from wood pulp fibres – is in better condition than twenty-year-old books today when not on acid free paper, the print is clear (much better than English books of even a century later), and there are numerous hand-written notes in Latin in the wide margins which although done with a quill pen are so small that I need a magnifying glass to read them, and presumably the writer needed one to write them. I had no idea that a quill pen could have such a fine point. From the sixteenth century I have, for example, a 1515 volume from the famous Aldine press in Venice, and a Quintillian printed in Paris in 1520, by now with a title page, and a number of others from the sixteenth, seventeenth, eighteenth and nineteenth centuries. I found them all over the place, mostly in the 1960s – at St Ives, Aylesbury, York, Cambridge, Norwich, Bath, Birmingham, even Valetta, Malta, as well as London. I bought many simply because they are old and interesting, but apart from that I was looking for early editions of philosophical works and have a number by Locke, Berkeley, Hume, Cudworth (*True Intellectual System of the Universe*), Pierre Bayle, Leibnitz's *Theodicée*, William King (*The Origin of Evil*), William Derham (*Astro-Theology*), Thomas Reid's *The Human Mind*, some of the Bridgewater Treatises. To my mind, if one is going to collect antiques there is a much more interesting difference between two books than two pieces of furniture. I don't spend a lot of time with my old books, but they are always there as familiar friends facing me in my study, the older ones bound in leather or calf (which I have treated occasionally with a leather preservative), connecting me with the past and occasionally with the first owner whose name plate is on the inside cover. I enjoy reading bits of Stowe's *Chronicles* of 1565, or the magic spells, including many on a signature of hand-written pages, in Henry Cornelius Agrippa's *Occult Philosophy* (1655), or King Charles I's (supposed) posthumous *Eikon Basilike* of 1648, or contemporary reports of the Crimean War in *The Graphic*, or some of Johnson's ingenious definitions in his Dictionary of which I have the two volume eighth edition of 1792. (How would you define 'net'? Johnson's simple but adequate solution is that a net is 'A texture woven with large interstices or meshes.') His definition of a philosopher – 'A man deep in knowledge, either moral or natural' – comes from the time when the sciences were called natural philosophy as distinguished from both moral philosophy and metaphysics. I also have a first edition of Johnson's *A Journey to the Western Islands of Scotland* (1775) previously owned by J.A. Stuart Wortley, and Edward Montagu Stuart Granville, Earl of Wharncliffe, both with book plates carrying their coats of arms, and more recently by one R.G. Neville.

From Birmingham Hazel and I made a number of visits on the continent to conferences etc. at which I was to speak – several times to Madrid and Barcelona, to Salzburg, Munich, Nachrodt in north Germany, Milan. It was at the concluding dinner of a conference at Milan that Wolfhart Pannenberg, a major German theologian who strongly disapproves of my views about religious pluralism, leaned over the table to me and said, 'I hope that on the last day the Lord will remember your time as a pastor'! What he disapproved of is what I have been saying over the years to a great many audiences in Britain and abroad, generally finding increasingly sympathetic hearers as time has gone on. I have presented this in different ways to different audiences, but usually including most of the following points.

Christian belief was developed over the centuries, and in the form in which it solidified and continued for many centuries in the western church it is a self-enclosed system, seeing the rest of humanity as being outside the ark of salvation. Since Christianity became the official religion of the Roman empire in the fourth century such contacts as there were with other religions were mostly hostile, externally in the Crusades and internally in the centuries-long persecution of the Jews; and in the period of the European empires the religions of the subject peoples were generally despised as heathen practices from which their people should be converted to the higher and saving truth of the gospel. But since the European Enlightenment of the eighteenth century, and particularly within the last hundred years or so, there has been a growing awareness in the west of the spiritual depth and power of the other world religions and it is no longer taken for granted by many people that Christianity is the one and only true faith and only locus of salvation. The issue became acute in the second half of the twentieth century as a result of large-scale immigration into the west, particularly from the Indian sub-continent. In Birmingham, for example, there are more than 80,000 Muslims whose parents or grandparents came from Pakistan or Bangladesh, and there are large Sikh and Hindu communities, as well as the small but long established Jewish community, and now Buddhist, Taoist and Bahá'í groups as well. Because a larger proportion of these than of the Christian – mostly of course only nominally Christian – population practice their faith, it is quite possible that about as many people each week attend the various non-Christian places of worship as the churches. Today probably the two most splendid new religious buildings in the city are the huge Sikh gurudwara on Soho Road, Handsworth, and the huge new mosque at Poet's Corner in Small Heath.

When we get to know our fellow citizens of other faiths – and we encounter them in every walk of life – and particularly when we know them individually as neighbours, colleagues, parents of children at the same school, and so on, we do not find that they are in general any less kindly, any less mutually caring in family and community, any less inclined to make sacrifices for the education of their children, any less likely to help a neighbour in need, any less law abiding, any less good citizens, any less faithful in the practice of their religion, than the Christian population of the city in general. Within all the different ethnic and religious populations there are both good and bad people in about the same proportions, and all face the same social problems, with an alarming number of alienated youth lost in drugs and crime, though with a higher unemployment rate among the black and brown than the white population. But it does not seem that Christians in general are morally and spiritually better people than non-Christians in general. Again, each faith seems to produce to a more or less equal extent the rare individuals whom we call saints. We have no statistics of saintliness but so far as one can tell there seem to be as many (per million of population) and as remarkable individuals of the kind who make religious faith easier for the rest of us, within Judaism, Islam, Hinduism, Sikhism and Buddhism and so on as within Christianity.

But is this what we would expect if the traditional Christian belief system is true? According to this system, Jesus was God (i.e. God the Son, second person of a divine Trinity) incarnate, so that Christianity alone among the religions of the world was founded by God in person and must therefore *ipso facto* be superior to all others. As Christians we supposedly have an uniquely close relationship to God, an uniquely full access to God through the sacraments of the church, and the presence of the Holy Spirit within us as members of the Body of Christ which is the church, and we have in Christ a direct knowledge of God's nature not available to others. As a result of all this should not the fruits of the Spirit, which St Paul listed as

'love, joy, peace, patience, kindness, goodness, faithfulness, gentleness, self-control' (Galatians 5:22–3), be more evident in the lives of
Christians generally than in those of non-Christians generally? And
yet this does not seem to be the case.

And so it seems to me reasonable to think that the great world
faiths are different but, so far as we can tell, equally effective (and
also equally ineffective) contexts of the salvific transformation from
natural self-centredness to a new orientation centred in God, the
Transcendent, the Ultimate, the Real, a recentering which frees
humans to value and love one another.

In that case the different ways of conceiving, and therefore of
experiencing, the Ultimate, reflect the different ways of being human
which are the great cultures of the earth. This in turn involves a
distinction between the Ultimate Reality in itself and that reality as
variously imaged by different human mentalities formed by different
earthly circumstances. (It is this latter suggestion that I developed
more technically in my epistemology of religion, sketched very
briefly in chapter 22).

But how is such a view possible for a Christian? Did not Jesus say
'I am the way, the truth, and the life. No one comes to the Father but
by me', 'I and the Father are one', 'He who has seen me has seen the
Father'? The answer is that almost certainly No, these are not words
of the historical Jesus but words put into his mouth by the writer of
St John's Gospel some sixty or seventy or more years after Jesus'
death, expressing the faith of the church as it had developed at that
time. It is the consensus of the great majority of New Testament
scholars today that Jesus himself did not claim to be God incarnate
and that his deification was the gradual work of the church. In the
earlier understanding of his disciples Jesus was 'a man attested to you
by God with mighty works and wonders and signs which God did
through him' (Acts 2:22). There are also grave and still unsolved
problems in trying to render coherent the idea that Jesus had both all
the divine attributes without which a being is not God and also all
the human attributes without which he is not human. But I have
written about all this more fully in *The Metaphor of God Incarnate*[4] and
this is not the place to repeat it.

Obviously all this is highly controversial within the churches,
although much more widely acceptable today than a generation ago.

But the leaders of all the denominations, whilst adopting an attitude of friendship and tolerance towards people of other faiths, still if pressed generally maintain the unique superiority of Christianity. However outside the churches there are a large number of people who are genuinely interested in real religious questions but totally unattracted, indeed often repelled, by the churches and the mental boxes in terms of which they want everyone to think. For such people awareness of other religions opens up a new range of fascinating possibilities. Thus the existence and power of the other great world faiths presents Christian thinking with a challenge comparable in magnitude to that posed by the nineteenth-century discovery of biological evolution and the continuity between human and the rest of animal life. It took two or three generations for the churches to accept the implication that the Bible is a human, culturally conditioned set of writings. We now have to recognise the continuity between our own Christian religious experience and that of humanity globally. It may well take another generation or two for the churches to accept that Christianity is one authentic religion amongst others, with the implications of this for the doctrines of Incarnation, Trinity and Atonement – none of which was taught by Jesus himself. And of course a corresponding challenge faces each of the other religious traditions. We all have to come to see that, in the Sufi poet Rumi's words, 'The lamps are different, but the Light is the same: it comes from Beyond.'⁵

Returning from theology to ordinary life, not long after retiring my old back problem   I had a 'slipped disk' operation at Princeton in 1962 – began to return, requiring two operations for a spinal stenosis, which however continues to limit mobility considerably. It was when I was in hospital in 1996 recovering from the first of these operations that Hazel suddenly suffered a massive stroke from which she never recovered consciousness, dying twenty four hours later. She usually visited me in the early evening but on this day did not. Pete had come down from Manchester to visit me in the Orthopaedic hospital – I being then the patient and Hazel seeming perfectly well – but he called in at the Tip first and found that he could not get in: he had a key but the outer door was bolted, as Hazel preferred to do at night. He climbed over a gate and peered in at the bedroom window. But it was dark and he could not see in properly. He rang

Mark, asking him to bring a torch, and they could see Hazel lying motionless on the bed. They broke in by breaking a glass pane in the front door and found her in a coma. They called an ambulance and she was taken to the nearby Selly Oak hospital and diagnosed as having had a brain stem stroke. I was able to be taken in the middle of the night to see her, but when we returned in the morning, Ele also arriving from Manchester, Hazel had just died. Her death was a complete surprise and shock. We had assumed that I would probably be the first to die since I am four years older and statistically women tend to live longer than men. And she had seemed well and had been very active. She was learning Urdu, the second language of Birmingham, and was teaching English to Asian women in their homes, and visiting care homes for the elderly as part of a team of lay inspectors on behalf of the City's Social Services department, as well as having served on rent tribunals and having been one of the lay assessors who sit with judges in race relations cases. A sudden loss of consciousness is of course a good way to die, but in her case, at the age of seventy, it was many years too early.

We all miss her a lot, for the family circle of Hazel and myself, Ele, Mark, and Pete, and earlier Mike, together with the 'children-in-law' and grandchildren, and sister Shirley, has always been a close one. I once said to her brother Michael and his wife Rosalind that the best thing I had ever done was to marry Hazel, and they told me that Hazel had said exactly the same thing to them the other way round. We are different, but complementary. Hazel was a natural pessimist, thinking it better to expect the worst and then sometimes be pleasantly surprised, whilst I am a natural optimist but liable on occasion to be disappointed. Sometimes one was right and sometimes the other, so that our outlooks balanced out. Another difference is that, perhaps because her father died when she was only fourteen leaving the family in a degree of financial insecurity, Hazel was always reluctant to spend money, whereas I had no such inhibition. But over the years we found an increasingly deep level of mutual love, trust, and care. Two years after her death I had this dream:

> This afternoon during my 10 minutes I slept and dreampt. I was sitting, eyes shut, I think at a table, when a hand touched me. I was aware somehow that it was Hazel, and kissed the hand. Then

she said (my eyes still shut) 'How I loved you in life!' I suddenly realised that she, dead, was there & opened my eyes, saw her for a split second, & then she was gone, & I woke up.

I miss her acutely at certain times, as indeed we all do.

Since settling in Birmingham again we were able to see much more of the 'Infantry', now of course in mid-career. I am proud of them all. I have spoken of the work of Mark and Pete in earlier chapters. As anyone knowing her would have expected, Ele rose rapidly in the teaching profession, and after being for some years a very successful primary school head in Manchester is now a special needs adviser in Lancashire, where she, Gareth, Rhiannon and Alexander live in a large former farm house in the country. They come down for weekends fairly often and it is fascinating to see how the children are growing – very rapidly! – as are the other two grandchildren, Mark's Jonathan and Emily, all in their own ways. Since Hazel's death six years ago Ele has been my 'guardian angel'. I am very fortunate in all my children and in the way in which they support both me and one another.

I have kept connections, which I value, with the University as a Fellow of its Institute for Advanced Research in Arts and Social Sciences, and the Open End discussion group, which continues to flourish mightily, and I use the Library, and the Staff House for lunches with friends. Having relied on computers operated by secretaries at Claremont I acquired one of my own when we came back to Birmingham and took a day course at the University on its use. Although I can only use it for probably a tenth of the jobs that it is capable of doing it is now indispensable for writing articles and chapters and for emailing. I wish however that the PC had been widely available years earlier, for I have files of handwritten letters from Kemp Smith, Donald MacKinnon and Ramu Gandhi which are almost undecipherable, as well as entirely readable ones from Jessop, Farmer, Price, John Robinson, Peter Heath and Charles Hartshorne. As well as getting computerised I have started a web site. I looked up my name on one of the search engines and found a mass of material, some supporting and much criticising my work, and thought I would add some new articles of my own to what is available (www.johnhick.org.uk).

Some of my time goes in what might be called, rather grandly, administering a literary estate. I have never had an agent and have always dealt with publishers myself. I don't know whether I would have done better with an agent. I have however sometimes operated in ways of which a professional agent would not approve. My policy has been to give higher priority to facilitating the spread of my ideas than to earning as much from them as possible. When university and college professors, nearly always American, have written to ask permission to reprint some article of mine in an anthology which they are editing for students – and I know of over fifty such books with more on the way – I have always granted permission without requiring any fee. On one occasion I made what any agent would have regarded as a bad mistake. I edited a book of readings on *The Existence of God* (1964) with a long Introduction for a fee of $1000 in lieu of royalties, and the book was reprinted many times and has sold well over a hundred thousand copies – which would have brought in much more than the amount of the fee. And when I have retained the translation rights of a book, which is however only the case with a few of them, I have encouraged foreign translations by genuine scholars in the subject by arranging for the royalties to go to the translator, and have written new Prefaces for various translations without any fee. I have thus missed a certain amount of money which I did not really need, but have encouraged the spread of my works. But I have also received quite large sums when my publishers, holding the rights, have arranged foreign translations. One or other of my books are now in Finnish, Swedish, Polish, German, Dutch, Danish, Italian, Spanish, Portuguese, Persian (Farsi), Arabic, Japanese, Chinese, Korean, Indonesian and, I am told, Hindi, and I receive correspondence (these days usually by email) from Japan, China, Germany, Turkey, India, Brazil, Australia, New Zealand, Canada, and a lot from the United States.

During this returned-to-Birmingham period I have written a book that I had long wanted to write, addressed not primarily to the academic world but to the many people, mostly outside the churches, who are genuinely interested in basic religious questions. This is *The Fifth Dimension* (1999) for which I found the ideal publisher in Oneworld of Oxford, led by Novin Doostdar, who has become a friend. Macmillan, still under Tim Farmiloe, wanted to publish it, with the largest advance they have ever offered me. But I wanted it to be as easy to buy as possible, and Oneworld matched the advance and have done well with the book, although US sales suffered between changing distributors. The book has so far been translated into Chinese, Japanese, Indonesian and Danish.

My most recent book, *Dialogues in the Philosophy of Religion* (2001), is an example of a kind of book which I have produced every ten years or so, gathering together a number of my articles and contributions to composite books which cohere reasonably well together.[6] In this particular case they have been replied to by others and I have replied to the replies, thus making the book dialogical. The next book will be in dialogue form, beginning with criticism of the pervasive naturalistic assumption of our culture, and involving the significance of religious experience, including discussion of its relation to brain states.

What of books read and enjoyed, for reading has been one of life's greatest pleasures? Among novels I have been relatively unadventurous, not often reading the latest success but re-reading many of the classics a number of times – for example, *Pride and Prejudice* fourteen times, *Sense and Sensibility* thirteen, *Emma* (probably, on reflection, Jane Austen's best) eleven, and her *Mansfield Park* and *Persuasion* ten times; much of George Eliot several times; Trollope's *Barchester* series and other books several times; *War and Peace* three times, and so on. I thoroughly enjoyed most of Scott and Dickens as a teenager, but have gone off them since. And when a little older, H.G. Wells and Aldous Huxley and P.G. Wodehouse. Like many other parents of my generation I enjoyed reading the C.S. Lewis and J.R.R. Tolkien stories to the children. Among modern classics E.M. Forster several times, Muriel Spark, Somerset Maughan, the ten novels of C.P. Snow's *Strangers and Brothers* series more than once, and C.S. Forrester's Hornblower books, and Gore Vidal. And among contemporary novelists I regard Vikram Seth's *A Suitable Boy* as of classic status, and think highly of Paul Scott's *Raj Quartet*, Joanne Harris (*Chocolat*), Jill Paton Walsh (*Knowledge of Angels*), Arundhati Roy (*The God of Small Things*), David Guterson, Robert Harris, David Lodge, Pat Barker, Umberto Eco, Richard Adams, Henry Porter. But I also read quite a lot of thrillers and detective stories, and in different genres James Michener, Ellis Peters, J.K. Rowling, and even Jeffrey Archer; and in science fiction not much, but some of Stephen Donaldson and Iain Banks.

Another large tranche of reading has been biography and auto-biography, mainly of writers, philosophers, politicians. Among the most outstanding, Roy Jenkins' *Gladstone* and *Churchill*, and also his autobiography *A Life at the Centre*, and Robert Skidelsky's three volume life of John Maynard Keynes, and Ray Monk's *Wittgenstein* and *Bertrand Russell* and Bryan Magee's *Confessions of a Philosopher*.

And among the poets, Fitzgerald's *Omar Kayyam* is a favourite, and Shakespeare's *Sonnets*, and Milton's *Paradise Lost*, T.S. Eliot's *Four Quartets*, and indeed a lot of Palgrave's Golden Treasury drawn from several centuries. Today's R.S. Thomas is intriguing, as was Auden. I read some poetry most weeks, but ought to read more. TV, except for occasional superb documentaries and films, has been a bad influence in usurping reading time.

In June 2001 I had an eightieth birthday party. The real date was in January 2002, but I wanted to invite quite a lot of people for a nice meal in a nice place in nice weather. The place was Birmingham's Botanical Gardens and it was in fact a beautiful warm sunny day. I had sent out about a hundred and fifty invitations (the card designed and made by a talented neighbour, David Barlow), hoping a little doubtfully that as many as ninety, the minimum number I was paying for, would come. But in the event a hundred and twenty-five came, filling the quite large room to its limits. It was a delight to see everyone, and the occasion went well. Amongst the many people whom it was a special treat to meet were two former Claremont students over from California. Maura O'Neill and her husband David Harnett brought gifts from friends within the LA Jewish-Christian–Muslim group. Tim Musgrove had arranged a business trip to London to fit in with the birthday party, and he later went out with the younger generation to a night club in the evening, and then came again the next day and spent more time with us, enjoyed by all. At the party itself, after the main part of the meal there were some short speeches, chaired by Mark. He first read a message from Desmond Tutu:

> Very dear Friend, Thank you for your kind invitation. You long passed your biblical allotted span and thank goodness for that since you have been such a splendid gift to God's world. I shan't

be able to come but will be with you in spirit recalling happy days at Claremont. God bless you richly and many happy returns, +Desmond.

Then Pete spoke, suitably funny but also sometimes serious. Then Clare Short, recalling AFFOR days and then our more recent discussions about religion. I wish we had recorded her confession of personal faith: goodness is God, i.e. human goodness, compassion, working for justice on earth for all is the ultimate value. She said that this did not satisfy me and that our discussions are ongoing – as they have been on several occasions. She remains unconvinced of a transcendent reality beyond the human. I hold that she is in fact responding in her life, as are many other people who are serving humanity without expressing their commitment in religious terms, to the universal presence of the Real. So much so that she is one of those who are so balanced and secure within themselves that they can take a genuine practical interest in others and their problems, as she does both in personal relationships and in her very productive work in International Development.

The next speaker was Keith Ward, with generous remarks about my influence in the philosophy of religion in general, and then Perry Schmidt-Leukel equally generous about religious pluralism in particular. I was in a bit of a daze during all these speeches and wish I had recorded them. I was very moved by the fact that so many people had taken the trouble to come, some from quite a distance. It was not possible to talk individually to everyone, but I have since had some long phone conversations to make up for this.

So life goes on, moving gradually towards its close in x years time. When I ask myself Nietzsche's ultimate challenging question, Would you be willing to live your life over again, just as it has been, with all its good and bad moments? I find that the answer is Yes. But I also believe, as part of a comprehensive religious philosophy, that this life is not the entirety of our existence, but an important part – the part that is important to us now – of a much larger and longer process and that its value is enhanced even further when seen in this light.

NOTES

1. I never knew Horace Alexander (b. 1889) but feel an affinity with him, not only because he was deeply influenced by Gandhi, but also in that he went to Bootham and was a c.o. during the First World War. He

taught at the Quaker Study Centre, Woodbrooke, Selly Oak for over twenty years from 1919. This house was built in the early 1920s, but I do not know in what years he occupied it.

2. Shops call them antiquarian books but this is clearly incorrect. There can be antiquarian book shops but not antiquarian books, except for books about antique books.

3. Printing from solid plates was first invented in China in the second century, where paper was also first manufactured, and with moveable print in the eleventh century.

4. *The Metaphor of God Incarnate*, London: SCM Press, and Louisville: Westminster/John Knox Press, 1993. Also available in Chinese, Japanese, Korean and Portuguese.

5. *Rumi, Poet and Mystic*, trans. R.A. Nicholson, in *A Rumi Anthology*, Oxford, Oneworld, 2000, p. 166.

6. The first of these collections was *God and the Universe of Faiths* (1973), then *God Has Many Names* (1980), *Problems of Religious Pluralism* (1985), *Disputed Questions in Theology and the Philosophy of Religion* (1993), *Dialogues in the Philosophy of Religion* (2001).

27

Philosophy of religion:
the state of the art

What is (or rather how do I see) the state of my subject, the philosophy of religion today? I am speaking of it as practised in the Anglo-American tradition, which is roughly called analytical (though post both logical positivism and linguistic analysis) in distinction from the typical style in continental Europe, though there has of late been an increasing mutual interest and interaction between the two. The first thing to say is that much the greater part of what is called philosophy of religion in the UK and USA is not this at all but is philosophical theology or, in the title of the Oxford chair, the philosophy of the Christian religion. The philosophy of religion proper is the philosophy of religion globally, not just of one particular tradition. This is now beginning increasingly to be done, but there is a far greater bulk of work in Christian philosophical theology. In Britain the leading figure is Richard Swinburne of Oxford, just recently retired. His main project began with an argument, using Bayes's probability theorem (about which in itself, without being a logician, I have no objection), for the existence of God conceived anthropomorphically as a person magnified to infinity but still with intentions and feelings and with moral rights and obligations in relation to the finite persons whom he has created. I do not share Richard's belief that the ultimate reality is an infinite person, or rather (as he also believes) three closely related infinite persons. But nevertheless this book is in my opinion his best and I used it several times very profitably as a basis for discussion in graduate seminars at Claremont. I do not however think that his probability argument for

God's existence succeeds and have criticised it elsewhere.[1] He has since gone on to apply the same method to the whole field of Christian doctrine, including the trinitarian nature of God, the problem of evil, and the atonement, and in seeking to show that the incarnation and the bodily resurrection of Christ are highly probable. I have, again, criticised some of this elsewhere.[2] At a recent (2001) conference Richard gave a paper concluding that the probability of the bodily resurrection of Jesus is ninety-seven per cent! His argument depends on estimated prior probabilities of God acting in this way and an estimate of the probability of the whole Christ phenomenon, including his resurrection, occurring without a theistic explanation. Everything depends, of course, on what one feeds into the calculus, which in this case included the data that Jesus claimed to be God incarnate, that he taught that his death was an atonement for human sin, and that he founded a church to make this known to the world through future ages. Since all these are today doubted by many NT scholars I asked what difference it would make to the outcome if they were omitted, and he allowed that this would reduce the resulting probability to less than half – so that the resurrection would then be more improbable than probable. However I do not think that the question can usefully be treated in this *a priori* way but rather by an examination of the NT evidence in the light of modern historical scholarship, something that Richard did not do in this paper, though he no doubt will in a forthcoming book on the subject.

His whole project reflects an immensely confident traditionally conservative religious stance and, believing as I do that this is too narrow and dogmatic to speak to the large majority in the west today, I watch his tremendous intellectual energy at work with awe but with regret that it is not better directed! In my contribution to Richard's *Festschrift* in 1994 I said,

> My own view is that this new summa, produced at the end of the twentieth century, is a vast anachronism, representing the thought-forms out of which Christianity is developing rather than the kind of new thinking that is needed as we approach the twenty-first century.[3]

It may seem strange to some that a colleague in the philosophy of religion world can be so rude in print about another's work and yet remain on thoroughly friendly terms with him. And yet this is not uncommon. I am sure that Richard would say something equally uncomplimentary about my own work, although we chat together perfectly amicably whenever we meet, and he came up from Oxford to my pre-eightieth birthday party in June 2001. However he never, so far as I know, replies directly to criticisms although he sometimes learns from them when returning later to the same subject.

As well as Swinburne there are other major figures. But much more profitable to my mind is the pioneering work of Keith Ward developing a global comparative theology, and the parallel philosophical work of Peter Byrne and others. Keith's four volume *magnum opus* is the most comprehensive attempt so far to produce a global theology on a Christian foundation – though it is of course that limited foundation about which I myself have reservations.

In the States the dominating, in the sense of the largest and most discussed, contribution is the 'Reformed epistemology' and its outworking introduced by Alvin Plantinga of Notre Dame (and formerly of Calvin College) and Nicholas Walterstorff, now retiring from Yale. The context is the wider religious situation in the States, where probably the majority of theologians and Christian philosophers are part of the very large evangelical constituency. Alvin himself comes out of the theologically very conservative, indeed virtually fundamentalist, part of the Dutch Calvinist tradition,[4] and his 'school', together with the many others who largely agree with him without all being themselves Calvinists, are also nearly always conservative evangelicals. These include such distinguished figures as Wolterstorff, Keith Yandell, George Mavrodes, Peter van Inwagen, Michael Peterson, William Hasker, Stephen Davis, Bruce Reichenbach, David Basinger, and many more. And there are a few, such as my brilliant one-time PhD student at Birmingham, Bill Craig, who support the most extreme possible evangelical/fundamentalist positions which evoke dissent even from some of their colleagues. But the USA, in which Christian fundamentalism is very strong, has produced the phenomenon of a combination of the highest intellectual gifts with what seems to some of us a startling lack of connection with the modern world.

Alvin presented the 'Reformed epistemology' in a programmatic paper in 1983,[5] and has gone on refining it ever since. A basic concept is that of proper basicality. Applied to religion this holds that belief in God can be held, not indirectly on the basis of evidence or reasoning but directly, as a basic belief such that in holding it we are not violating any valid epistemological rules. But properly basic beliefs, although not based on evidence, do have grounds. Thus the experience of 'seeing a tree' is generally a good justifying ground for the basic belief that I am seeing a tree. And such propositions as 'God is speaking to me', 'God has created all this', 'God disapproves of what I have done', 'God forgives me' are properly basic because based on my experience of God speaking to me, etc., so that the presupposed proposition that God exists is likewise properly basic.[6]

More recently however Alvin has made more central Calvin's notion of the *sensus divinitatis*, and the concept of warranted propositional beliefs, emphasising less the question of their basis in religious experience.[7] He thus takes a different position to that of Bill Alston and myself. I have met and corresponded with Alvin and like him, and he has after some hesitation – because my religious pluralism challenges his own Christian exclusivism[8] so directly – offered a twenty page critique of it (which he sent me in advance for my comments) in his latest book.[9]

William Alston's enormously important contribution, developed over the years in many articles, found its definitive expression in his *Perceiving God*.[10] But the first modern philosophical (as distinguished from theological) expression of the position that belief in God is not properly based on philosophical arguments but on the religious person's experience of God's presence, or of being in God's presence, came in my own *Faith and Knowledge* in 1957. The role of philosophical argument is not to prove or to probabilify God's existence but to establish our right, as rational beings, to trust our religious experience as we trust our other modes of experience, except in each case when we have good reason to doubt them. Bill Alston has acknowledged in several places the large influence that this had on his own thinking.[11] We have worked along parallel lines, though in different styles, he presenting his argument in the rigorous logical form favoured by many today, particularly in the States, and I more in the tradition of the English empiricists, Locke, Berkeley and Hume and, in the twentieth century, Russell and others. But we have in fact presented what is at root essentially the same defence of the rational permissibility of religious belief. Over the years Bill has had an enormous influence in the US, many of the other significant figures having been at some time his students.

Other major philosophers of religion in the States include Robert and Marilyn Adams (whom I have known for many years, Bob since Princeton days), Bill Rowe, with whom I have had very useful email debates, Bill Wainwright (also an email correspondent), Eleanor Stump, Philip Quinn, Robert Audi, Fred Ferré, Linda Zagzebski, and Terence Penelhum and Kai Nielsen in Canada, and many others.

Another major movement in the philosophy of religion stems from the work of Ludwig Wittgenstein. His thoughts about religion can be variously interpreted, but the movement which has grown up and flourished is represented most prominently by my friend and successor at Claremont, Dewi (D.Z.) Phillips. From my point of view its key position is non-realism concerning the reality of God: God – or the Transcendent/the Ultimate Reality/the Real – exists only as a human concept, operative in human language and in religious forms of life. However Dewi always claims in discussion that the realist/ non-realist question is a mistaken question, although he does not explain why. So we have a longstanding and probably unresolvable dispute about this. But Dewi does point very interestingly to religious ideas embedded in poetry (particularly the powerful and fiery Welsh poet R.S. Thomas) and in novels and films. He is also great fun as a companion, and is the greatest humorous story teller I know, able to entertain his listeners for a whole evening without ever repeating himself. But lest this should give a misleading impression, he is also a very serious and substantial philosopher with a growing influence on both sides of the Atlantic. His non-realist theological counterpart is Don Cupitt, particularly in his writings of twenty years ago, beginning with *Taking Leave of God* (1980), in which he argued (like Feuerbach, though he does not like my pointing this out) that God is a symbolic personification of our moral ideals. This book, and a very successful TV series – Don has been a superb TV presenter – launched the Sea of Faith movement. More recently however, continuing to publish a book a year, he has spun off into realms in which few can follow him, in both senses of 'follow'. But no one who knows Don personally can fail to admire him and to wish him well. And the Sea of Faith has been a liberating movement for many who have received from it a liberal and undogmatic Christian outlook, often without fully appreciating and taking on board the full anti-realist proposal.

Another quite different movement, particularly in the States, is process theology, arising from the metaphysical writings of A.N. Whitehead after he had moved from Cambridge, England to Cambridge, Massachussets. The entire system is very complex, and I make no attempt to summarise it here, but it involves the distinction between an eternal abstract deity and an available limited deity who is himself part of the universal process of life. At one time, as a teenager, I read virtually the whole of the Whitehead corpus, now treated as almost holy writ within the process movement, including his famous but very difficult Gifford lectures, *Process and Reality* (1929), but I now find the 'wisdom literature' within the process scriptures, such as *Adventures of Ideas* and Whitehead's *Dialogues*, the most valuable. The movement's leading figure – it was not a movement in Whitehead's own time – has been Charles Hartshorne, who died recently at the age of over a hundred, and its headquarters is the Center for Process Studies within the South Californian School of Theology at Claremont. Here the leading figure has been John Cobb, followed as Director of the Center by David Griffin. They were both academic neighbours and friends at Claremont. John had (indeed has) a broad vision and open mind, and a deep concern for the world's environmental problems and the church's regressive theological turn, and gave his students space to think for themselves. David, though a powerful thinker, was much more dogmatic and intellectually aggressive, and sometimes even dictatorial towards students. John has enabled me to recognise some valuable insights within process thought, which I would probably not have been able to receive from David. But the movement has been much more influential among theologians than among philosophers, and I do not include it here as a major element within contemporary philosophy of religion.

Nor – though fearing the wrath to come from some good friends in California! – do I see feminist philosophy of religion as a major development. Feminist *theology* has a great deal of importance to say and we ought all to heed its messages. For the traditional monotheistic concept of God was created by males in their own image, in terms of overwhelming power and authority, using typically male images of lordship, fatherhood, kingship, and this together with its ramifications through the whole body of Christian doctrine needs radical correction. Thus the feminist movement in religious thinking is extremely important. But I, personally, have not found specifically feminist philosophy illuminating. There are major women philosophers of religion – such as Marilyn Adams, Eleanor Stump, Janet Soskice, Marjorie Suchocki, Linda Zagzebski, and many others – but they are not doing a distinctively feminine form of philosophy of religion. I can see very clearly the importance of female forms of religious experience and of the enormous contributions of female mystics through the centuries – my own favourite being the thirteenth/fourteenth century English Julian of Norwich.[12] However in the comprehensive *Companion to Philosophy of Religion*, edited by Philip Quinn and Charles Taliaferro[13], one of the three 'New Direct ions in Philosophy of Religion' is Feminism, discussed and defended by Sarah Coakley.

The other two new directions treated in the *Companion* are religious pluralism and comparative philosophy of religion. These are closely related and I can discuss them together. The pioneers of religious pluralism within the philosophy of religion were William Christian of Yale,[14] and Ninian Smart. Ninian was my predecessor in the H.G. Wood chair at Birmingham, and then a neighbour (in terms of the American sense of distance) at Santa Barbara whilst I was at Claremont, and was a good friend for many years until his death last year.

And, although not a philosopher, Wilfred Cantwell Smith contributed very importantly to our understanding of the nature of religion.[15] The religious pluralism issue centres on the question of the relationship between religions. This has of course long been treated theologically, but the philosophical discussion of it in the west (Rhadakrishnan and others had discussed it in India) is comparatively recent, and I suppose it is true (if immodest) to say that my *An Interpretation of Religion* is one of the books that scholars now writing in this area feel they have to come to terms with. Other major contributors include Huston Smith, Steven Katz, Keith Ward, Schmidt-Leukel, Gordon Kaufman, Mark Heim, James Kellenberger, Joseph Runzo, Alan Race, Hendrik Vroom and his group at the Free

University of Amsterdam, and a growing number of others, including Paul Griffiths who in the *Handbook* writes the article about comparative philosophy of religion – an area that deserves and will I am sure receive continuing development.

So the philosophy of religion in a variety of forms is a very active subject today, pursued more in philosophy than in religion departments, and much more in the States than in Britain. I am sad that the theology department here at Birmingham University has until recently had no courses in the philosophy of religion (though there was for a while one in philosophical theology) since I left over twenty years ago. And this lack is typical of such departments around the country, though I hope there are more exceptions than the few I know of, namely at Oxford, Cambridge and London.

But the philosophy of religion is an absolutely fascinating subject. Nearly all the major philosophers of the past have had something to say about it, many of them a great deal to say. But today too many theologians lack a philosophical training, and too many philosophers have turned their backs on the big issues that are of concern to their fellow human beings.

NOTES

1. See *An Interpretation of Religion*, pp. 104–9.
2. *Reason and the Christian Religion: Essays in Honour of Richard Swinburne*, edited by Alan Padgett, Oxford: Clarendon Press, 1994, chap. 11.
3. Ibid., p. 247, and in an extended review of Swinburne's 'Providence and the Problem of Evil' in the *International Journal for Philosophy of Religion*, Feb. 2000.
4. See Alvin's 'When Faith and Reason Clash: Evolution and the Bible' in *Christian Scholar's Review*, vol. 21, no. 1 (September 1991), denying the emergence of humanity out of the evolution of the forms of life.
5. Alvin Plantinga in Plantinga & Wolterstorff, eds., *Faith and Rationality*, University of Notre Dame Press, 1983.
6. Ibid., p. 81.
7. Alvin Plantinga, *Warranted Christian Belief*, OUP, 2000, see particularly pp. 180–84.
8. Alvin Plantinga, 'A Defence of Religious Exclusivism' in Thomas Senor, ed., *The Rationality of Belief and the Plurality of Faith*, Ithaca: Cornell University Press, 1995.
9. Alvin Plantinga, *Warranted Christian Belief*, in chap. 2.
10. William Alston, *Perceiving God*, Ithaca: Cornell University Press, 1991.

11. See chapter 11 above.
12. On mysticism in general (and Julian in particular) see *The Fifth Dimension*, which gives it a central place.
13. London and Cambridge, MA: Blackwell, 1997.
14. William Christian, *Oppositions of Religious Doctrines*, London: Macmillan and New York: Herder & Herder, 1972, and *Doctrines of Religious Communities: A Philosophical Study*, Yale University Press, 1987.
15. More about Wilfred in chapter 23.

28

Epilogue:
Write your own pre-obituary!

I have long thought that it would be a valuable exercise for people to try to write an obituary of themselves as they think it might be written by someone else, not a personal friend, in X years' time. Of course, although intended to be objective it can really only be subjective, and the more so because obituaries are customarily appreciative rather than critical! So here is mine:

John Hick, who has died at the age of XX, was one of the most influential philosophers of religion of his generation in the English-speaking world. In a writing career of over forty-five years he introduced several new but now familiar concepts – epistemic distance, experiencing-as, the Irenaean type of theodicy, the replica theory, pareschatology, eschatological verification, the transcategorial Real. His text, *Philosophy of Religion*, selling well over 600,000 copies in several languages, has been used in its successive editions by generations of students. Among his nearly thirty authored and edited publications his major original works, *Faith and Knowledge* (1957, 1966), *Evil and the God of Love* (1966, 1977), *Death and Eternal Life* (1976), and *An Interpretation of Religion* (1989), containing his Gifford Lectures and receiving the Grawemeyer Award for significant new thinking in religion, are classics in the debased modern sense in which books less than a century old can be described as classics. In theology his edited *The Myth of God Incarnate* (1977), in collaboration with other major UK theologians, caused a considerable stir in Britain which his own later more unitary *The Metaphor of God Incarnate* (1993) did not – the shocking ideas of 1977 were no longer so shocking sixteen years later. His books have, between them, been translated into sixteen languages.

His work on religious pluralism in particular was highly controversial and he was attacked from different quarters as anti-Christian, as too narrowly Christian, as an atheist, a polytheist, a postmodernist, and as not postmodernist enough! In the United States he was strongly opposed and resented by many fundamentalists and evangelicals. He did however stir some more moderate evangelicals to think afresh about the problem of religious plurality. Whilst teaching in the States two attempts were made to exclude him from the ministry of the Presbyterian Church, first at Princeton over the Virgin Birth doctrine, and later at Claremont, California, over his attitude to other religions. In the first case his membership of the local Presbytery was eventually, after appeal to the General Assembly, sustained, and in the second case he was asked to withdraw his application to join the local Presbytery to avoid a split in the church, and readily did so. In Britain he was the object of sustained criticism from a generally more civilised breed of evangelicals.

Hick's work has been at least as influential in the United States as in Britain, indeed probably more so. It was he who first made the generally theologically conservative philosophy of religion community there face the problems of religious diversity, so that today every new students' text on the subject has its chapter on the subject, almost all including a discussion of his pluralist hypothesis. The breadth of his interests, comprising epistemology, metaphysics, theodicy, Christology, eschatology (including parapsychology), the world religions, mysticism, religious experience and its relation to neuroscience, was exceptional. As a result he is often still known in different academic circles for different reasons, in some as a philosopher of religion writing about the religious ambiguity of the universe, the inadequacy of physicalist naturalism, the epistemology of faith, the validity of religious experience, and in other circles as a theologian writing about the problem of evil and about the metaphorical character of the concept of divine incarnation. But he is probably most widely known today for his work during the last twenty or so years advocating an understanding of the world religions as different culturally formed responses to an ineffable transcendent reality which he called the Real. The biggest single influence on his philosophical thought was Immanuel Kant.

His main academic limitation was that he was not a scholar in the sense of one who studies the ancient texts of different traditions in their original languages. He had neither the linguistic equipment nor the inclination for this. His knowledge of other religions was based not only on reading but also on time spent in India, Sri Lanka and Japan, as well as in multi-faith Birmingham and Los Angeles, and he relied on the work of specialists on the Sanscrit, Pali, Chinese and Arabic texts. And his influence was probably limited by the fact that he never taught continuously for several decades at any one major university so as to create a local school of thought propagating his ideas. Although he had some first-rate individual graduate students who have since become well known, his influence has come mainly through his writings, public lectures and conference presentations.

The clarity of Hick's writings made them readily available for critical attention and they have provoked more than twenty books, more than fifty academic dissertations, and well over two hundred journal articles devoted to discussing and very often criticising them. He welcomed informed and responsible criticisms, responded to them, and developed many of his theories as a result. Within the comparatively small international philosophy of religion world most of the critics were also friends. Only time will tell how lasting his contributions turn out to be. His own view was that his theological work, presenting Christianity as one great world faith amongst others rather than as the one and only true faith, will become redundant as Christian thinking, except on its continuing, probably large, fundamentalist wing, comes to embrace a pluralist point of view, but he hoped that some of his contributions to the philosophy of religion will remain part, as they already are, of the continuing development of the subject.

Hick's concern for the constructive development of inter-faith, inter-ethnic, and inter-cultural human relations was practical as well as theoretical and he had friends of different faiths in many parts of the world. He was involved in inter-religious dialogue, particularly Jewish–Christian–Muslim and Buddhist–Christian, and also in race relations work, incurring threats from the neo-Nazi National Front in Britain and the banning in South Africa of his account of apartheid, based on time spent there. The biggest influence on this side of his life was Mahatma Gandhi.

John Harwood Hick was born in Scarborough, England in 1922, the son of a solicitor. He intended to follow the same career, but as a law student he experienced a strong evangelical conversion and trained for the ministry of the Presbyterian Church of England (now United Reformed Church). He only gradually moved away from his student fundamentalist beliefs. During the Second World War he served as a conscientious objector in the Friends Ambulance Unit. After a First in his philosophy degree at Edinburgh, a doctorate in the philosophy faculty at Oxford, and theological training at Westminster College, Cambridge, he was ordained in 1953, serving as minister of Belford Presbyterian Church in Northumberland. From there he was called to teach as an assistant professor in the philosophy department of Cornell University, then as Stuart professor at Princeton Theological Seminary, then briefly as a lecturer in the philosophy of religion at Cambridge, then to the H.G. Wood chair at Birmingham for fifteen years, and finally for ten years to the Danforth chair at the Claremont Graduate University in California.

His gradually developed personal faith, expressed in *The Fifth Dimension* (1999), was of a more universal than exclusively Christian kind. He practised a form of Buddhist meditation, and was an irregular attender of both URC church services and Quaker meetings for worship. Either religion or temperament or both produced in him a certain serenity, and his practical outlook on life was always positive and optimistic, strongly supported by a close family life. His wife Hazel (née Bowers), who he married in 1953, and to whom he was married for forty-four years, predeceased him. He leaves a daughter and two sons (a third son died in a mountain accident when young), and four grandchildren.

Index